Alfred Thayer Mahan

From Sail to Stream

Alfred Thayer Mahan

From Sail to Stream

ISBN/EAN: 9783954273416
Erscheinungsjahr: 2013
Erscheinungsort: Bremen, Deutschland

© maritimepress in Europäischer Hochschulverlag GmbH & Co. KG, Fahrenheitstr. 1, 28359 Bremen. Alle Rechte beim Verlag und bei den jeweiligen Lizenzgebern.

www.maritimepress.de | office@maritimepress.de

Bei diesem Titel handelt es sich um den Nachdruck eines historischen, lange vergriffenen Buches. Da elektronische Druckvorlagen für diese Titel nicht existieren, musste auf alte Vorlagen zurückgegriffen werden. Hieraus zwangsläufig resultierende Qualitätsverluste bitten wir zu entschuldigen.

Alfred Thayer Mahan

From Sail to Stream

PREFACE

When I was a boy, some years before I obtained my appointment in the navy, I spent many of those happy hours that only childhood knows poring over the back numbers of a British service periodical, which began its career in 1828, with the title *Colburn's United Service Magazine*; under which name, save and except the Colburn, it still survives. Besides weightier matters, its early issues abounded in reminiscences by naval officers, then yet in the prime of life, who had served through the great Napoleonic wars. More delightful still, it had numerous nautical stories, based probably on facts, serials under such entrancing titles as "Leaves from my Log Book," by Flexible Grommet, Passed Midshipman; a pen-name, the nautical felicity of which will be best appreciated by one who has had the misfortune to handle a grommet[1] which was not flexible. Then there was "The Order Book," by Jonathan Oldjunk; an epithet so suggestive of the waste-heap, even to a landsman's ears, that one marvels a man ever took it unto himself, especially in that decline of life when we are more sensitive on the subject of bodily disabilities than once we were. Old junk, however, can yet be "worked up," as the sea expression goes, into other uses, and that perhaps was what Mr. Oldjunk meant; his early adventures as a young "luff" were, for economical reasons, worked up into their present literary shape, with the addition of a certain amount of extraneous matter – love-making, and the like. Indeed, so far from uselessness, that veteran seaman and rigid economist, the Earl of St. Vincent, when First Lord of the Admiralty, had given to a specific form of old junk – viz., "shakings" – the honors of a special order, for the preservation thereof, the which forms the staple of a comical anecdote in Basil Hall's *Fragments of Voyages and Travels*; itself a superior example of the instructive "recollections," of less literary merit, which but for Colburn's would have perished.

Any one who has attempted to write history knows what queer nuggets of useful information lie hidden away in such papers; how they often help to reconstruct an incident, or determine a mooted point. If the Greeks, after the Peloponnesian war, had had a Colburn's, we should have a more certain, if not a perfect, clew to the reconstruction of the trireme; and probably even could deduce with some accuracy the daily routine, the several duties, and hear the professional jokes and squabbles, of their officers and crews. The serious people who write history can never fill the place of the gossips, who pour out an unpremeditated mixture of intimate knowledge and idle trash.

Trash? Upon the whole is not the trash the truest history? perhaps not the most valuable, but the most real? If you want contemporary color, contemporary atmosphere, you must seek it among the impressions which can be obtained only from those who have lived a life amid particular surroundings, which they breathe and which colors them – dyes them in the wool. However skilless, they cannot help reproducing, any more than water poured from an old ink-bottle can help coming out more or less black; although, if suffi-

ciently pretentious, they can monstrously caricature, especially if they begin with the modest
time-worn admission that they are more familiar
with the marling-spike than with the pen. But
even the caricature born of pretentiousness will
not prevent the unpremeditated betrayal of conditions, facts, and incidents, which help reconstruct
the *milieu*; how much more, then, the unaffected
simplicity of the born story-teller. I do not know
how Froissart ranks as an authority with histori-
ans. I have not read him for years; and my recollections are chiefly those of childhood, with all the
remoteness and all the vividness which memory
preserves from early impressions. I think I now
might find him wearisome; not so in boyhood. He
was to me then, and seems to me now, a glorified
Flexible Grommet or Jonathan Oldjunk; ranking,
as to them, as Boswell does towards the common
people of biography. That there are many solid
chunks of useful information to be dug out of him
I am sure; that his stories are all true, I have no
desire to question; but what among it all is so instructive, so entertaining, as the point of view of
himself, his heroes, and his colloquists – the particular contemporary modification of universal
human nature in which he lived, and moved, and
had his being?

   If such a man has the genius of his business, as
had Froissart and Boswell, he excels in proportion
to his unconsciousness of the fact; his colors run
truer. For lesser gobblers, who have not genius,
the best way to lose consciousness is just to IT
themselves go; if they endeavor to paint artisti-
cally the muddle will be worse. To such the prov-

erb of the cobbler and his last is of perennial warning. As a barber once sagely remarked to me, "You can't trim a beard well, unless you're born to it." It is possible in some degree to imitate Froissart and Boswell in that marvellous diligence to accumulate material which was common to them both; but, when gathered, how impossible it is to work up that old junk into permanent engrossing interest let those answer who have grappled with ancient chronicles, or with many biographies. So, with a circumlocution which probably convicts me in advance of decisive deficiency as a narrator, I let myself go. I have no model, unless it be the old man sitting in the sun on a summer's day, bringing forth out of his memories things new and old – mostly old.

A. T. MAHAN.

INTRODUCING MYSELF

While extracts from the following pages were appearing in *Harper's Magazine*, I received a letter from a reader hoping that I would say something about myself before entering the navy. This had been outside my purpose, which was chiefly to narrate what had passed around me that I thought interesting; but it seems possibly fit to establish in a few words my antecedents by heredity and environment.

I was born September 27, 1840, within the boundaries of the State of New York, but not upon its territory; the place, West Point on the Hudson River, having been ceded to the General Government for the purposes of the Military Academy, at which my father, Dennis Hart Mahan, was then Professor of Engineering, as well Civil as Military. He himself was of pure Irish blood, his father and mother, already married, having emigrated together from the old country early in the last century; but he was also American by birthright, having been born in April, 1802, very soon after the arrival of his parents in the city of New York. There also he was baptized into the Roman Catholic Church, in the parish of St. Peter's, the church building of which now stands far down town, in Barclay Street. It is not, I believe, the same that existed in 1802.

Very soon afterwards, before he reached an age to remember, his parents removed to Norfolk, Virginia, where he grew up and formed his earliest associations. As is usual, these colored his whole life; he was always a Virginian in attachment and preference. In the days of crisis he remained firm to the Union, by conviction and affection; but he broke no friendships, and to the end there continued in him that surest positive indication of local fondness, admiration for the women of what was to him his native land. In beauty, in manner, and in charm, they surpassed. "Your mother is Northern," he once said to me, "and very few can approach her; but still, in the general, none compare for me with the Southern woman." The same causes, early association, gave him a very pronounced dislike to England; for he could remember the War of 1812, and had experienced the embittered feeling which was probably nowhere fiercer than around the shores of the Chesapeake, the scene of the most wide-spread devastation inflicted, partly from motives of policy, partly as measures of retaliation. Spending afterwards three or four years of early manhood in France, he there imbibed a warm liking for the people, among whom he contracted several intimacies. He there knew personally Lafayette and his family; receiving from them the hospitality which the Marquis' service in the War of Independence, and his then recent ovation during his tour of the United States in 1825, prompted him to extend to Americans. This communication with a man who could tell, and did tell him, intimate stories of intercourse with Washington doubtless emphasized my father's patriotic prejudices as well as his patriotism. When he revisited France, in 1856, he found many former friends still alive, and when I myself went there for the first time, in 1870, he asked me too to hunt them up; but they had all then disappeared. His fondness for the French doubtless accentuated his repugnance to the English, at that time still their traditional enemy. The combination of Irish and French prepossession could scarcely have resulted otherwise; and thus was evolved an atmosphere in which I was brought up, not only passively absorbing, but to a certain degree actively impressed with love for France and the Southern section of the United States, while learning to look askance upon England and abolitionists. The experiences of life, together with subsequent reading and reflection, modified and in the end entirely overcame these early prepossessions.

My father was for over forty years professor at West Point, of which he had been a graduate. In short, the Academy was his life, and he there earned what I think I am modest in calling a distinguished reputation. The best proof of this perhaps is that at even so early a date in our national history as his graduation from the Academy, in 1824, he was thought an officer of such promise as to make it expedient to send him to France for the higher military education in which the country of Napoleon and his marshals then stood pre-eminent. From 1820, when he entered the Academy as a pupil, to his death in 1871, he was detached from it only these three or four years. Yet this determination of his life's work proceeded from a mere accident, scarcely more than a boy's fancy. He had begun the study of medicine, under Dr. Archer, of Richmond; but he had a very strong wish to learn drawing. In those primitive days the opportunity of instruction was wanting where he lived; and hearing that it was taught at the Military Academy he set to work for an appointment, not from inclination to the calling of a soldier, but as a means to this particular end. It is rather singular that he should have had no bias towards the profession of arms; for although he drifted almost from the first into the civil branch, as a teacher and then professor, I have never known a man of more strict and lofty military ideas. The spirit of the profession was strong in him, though he cared little for its pride, pomp, and circumstance. I believe that in this observation others who knew him well agreed with me.

The work of a teacher, however important and absorbing in itself, does not usually offer much of interest to readers. My father, by the personal contact of teacher and taught, knew almost every one of the distinguished generals who fought in the War of Secession, on either the Union or the Confederate side. With scarcely an exception, they had been his pupils; but his own life was uneventful. He married, in 1839, Mary Helena Okill, of New York City. My mother's father was English, her mother an American, but with a strong strain of French blood; her maiden name, Mary Jay, being that of a Huguenot family which had left France under Louis XIV. By the time of her birth, in 1786, a good deal of American admixture had doubtless qualified the original French; but I remember her well, and though she lived to be seventy-three, she had up to the last a vivacity and keen enjoyment of life, more French than American, reflected from quick black eyes, which fairly danced with animation through her interest in her surroundings.

From my derivation, therefore, I am a pretty fair illustration of the mix-up of bloods which seems destined to bring forth some new and yet undecipherable combination on the North American continent. One-half Irish, one-fourth English, and a good deal more than "a trace" of French, would appear to be the showing of a quantitative analysis. Yet, as far as I understand my personality, I think to see in the result the predominance which the English strain has usually asserted for itself over others. I have none of the gregariousness of either the French or Irish; and while I have no difficulty in entering into civil conversation with a stranger who addresses me, I rarely begin, having, upon the whole, a preference for an introduction. This is not perverseness, but lack of facility; and I believe Froissart noted something of the same in the Englishmen of five hundred years ago. I have, too, an abhorrence of public speaking, and a desire to slip unobserved into a back seat wherever I am, which amount to a mania; but I am bound to admit I get both these dispositions from my father, whose Irishry was undiluted by foreign admixture.

In my boyhood, till I was nearly ten, West Point was a very sequestered place. It was accessible only by steam-boats; and during great part of the winter months not by them, the Hudson being frozen over most of the season as far as ten to twenty miles lower down. The railroad was not running before 1848, and then it followed the east bank of the river. One of my early recollections is of begging off from school one day, long enough to go to a part of the post distant from our house, whence I caught my first sight of a train of cars on the opposite shore. Another recollection is of the return of a company of engineer soldiers from the War with Mexico. The detachment was drawn up for inspection where we boys could see it. One of the men had grown a full beard, a sight to me then as novel as the railroad, and I announced it at home as a most interesting fact. I had as yet seen only clean-shaven faces. Among my other recollections of childhood are, as superintendent of the Academy, Colonel Robert E. Lee, afterwards the great Confederate leader; and McClellan, then a junior engineer officer.

As my boyhood advanced the abolition movement was gaining strength, to the great disapprobation and dismay of my father, with his strong Southern and Union sympathies. I remember that when *Uncle Tom's Cabin* came out, in my twelfth year, the master of the school I attended gave me a copy; being himself, I presume, one of the rising party adverse to slavery. My father took it out of my hands, and I came to regard it much as I would a bottle labelled "Poison." In consequence I never read it in the days of its vogue, and I have to admit that since then, in mature years, I have not been able to continue it after beginning. The same motives, in great part, led to my being sent to a boarding-school in Maryland, near Hagerstown, which drew its pupils very largely, though not exclusively, from the South. The environment would be upon the whole Southern. I remained there, however, only two years, my father becoming dissatisfied with my progress in mathematics. In 1854, therefore, I matriculated as a freshman at Columbia College in the city of New York, where I remained till I went to the Naval Academy.

My entrance into the navy was greatly against my father's wish. I do not remember all his arguments, but he told me he thought me much less fit for a military than for a civil profession, having watched me carefully. I think myself now that he was right; for, though I have no cause to complain of unsuccess, I believe I should have done better elsewhere. While thus more than dissenting from my choice, he held that a child should not be peremptorily thwarted in his scheme of life. Consequently, while he would not actively help me in the doubtful undertaking of obtaining an appointment, which depended then as now upon the representative from the congressional district, he gave me the means to go to Washington, and also two or three letters to personal friends; among them Jefferson Davis, then Secretary of War, and James Watson Webb, a prominent character in New York journalism and in politics, both state and national.

Thus equipped, I started for Washington on the first day of 1856, being then three months over fifteen. As I think now of my age, and more than usual diffidence, and of my omission, to win the favor of a politician who had constituents to reward, whereas to all my family practical politics were as foreign as Sanskrit, I know not whether the situation were more comical or pathetic. On the way I foregathered with a Southern lad, some three years my senior, returning home from England, where he had been at school. He beguiled the time by stories of his experiences, to me passing strange; and I remember, in crossing the Susquehanna, which was then by ferry-boat, looking at the fields of ice fragments, I said it would be unpleasant to fall in. "I would sooner have a knife stuck into me," he replied. I wonder what became of him, for I never knew his name. Of course he entered the Confederate army; but what besides?

I remember my week's stay in Washington much as I suppose a man overboard remembers the incidents of that experience. Memory is an odd helpmate; why some circumstances take hold and others not is "one of those things no fellow can find out." I saw the member of Congress, who I find by reference to have been Ambrose S. Murray, representative of the district within which West Point lay. He received me kindly, but with the reserve characteristic of most interviews where one party desires a favor for which he has nothing in exchange to offer. I think, however, that Mr. Webb, with whom and his family I breakfasted one day, said some good words for me. Jefferson Davis was a graduate of the Military Academy, of 1827; and although his term there had overlapped my father's by only one year, his interest in everything pertaining to the army had maintained between them an acquaintance approaching intimacy. He therefore was very cordial to the boy before him, and took me round to the office of the then Secretary of the Navy, Mr. James C. Dobbin, of North Carolina; just why I do not understand yet, as the Secretary could not influence my immediate object. Perhaps he felt the need of a friendly chat; for I remember that, after presenting me, the two sat down and discussed the President's Message, of which Davis expressed a warm approval. This being the time of the protracted contest over the Speakership, which ended in the election of Banks, I suppose the colleagues were talking about a document which was then ready, and familiar to them, but which was not actually sent to Congress until it organized, some weeks after this interview. Probably their conversation was the aftermath of a cabinet meeting.

I returned home with fairly sanguine hopes, which on the journey received a douche of cold water from an old gentleman, a distant connection of my family, to visit whom I stopped a few hours in Philadelphia. He asked about my chance of the appointment; and being told that it seemed good, he rejoined, "Well, I hope you won't get it. I have known many naval officers, captains and lieutenants, in different parts of the world" – for his time, he was then nearly eighty, he had travelled extensively – "I have talked much with them, and know that it is a profession with little prospect." Then he quoted Dr. Johnson: "No man will be a sailor who has contrivance enough to get himself into jail; for being in a ship is being in a jail with the chance of being drowned"; and further to overwhelm me, he clinched the saying by a comment of his own. "In a ship of war you run the risk of being killed as well as that of being drowned." The interview left me a perplexed but not a wiser lad.

Late in the ensuing spring Mr. Murray wrote me that he would nominate me for the appointment. Just what determined him in my favor I do not certainly know; but, as I remember, Mr. Davis had authorized me to say to him that, if the place were given me, he would use his own influence with President Pierce to obtain for a nominee from his district a presidential appointment to the Military Academy. Mr. Murray replied that such a proposition was very acceptable to him, because the tendency among his constituents was much more to the army than to the navy. At that day, besides one cadet at West Point for each congressional district, which was in the gift of the representative, the law permitted the President a certain number of annual appointments, called "At Large"; the object being to provide for sons of military and naval officers, whose lack of political influence made it difficult otherwise to enter the school. This presidential privilege has since been extended to the Naval Academy, but had not then. The proposed interchange in my case, therefore, would be practically to give an officer's son an appointment at large in the navy. Whether this arrangement was actually carried out, I have never known nor inquired; but it has pleased me to believe, as I do, that I owed my entrance to the United States navy to the interposition of the first and only President of the Southern Confederacy, whose influence with Mr. Pierce is a matter of history.

I entered the Naval Academy, as an "acting midshipman," September 30, 1856.

I
NAVAL CONDITIONS BEFORE
THE WAR OF SECESSION

THE OFFICERS AND SEAMEN

Naval officers who began their career in the fifties of the past century, as I did, and who survive till now, as very many do, have been observant, if inconspicuous, witnesses of one of the most rapid and revolutionary changes that naval science and warfare have ever undergone. It has been aptly said that a naval captain who fought the Invincible Armada would have been more at home in the typical war-ship of 1840, than the average captain of 1840 would have been in the advanced types of the American Civil War.[2] The twenty years here chosen for comparison cover the middle period of the century which has but recently expired. Since that time progress has gone on in accelerating ratio; and if the consequent changes have been less radical in kind, they have been more extensive in scope. It is interesting to observe that within the same two decades, in 1854, occurred the formal visit of Commodore Perry to Japan, and the negotiations of the treaty bringing her fairly within the movement of Western civilization; starting her upon the path which has resulted in the most striking illustration yet given of the powers of modern naval instruments, ships and weapons, diligently developed and elaborated during the period that has since elapsed.

When I received my appointment to the Naval School at Annapolis, in the early part of the year

1856, the United States navy was under the influence of one of those spasmodic awakenings which, so far as action is concerned, have been the chief characteristic of American statesmanship in the matter of naval policy up to twenty years ago. Since then there has been a more continuous practical recognition of the necessity for a sustained and consistent development of naval power. This wholesome change has been coincident with, and doubtless largely due to, a change in appreciation of the importance of naval power in the realm of international relations, which, within the same period, has passed over the world at large. The United States of America began its career under the Constitution of 1789 with no navy; but in 1794 the intolerable outrages of the Barbary pirates, and the humiliation of having to depend upon the armed ships of Portugal for the protection of American trade, aroused Congress to vote the building of a half-dozen frigates, with the provision, however, that the building should stop if an arrangement with Algiers were reached. Not till 1798 was the navy separated from the War Department. The President at that date, John Adams, was, through his New England origin, in profound sympathy with all naval questions; and, while minister to Great Britain, in 1785, had had continual opportunity to observe the beneficial effect of maritime activity and naval power upon that kingdom. He had also bitter experience of the insolence of its government towards our interests, based upon its conscious control of the sea. He thus came into office strongly biassed towards naval development. To the impulse given by him contributed also the outrageous course towards our commerce initiated by the French Directory, after Bonaparte's astounding campaigns in Italy had struck down all opposition to France save that of the mistress of the seas. The nation, as represented in Congress, woke up, rubbed, its eyes, and built a small number of vessels which did exemplary service in the subsequent quasi war with France. Provision was made for a further increase; and it is not too much to say that this beginning, if maintained, might have averted the War of 1812. But within four years revulsion came. Adams gave place to Jefferson and Madison, the leaders of a party which frankly and avowedly rejected a navy as an element of national strength, and saw in it only a menace to liberty. Save for the irrepressible marauding of the Barbary corsairs, and the impressment of our seamen by British ships-of-war, the remnant of Adams' ships would not improbably have been swept out of existence. This result was feared by naval officers of the day; and with what good reason is shown by the fact that, within six months of the declaration of the War in 1812, and when the party in control was determined that war there should be, a proposition to increase the navy received but lukewarm support from the administration, and was voted down in Congress. The government, awed by the overwhelming numbers of the British fleet, proposed to save its vessels by keeping them at home; just as a few years before it had undertaken to save its commerce by forbidding its merchant-ships to go to sea.

Such policy with regard to a military service means to it not sleep, but death. The urgent remonstrances of three or four naval captains obtained a change of plan; and at the end of the year the President admitted that, for the very reasons advanced by them, the activity of a small squadron, skilfully directed, had insured the safe return of much the most part of our exposed merchant-shipping. It is not, however, such broad general results of sagacious management that bring conviction to nations and arouse them to action. Professionally, the cruise of Rodgers's squadron, unsuccessful in outward seeming, was a much more significant event, and much more productive, than the capture of the *Guerrière* by the *Constitution*; but it was this which woke up the people. The other probably would not have turned a vote in either House. As a military exploit the frigate victory was exaggerated, and not unnaturally; but no words can exaggerate its influence upon the future of the American navy. Here was something that men could see and understand, even though they might not correctly appreciate. Coinciding as the tidings did with the mortification of Hull's surrender at Detroit, they came at a moment which was truly psychological. Bowed down with shame at reverse where only triumph had been anticipated, the exultation over victory where disaster had been more naturally awaited produced a wild reaction. The effect was decisive. Inefficient and dilatory as was much of the subsequent administration of the navy, there was never any further question of its continuance. And yet, from the ship which thus played the

most determining part in the history of her service, it has been proposed to take her name, and
give it to another, of newer construction; as
though with the name could go also the association. Could any other *Victory* be Nelson's *Victory*
to Great Britain? Can calling a man George
Washington help to perpetuate the services of the
one Washington? The last much-vaunted addition
to the British fleet, the *Dreadnaught*, bears a family
name extending back over two centuries, or more.
She is one of a series reasonably perpetuated, ship
after ship, as son after sire; a line of succession
honored in the traditions of the nation. So there
were *Victorys*, before the one whose revered hulk
still maintains a hallowed association; but her individual connection with one event has set her
apart. The name might be transferred, but with it
the association cannot be transmitted. But not
even the *Victory*, with all her clinging memories,
did for the British navy what the *Constitution* did
for the American.

There was thenceforward no longer any question about votes for the navy. Ships of the line,
frigates, and sloops, were ordered to be built, and
the impulse thus received never wholly died out.
Still, as with all motives which in origin are emo-
tional rather than reasoned, there was lack of
staying power. As the enthusiasm of the moment
languished, there came languor of growth; or,
more properly, of development. Continuance became routine in character, tending to reproduce
contentedly the old types consecrated by the War
of 1812. There was little conscious recognition of
national exigencies, stimulating a demand that the

navy, in types and numbers, should be kept abreast of the times. In most pursuits of life American intelligence has been persistently apt and quick in search of improvement; but, while such characteristics have not been absent from the naval service, they have been confined chiefly, and naturally, to the men engaged in the profession, and have lacked the outside support which immediate felt needs impart to movements in business or politics. Few men in civil life could have given an immediate reply to the question, Why do we need a navy? Besides, although the American people are aggressive, combative, even warlike, they are the reverse of military; out of sympathy with military tone and feeling. Consequently, the appearance of professional pride, the insistence upon the absolute necessity for professional training, which in the physician, lawyer, engineer, or other civil occupation is accepted as not only becoming, but conducive to uplifting the profession as a whole, is felt in the military man to be the obtrusion of an alien temperament, easily stigmatized as the arrogance of professional conceit and exclusiveness. The wise traditional jealousy of any invasion of the civil power by the military has no doubt played some part in this; but a healthy vigilance is one thing, and morbid distrust another. Morbid distrust and unreasoned prepossession were responsible for the feebleness of the navy in 1812, and these feelings long survived. An adverse atmosphere was created, with results unfortunate to the nation, so far as the navy was important to national welfare or national progress.

Indeed, between the day of my entrance into the service, fifty years ago, and the present, nowhere is change more notable than in the matter of atmosphere; of the national attitude towards the navy and comprehension of its office. Then it was accepted without much question as part of the necessary lumber that every adequately organized maritime state carried, along with the rest of a national establishment. Of what use it was, or might be, few cared much to inquire. There was not sufficient interest even to dispute the necessity of its existence; although, it is true, as late as 1875 an old-time Jeffersonian Democrat repeated to me with conviction the master's dictum, that the navy was a useless appendage; a statement which its work in the War of Secession, as well on the Confederate as on the Union side, might seem to have refuted sufficiently and with abundant illustration. To such doubters, before the war, there was always ready the routine reply that a navy protected commerce; and American shipping, then the second in the world, literally whitened every sea with its snowy cotton sails, a distinctive mark at that time of American merchant shipping. In my first long voyage, in 1859, from Philadelphia to Brazil, it was no rare occurrence to be becalmed in the doldrums in company with two or three of these beautiful semi-clipper vessels, their low black hulls contrasting vividly with the tall pyramids of dazzling canvas which rose above them. They needed no protection then, and none foresaw that within a decade, by the operations of a few small steam-cruisers, they would be swept from the seas, never to return. Everything was taken for granted, and not least that war was a barbarism of the past. From 1815 to 1850, the lifetime of a generation, international peace had prevailed substantially unbroken, despite numerous revolutionary movements internal to the states concerned; and it had been lightly assumed that these conditions would thenceforth continue, crowned as they had been by the great sacrament of peace, when the nations for the first time gathered under a common roof the fruits of their several industries in the World's Exposition of 1851. The shadows of disunion were indeed gathering over our own land, but for the most of us they carried with them no fear of war. American fight American? Never! Separation there might be, and with a common sorrow officers of both sections thought of it; but, brother shed the blood of brother? No! By 1859 the Crimean War had indeed intervened to shake these fond convictions; but, after all, rules have exceptions, and in the succeeding peace the British government, consistent with the prepossessions derived from the propaganda of Cobden, yielded perfectly gratuitously the principle that an enemy's commerce might be freely transported under a neutral flag, thereby wrenching away prematurely one of the prongs of Neptune's trident. Surely we were on the road to universal peace.

San Francisco before and after its recent earthquake – at this moment of writing ten days ago – scarcely presented a greater contrast of experience than that my day has known; and the political condition and balance of the world now is as different from that of the period of which I have been writing as the new city will be from the old one it will replace at the Golden Gate. Of this universal change and displacement the most significant factor – at least in our Western civilization – has been the establishment of the German Empire, with its ensuing commercial, maritime, and naval development. To it certainly we owe the military impulse which has been transmitted everywhere to the forces of sea and land – an impulse for which, in my judgment, too great gratitude cannot be felt. It has braced and organized Western civilization for an ordeal as yet dimly perceived. But between 1850 and 1860 long desuetude of war, and confident reliance upon the commercial progress which freedom of trade had brought in its train, especially to Great Britain, had induced the prevalent feeling that to-morrow would be as to-day, and much more abundant. This was too consonant to national temperament not to pervade America also; and it was promoted by a distance from Europe and her complications much greater than now exists, and by the consistent determination not to be implicated in her concerns. All these factors went to constitute the atmosphere of indifference to military affairs in general; and particularly to those external interests of which a navy is the outward and visible sign and champion.

I do not think there is error or exaggeration in this picture of the "environment" of the navy in popular appreciation at the time I entered. Under such conditions, which had obtained substantially since soon after the War of 1812, and which long disastrously affected even Great Britain, with all

her proud naval traditions and maritime and co-
lonial interests, a military service cannot thrive.
Indifference and neglect tell on most individuals,
and on all professions. The saving clauses were
the high sense of duty and of professional integrity, which from first to last I have never known
wanting in the service; while the beauty of the
ships themselves, quick as a docile and intelligent
animal to respond to the master's call, inspired
affection and intensified professional enthusiasm.
The exercises of sails and spars, under the varying
exigencies of service, bewildering as they may
have seemed to the uninitiated, to the appreciative
possessed fascination, and were their own sufficient reward for the care lavished upon them. In
their mute yet exact response was some compen-
sation for external neglect; they were, so to say,
the testimony of a good conscience; the assurance
of professional merit, and of work well done, if
scantily recognized. Poor and beloved sails and
spars – *la joie de la manoeuvre*, to use the sympathetic phrase of a French officer of that day – gone
ye are with that past of which I have been speaking, and of which ye were a goodly symbol; but
like other symptoms of the times, had we listened
aright, we should have heard the stern rebuke: Up
and depart hence; this is not the place of your rest.

The result of all this had been a body of officers, and of men-of-war seamen, strong in professional sentiment, and admirably qualified in the
main for the duties of a calling which in many of
its leading characteristics was rapidly becoming
obsolete. There was the spirit of youth, but the
body of age. As a class, officers and men were

well up in the use of such instruments as the country gave them; but the profession did not wield the corporate influence necessary to extort better instruments, and impotence to remedy produced acquiescence in, perhaps, more properly, submission to, an arrest of progress, the evils of which were clearly seen. Yet the salt was still there, nor had it lost its savor. The military professions are discouraged, even enjoined, against that combined independent action for the remedy of grievances which is the safeguard of civil liberty, but tends to sap the unquestioning obedience essential to unity of action under a single will – at once the virtue and the menace of a standing army. Naval officers had neither the privilege nor the habits which would promote united effort for betterment; but when individuals among them are found, like Farragut, Dupont, Porter, Dahlgren – to mention only a few names that became conspicuous in the War of Secession – there will be found also in civil and political life men who will become the channels through which the needs of the service will receive expression and ultimately obtain relief. The process is overslow for perfect adequacy, but it exists. It may be asked, Was not the Navy Department constituted for this special purpose? Possibly; but experience has shown that sometimes it is effective, and sometimes it is not. There is in it no provision for a continuous policy. No administrative period of our naval history since 1812 has been more disastrously stagnant and inefficient than that which followed closely the War of Secession, with its extraordinary, and in the main well-directed, administrative energy.

The deeds of Farragut, his compeers, and their followers, after exciting a moment's enthusiasm, were powerless to sustain popular interest. Reaction ruled, as after the War of 1812.

To whomsoever due, in the decade immediately preceding the War of Secession there were two notable attempts at regeneration which had a profound influence upon the fortunes of that contest. Of these, one affected the personnel of the navy, the other the material. It had for some time been recognized within the service that, owing partly to easy-going toleration of offenders, partly to the absence of authorized methods for dealing with the disabled, or the merely incompetent, partly also, doubtless, to the effect of general professional stagnation upon those naturally inclined to worthlessness, there had accumulated a very considerable percentage of officers who were useless; or, worse, unreliable. In measure, this was also due to habits of drinking, much more common in all classes of men then than now. Even within the ten years with which I am dealing, an officer not much my senior remarked to me on the great improvement in this respect in his own experience; and my contemporaries will bear me out in saying that since then the advance has been so sustained that the evil now is practically non-existent. But then the compassionate expression, "A first-rate officer when he is not drinking," was ominously frequent; and in the generation before too little attention had been paid to the equally significant remark, that with a fool you know what to count on, but with one who drank you never knew.

But drink was far from the only cause. There were regular examinations, after six years of service, for promotion from the warrant of midshipman to a lieutenant's commission; but, that successfully passed, there was no further review of an officer's qualifications, unless misconduct brought him before a court-martial. Nor was there any provision for removing the physically incompetent. Before I entered the navy I knew one such, who had been bed-ridden for nearly ten years. He had been a midshipman with Farragut under Porter in the old *Essex*, when captured by the *Phoebe* and *Cherub*. A gallant boy, specially named in the despatch, he had such aptitude that at sixteen, as he told me himself, he wore an epaulette on the left shoulder – the uniform of a lieutenant at that time; and a contemporary assured me that in handling a ship he was the smartest officer of the deck he had ever known. But in early middle life disease overtook him, and, though flat on his back, he had been borne on the active list because there was nothing else to do with him. In that plight he was even promoted. There was another who, as a midshipman, had lost a foot in the War of 1812, but had been carried on from grade to grade for forty years, until at the time I speak of he was a captain, then the highest rank in the navy. Possibly, probably, he never saw water bluer than that of the lakes, where he was wounded. The undeserving were not treated with quite the same indulgence. Those familiar with the *Navy Register* of those days will recall some half-dozen old die-hards, who figured from year to year at the head of the lieutenant's list; continuously "overslaughed," never promoted, but never dismissed. To deal in the same manner with such men as the two veterans first mentioned would have been insulting; the distinction of promotion had to be conceded.

But there were those also who, despite habits or inefficiency, slipped through even formal examination; commanders whose ships were run by their subordinates, lieutenants whose watch on deck kept their captains from sleeping, midshipmen whose unfitness made their retention unpardonable; for at their age to re-begin life was no hardship, much less injustice. Of one such the story ran that his captain, giving him the letter required by regulation, wrote, "Mr. So and So is a very excellent young gentleman, of perfectly correct habits, but nothing will make an officer of him." He answered his questions, however; and the board considered that they could not go beyond that fact. They passed him in the face of the opinion of a superior of tried efficiency who had had his professional conduct under prolonged observation. I never knew this particular man professionally, but the general estimate of the service confirmed his captain's opinion. Twenty or thirty years later, I was myself one of a board called to deal with a precisely similar case. The letter of the captain was explicitly condemnatory and strong; but the president of the board, a man of exemplary rectitude, was vehement even in refusing to act upon it, and his opinion prevailed. Some years afterwards the individual came under my command, and proved to be of so eccentric worthlessness that I thought him on the border-line of insanity. He afterwards disappeared, I do not know how.

Talking of examinations, a comical incident came under my notice immediately after the War of Secession, when there were still employed a large number of those volunteer officers who had honorably and usefully filled up the depleted ranks of the regular service – an accession of strength imperatively needed. There were among them, naturally, inefficients as well as efficients. One had applied for promotion, and a board of three, among them myself, was assembled to examine. Several commonplace questions in seamanship were put to him, of which I now remember only that he had no conception of the difference between a ship moored, and one lying at single anchor – a subject as pertinent to-day as a hundred years ago. After failing to explain this, he expressed his wish not to go further; whereupon one of the board asked why, if ignorant of these simple matters, he had applied for examination. His answer was, "I did not apply for examination, I applied for promotion." Even in this case, when the applicant had left the room, the president of the board, then a somewhat notorious survival of the unfittest, long since departed this life, asked whether we refused to pass him. The third member, himself a volunteer officer, and myself, said we did. "Well," he rejoined, "you know this man may get a chance at *you* some day." This prudent consideration, however, did not save him.

Such tolerance towards the unfit, the reluctance to strike the individual in the interests of the community, was but a special, and not very flagrant, instance of the sympathy evoked for much worse offenders – murderers, and defrauders – in civil life. In such cases, the average man, except when personally affected, sides unreasonably with the sufferer and against the public; witness the easily signed petitions for pardon which flow in. It can be understood that in a public employment, civil or military, there will usually be reluctance to punish, and especially to take the bread out of the mouths of a man and his family by ejection. Usually only immediate personal interest in efficiency can supply the needed hardness of heart. Speaking after a very extensive and varied inside experience of courts-martial, I can say most positively that their tendency is not towards the excessive severity which I have heard charged against them by an eminent lawyer. On the contrary, the difficulty is to keep the members up to the mark against their natural and professional sympathies. Their superiors in the civil government have more often to rebuke undue leniency. How much more hard when, instead of an evil-doer, one had only to deal with a good-tempered, kindly ignoramus, or one perhaps who drew near the border-line of slipshod adequacy; and especially when to do so was to initiate action, apparently invidious, and probably useless, as in cases I have cited. It was easier for a captain or first lieutenant to nurse such a one along through a cruise, and then dismiss him to his home, thanking God, like Dogberry, that you are rid of a fool, and trusting you may see him no more. But this confidence may be misplaced; even his ghost may return to plague you, or your conscience. Basil Hall tells an interesting story in point. When himself about to pass for lieutenant, in 1808, while in an ante-room awaiting his summons, a candidate came out flushed and perturbed. Hall was called in, and one of the examining captains said to him, "Mr. ----, who has just gone out, could not answer a question which we will put to you." He naturally looked for a stunner, and was surprised at the extremely commonplace problem proposed to him. From the general incident he presumed his predecessor had been rejected, but when the list was published saw his name among the passed. Some years later he met one of the examiners, who in the conversation recalled to him the circumstances. "We hesitated," he said, "whether to let him go through: but we did, and I voted for him. A few weeks later I saw him gazetted second lieutenant of a sloop-of-war, and a twinge of compunction seized me. Not long afterwards I read also the loss of that ship, with all on board. I never have known how it happened, but I cannot rid myself of an uneasy feeling that it may have been in that young man's watch." He added, "Mr. Hall, if ever you are employed as I then was, do not take your duties as lightly as I did."

Sometimes retribution does not assume this ghastly form, but shows the humorous side of her countenance; for she has two faces, like the famous ship that was painted a different color on either side and always tacked at night, that the enemy might imagine two ships off their coast. I recall – many of us recall – a well-known character in the service, "Bobby," who was a synonyme for inefficiency. He is long since in his grave, where reminiscence cannot disturb him; and the Bobby can reveal him only to those who knew him as well and better than I, and not to an unsympathetic public. Well, Bobby after much indulgence had been retired from active service by that convulsive effort at re-establishment known as the Retiring Board of 1854-55, to which I am coming if ever I see daylight through this thicket of recollections that seems to close round me as I proceed, instead of getting clearer. The action of that board was afterwards extensively reviewed, and among the data brought before the reviewers was a letter from a commander, who presumably should have known better, warmly endorsing Bobby. In consequence of this, and perhaps other circumstances, Bobby was restored to an admiring service; but the Department, probably through some officer who appreciated the situation, sent him to his advocate as first lieutenant – that is, as general manager and right-hand man. The joke was somewhat grim, and grimly resented. It fell to me a little later to see the commander on a matter of duty. He received me in his cabin, his feet swathed on a chair, his hands gnarled and knotted with gout or rheumatism, from which he was a great sufferer. Business despatched, we drifted into talk, and got on the subject of Bobby. His face became distorted. "I suppose the Department thinks it has done a very funny thing in sending me him as first lieutenant; but I tell you, Mr. Mahan, every word I wrote was perfectly true. There is nothing about a ship from her hold to her trucks that Bobby don't know; but – " here fury took possession of him, and he vociferated – "put him on deck, handling men, he is the d----dest fool that ever man laid eyes on." How far his sense of injury biassed his judgments as to the acquirements of his protégé, I cannot say; but a cruise or two before I had happened to hear from eye-witnesses of Bobby's appearance in public after his restoration as first lieutenant in charge of the deck. On the occasion in question he was to exercise the whole crew at some particular manoeuvre. Taking his stand on the hawse-block, he drew from his pocket a small note-book, cast upon it his eye and announced – doubtless through the trumpet – "Man the fore-royal braces!" Again a pause, and further reference. "Man the main-royal braces!" Again a pause: "Man the mizzen-royal braces – Man *all* the royal braces." It is quite true, however, that there may be plenty of knowledge with lack of power to apply it professionally – a fact observable in all callings, but one which examination alone will not elicit. I knew such a one who said of himself, "Before I take the trumpet I know what ought to be said and done, but with the trumpet in my hand everything goes away from me." This was doubtless partly stage-fright; but stage-fright does not last where there is real aptitude. This man, of very marked general ability, esteemed and liked by all, finally left the navy; and probably wisely. On the other hand, I remember a very excellent seaman – and officer – telling me that the poorest officer he had ever known tacked ship the best. So men differ.

Thus it happened, through the operation of a variety of causes, that by the early fifties there had accumulated on the lists of the navy, in every grade, a number of men who had been tried in the balance of professional judgment and found distinctly wanting. Not only was the public – the nation – being wronged by the continuance in positions of responsibility of men who could not meet an emergency, or even discharge common duties, but there was the further harm that they were occupying places which, if vacated, could be at once filled by capable men waiting behind them. Fortunately, this had come to constitute a body of individual grievance among the deserving, which counterbalanced the natural sympathy with the individual incompetent. The remedy adopted was drastic enough, although in fact only an application of the principle of selection in a very guarded form. Unhappily, previous neglect to apply selection through a long series of years had now occasioned conditions in which it had to be used on a huge scale, and in the most invidious manner – the selecting out of the unfit. It was therefore easy for cavillers to liken this process to a trial at law, in which unfavorable decision was a condemnation without the accused being heard; and, of course, once having received this coloring, the impression could not be removed, nor the method reconciled to a public having Anglo-Saxon traditions concerning the administration of justice. A board of fifteen was constituted – five captains, five commanders, and five lieutenants. These were then the only grades of commissioned officers, and representation from them all insured, as far as could be, an adequate acquaintance with the entire personnel of the navy. The board sat in secret, reaching its own conclusions by its own methods; deciding who were, and who were not, fit to be carried longer on the active list. Rejections were of three kinds: those wholly removed, and those retired on two different grades of pay, called "Retired," and "Furloughed." The report was accepted by the government and became operative.

This occurred a year or two before I entered the Naval School: and, as I was already expecting to do so, I read with an interest I well recall the lists of person unfavorably affected. Of course, neither then nor afterwards had I knowledge to form an independent opinion upon the merits of the cases; but as far as I could gather in the immediately succeeding years, from different officers, the general verdict was that in very few instances had injustice been done. Where I had the opportunity of verifying the mistakes cited to me, I found instead reason rather to corroborate than to impugn the action of the board; but, of course, in so large a review as it had to undertake, even a jury of fifteen experts can scarcely be expected never to err. In the navy it was a first, and doubtless somewhat crude, attempt to apply the method of selection which every business man or corporation uses in choosing employés; an arbitrary conclusion, based upon personal knowledge and observation, or upon adequate information. But in private affairs such decisions are not regarded as legal judgment, nor rejection as condemnation; and there is no appeal. The private interest of the employer is warrant that he will do the best he can for his business. This presumption does not lie in the case of public affairs, although after the most searching criticism the action of the board of fifteen might probably be quoted to prove that selection for promotion could safely be trusted at all times to similar means. I mean, that such a body would never recommend an unfit man for promotion, and in three cases out of five would choose very near the best man. But no such system can work unless a government have the courage of its findings; for private and public opinion will inevitably constitute itself a court of appeal. In Great Britain, where the principle of selection has never been abandoned, in the application the Admiralty is none the less constrained – browbeaten, I fancy, would hardly be too strong a word – by opinion outside. P. has been promoted, say the service journals; but why was A. passed over, or F., or K.? Choice is difficult, indeed, in peace times; but years sap efficiency, and for the good of the nation it is imperative to get men along while in the vigor of life, which will never be effected by the slow routine in which each second stands heir to the first. P. possibly may not be better than A. or K., but the nation will profit more, and in a matter vital to it, than if P., whose equality may be conceded, has to wait for the whole alphabet to die out of his way. The injustice, if so it be, to the individual must not be allowed to impede the essential prosperity of the community.

In 1854-55, the results of a contrary system had reached proportions at once disheartening and comical. It then required fourteen years after entrance to reach a lieutenant's commission, the lowest of all. That is, coming in as a midshipman at fifteen, not till twenty-nine, after ten to twelve years probably on a sea-going vessel, was a man found fit, by official position, to take charge of a ship at sea, or to command a division of guns. True, the famous Billy Culmer, of the British navy, under a system of selection found himself a midshipman still at fifty-six, and then declined a commission on the ground that he preferred to continue senior midshipman rather than be the junior lieutenant;[3] but the injustice, if so it were, to Billy, and to many others, had put the ships into the hands of captains in the prime of life. Of the historic admirals of that navy, few had failed to reach a captaincy in their twenties. *Per contra*, I was told the following anecdote by an officer of our service whose name was – and is, for he still lives – a synonyme for personal activity and professional seamanship, but who waited his fourteen years for a lieutenancy. On one occasion the ship in which he returned to Norfolk from a three-years' cruise was ordered from there to Portsmouth, New Hampshire, to go out of commission. For some cause almost all the lieutenants had been detached, the cruise being thought ended. It became necessary, therefore, to intrust the charge of the deck to him and other "passed" midshipmen, and great was the shaking of heads among old stagers over the danger that ship was to run. If this were exceptional, it would not be worth quoting, but it was not. A similar routine in the British navy, in a dry-rot period of a hundred years before, had induced a like head-wagging and exchange of views when one of its greatest admirals, Hawke, was first given charge of a squadron; being then already a man of mark, and

41

four years older than Nelson at the Nile. But he was younger than the rule, and so distrusted.

The vacancies made by the wholesale action of 1854 remedied this for a while. The lieutenants who owed their rank to it became such after seven or eight years, or at, twenty-three or four; and this meant really passing out of pupilage into manhood. The change being effected immediately, anticipated the reaction in public opinion and in Congress, which rejected the findings of the board and compelled a review of the whole procedure. Many restorations were made; and, as these swelled the lists beyond the number then authorized by law, there was established a reduced pay for those whose recent promotion made them in excess. For them was adopted, in naval colloquialism, the inelegant but suggestive term "jackass" lieutenants. It should be explained to the outsider, perhaps even many professional readers now may not know, that the word was formerly used for a class of so-called frigates which intervened between the frigate-class proper and the sloop-of-war proper, and like all hybrids, such as the armored cruiser, shared more in the defects than in the virtues of either. It was therefore not a new coinage, and its uncomplimentary suggestion applied rather to the grudging legislation than to the unlucky victims. Of course, promotion was stopped till this block was worked off; but the immediate gain was retained. Before the trouble came on afresh the War of Secession, causing a large number of Southerners to leave the service, introduced a very different problem; – namely, how to find officers enough to meet the expansion of the navy caused by the vast demands of the contest. The men of my time became lieutenants between twenty and twenty-three. My own commission was dated a month before my twenty-first birthday, and with what good further prospects, even under the strict rule of seniority promotion, is evident, for before I was twenty-five I was made lieutenant-commander, corresponding to major in the army. Those were cheerful days in this respect for the men who struck the crest of the wave; but already the symptoms of inevitable reaction to old conditions of stagnancy were observable to those careful to heed.

It would be difficult to exaggerate the benefit of this measure to the nation, through the service, despite the subsequent reactionary legislation. By a single act a large number of officers were advanced from the most subordinate and irresponsible positions to those which called all their faculties into play. "Responsibility," said one of the most experienced admirals the world has known, "is the test of a man's courage"; and where the native fitness exists nothing so educates for responsibility as the having it. The responsibility of the lieutenant of the watch differs little from that of the captain in degree, and less in kind. To early bearing of responsibility Farragut attributed in great part his fearlessness in it, which was well known to the service before his hour of strain. It was much that the government found ready for the extreme demands of the war a number of officers, who, instead of supervising the washing of lower decks and stowing of holds during their best years, had been put betimes in charge of the ship. From there to the captain's berth was but a small step. "Passed midshipman," says one of Cooper's characters, "is a good grade to reach, but a bad one to stop in." From a fate little better than this a large and promising number of young officers were thus rescued for the commands and responsibilities of the War of Secession.

II
NAVAL CONDITIONS BEFORE
THE WAR OF SECESSION

THE VESSELS

Less far-reaching, because men are greater than ships, but still of immense timeliness as a preparative to the war, was the reconstitution of the material of the navy, practically coincident with the regeneration of the personnel. The causes which led to this are before my time, and beyond my contemporary knowledge. They therefore form no part of my theme; but the result, which is more important than the process, was strictly contemporary with me. It marked a definite parting with sails as the motive reliance of a ship-of-war, but at the same time was characterized by an extreme conservatism, which then was probably judicious, and certainly represented the naval opinion of the day. It must be remembered that the Atlantic was first crossed under steam in 1837, a feat shortly before thought impossible on account of coal consumption, and that the screw-propeller was not generally adopted till several years afterwards. In 1855 the transatlantic liners were still paddlers; but the paddle-wheel shaft was far above the water, and so, in necessary consequence, was much of the machinery which transmitted power from the boilers to the wheel. All battle experience avouched the probability of disabling injury under such exposure; not more certain, but probably more fatal, than that to spars and sails of sailing-ships. Despite this drawback, paddle wheel men-of-war were being built between 1840 and 1850. Our own navy had of these two large and powerful vessels, sisters, the *Missouri* and the *Mississippi*. Singularly enough, both met the same end, by fire; the *Missouri* being burned in the Bay of Gibraltar in 1843, the *Mississippi* in the river whence she took her name, in the course of Farragut's passage of the batteries at Port Hudson in 1863. This engagement marked the end of the admiral's achievements in the river, throughout which, beginning with the passage of the forts and the capture of New Orleans, the *Mississippi* had done good work. At the time of her destruction, the present Admiral Dewey was her first lieutenant. Besides these two we had the *Susquehanna*, "paddle-wheel steam-frigate," which also served manfully through the war, and was in commission after it. It was she that carried General Sherman on his mission to Mexico in 1866. As usual, the principal European navies had built many more of these vessels; that is, had adopted improvements more readily than we did. During my first cruise after graduation, on the coast of Brazil, 1859-61, the British squadron there was composed chiefly of paddlers; the flag-ship *Leopard* being one. As I remember, there was only one screw-steamer, the sloop-of-war *Curaçao*.

By that time, however, the paddlers were only survivals; but it may be noted, in passing, with reference to the cry of obsolescence so readily raised in our day, that these survivals did yeoman service in the War of Secession. It is possible to be too quick in discarding, as well as too slow in adopting. By 1850 the screw had made good its position; and the difficulty which had impeded the progress of steam in men-of-war disappeared when it became possible to place all machinery below water. There were, however, many improvements still to come, before it could be frankly and fully accepted as the sole motive power. It is not well to let go with one hand till sure of your grip with the other. So in the early days of electric lighting prudent steamship companies kept their oil-lamps trimmed and filled in the brackets alongside of the electric globes. Apart from the problem experienced by the average man – and governments are almost always averages in adjusting his action to novel conditions, the science of steam-enginery was still very backward. Notably, the expenditure of coal was excessive; to produce a given result in miles travelled, or speed attained, much more had to be burned than now, a condition to which contributed also the lack of rigidity in the wooden hulls, which still held their ground. Sails were very expensive articles, as I heard said by an accomplished officer of the olden days; but they were less costly than coal. Steam therefore was accepted at the first only as an accessory, for emergencies. It was too evident for question that in battle a vessel independent of the wind would have an unqualified advantage over one dependent; though an early acquaintance of mine, a sailmaker in the navy, a man of unusual intelligence and tried courage, used to maintain that steam would never prevail. Small steamers, he contended, would accompany sailing fleets, to tow vessels becalmed, or disabled in battle; a most entertaining instance of professional prepossession. What would be his reflections, had he survived till this year of grace, to see only six sail-makers on the active list of the navy, the last one appointed in 1888, and not one of them afloat. Likewise, in breasting the continuous head-winds which mark some ocean districts, or traversing the calms of others, there would be gain; but for the most part sailing, it was thought, was sufficiently expeditious, decidedly cheaper, and more generally reliable; for steamers "broke down." Admiral Baudin; a French veteran of the Napoleonic period, was very sarcastic over the uncertainties of action of the steamers accompanying his sailing frigates, when he attacked Fort San Juan de Ulloa, off Vera Cruz in 1839; and since writing these words I have come across the following quotation, of several years later, from the London *Guardian*, which is republishing some of its older news under the title "'Tis Sixty Years Since."

"Naval manoeuvres in 1846. The Squadron of Evolution is one of the topics of the present week (June 10, 1846). Its arrival in the Cove of Cork, after a cruise which has tested by every variety of weather the sailing qualities of the vessels, has furnished the world with a few particulars of its doings, and with some materials for speculating on the problems it was sent out to solve. The result, as far as it goes, is certainly unfavorable to the exclusive prevalence of steam agency in naval warfare. Sailing ships, it is seen, can do things which steamers, as at present constructed, cannot accomplish. They can keep the sea when steamers cannot. But the screw-steamer, which is reported to have astonished everybody, is certainly an exception. Perhaps by this contrivance the rapidity and convenience of steam locomotion may be combined with the power and stability of our huge sailing batteries."

Under convictions thus slowly recasting, the first big steam ships-of-war carried merely "auxiliary" engines; were in fact sailing vessels, of the types in use for over a century, into which machinery was introduced to meet occasional emergencies. In some cases, probably in many, ships already built as sailers were lengthened and engined. As late as 1868 we were station-mates with one such, the *Rodney*, of 90 guns, then the flag-ship of the British China squadron; and we had already met, another, the *Princess Royal*, at the Cape of Good Hope, homeward bound. She, however, had been built as a steamer. She was a singularly handsome vessel, of her majestic type; and, as she lay close by us, I remember commenting on her appearance to one of my messmates, poor Stewart, who afterwards went down in the *Oneida*. "Yes," he replied, "she possesses several elements of the sublime." They were certainly imposing creations, with their double and treble tiers of guns, thrusting their black muzzles through the successive ports which, to the number of fifteen to twenty, broke through the two broad white hands that from bow to stern traversed the blackness of their hulls; above which rose spars as tall and broad as ever graced the days of Nelson. To make the illusion of the past as complete as possible, and the dissemblance from the sailing ship as slight, the smoke-stack – or funnel – was telescopic, permitting it to be lowered almost out of sight.

For those who can recall these predecessors of the modern battle-ships, the latter can make slight claim to beauty or impressiveness; yet, despite the ugliness of their angular broken sky-line, they have a gracefulness all their own, when moving slowly in still water. I remember a dozen years ago watching the French Mediterranean fleet of six or eight battle-ships leaving the harbor of Villefranche, near Nice. There was some manoeuvring to get their several stations, during which, here and there, a vessel lying quiet waiting her opportunity would glide forward with a dozen slow turns of the screws, not agitating the water beyond a light ripple at the bows. The bay at the moment was quiet as a mill-pond, and it needed little imagination to prompt recognition of the identity of dignified movement with that of a swan making its leisurely way by means equally unseen; no turbulent display of energy, yet suggestive of mysterious power.

Before the War of Secession, and indeed for twenty years after it, the United States never inclined to the maintenance of squadrons, properly so-called. It is true, a dozen fine ships-of-the-line were built during the sail period, but they never sailed together; and the essence of the battle-ship, in all eras, is combined action. Our squadrons, till long after I entered the navy, were simply aggregations of vessels, no two of which were necessarily of the same size or class. When a ship-of-the-line went to sea – which never happened in my time – she went without mates, a palpable paradox; a ship-of-the-line, which to no line belonged. Ours was a navy of single, isolated cruisers; and under that condition we had received a correct tradition that, whatever the nominal class of an American ship-of-war, she should be somewhat stronger than the corresponding vessels built by other nations. Each cruiser, therefore, would bring superior force to any field of battle at all possible to her. This was a perfectly just military conception, to which in great measure we owed our successes of 1812. The same rule does not apply to fleets, which to achieve the like superiority rely upon united action, and upon tactical facility obtained by the homogeneous qualities of the several ships, enabling them to combine greater numbers upon a part of the enemy. Therefore Great Britain, which so long ruled the world by fleets, attached less importance to size in the particular vessel. Class for class, her ships were weaker than those of her enemies, but in fleet action they usually won. At the period of which I am writing, the screw-propeller, having fairly established its position, prompted a reconstruction of the navy, with no change of the principles just mentioned. The cruiser idea dictated the classes of vessels ordered, and the idea of relative size prescribed their dimensions. There were to be six steam-frigates of the largest class, six steam-sloops, and six smaller vessels, a precise title for which I do not know. I myself have usually called them by the French name corvette, which has a recognized place in English marine phraseology, and means a sloop-of-war of the smaller class. A transfer of terms accompanying a change of system is apt to be marked by anomalies.

These eighteen vessels were the nucleus of the fighting force with which the government met the war of 1861. In the frigates and sloops steam was purely auxiliary; they had every spar and sail of the sailing ships to which they corresponded. Four of the larger sloops – the *Hartford*, *Richmond*, *Brooklyn*, and *Pensacola* – constituted the backbone of Farragut's fleet throughout his operations in the Mississippi. The *Lancaster*, one of the finest of these five sisters, was already in the Pacific, and there remained throughout the contest; while the *San Jacinto*, being of different type and size, was employed rather as a cruiser than for the important operations of war. It was she that arrested the Confederate commissioners, Slidell and Mason, on board the British mail-steamer *Trent*, in 1861. The corvettes for the most part were also employed as cruisers, being at once less effective in battery, for river work, and swifter. They alone of the vessels built in the fifties were engined for speed, as speed went in those days; but their sail power also was ample, though somewhat reduced. One of them, the *Iroquois*, accompanied Farragut to New Orleans, as did a sister ship to her, the *Oneida*, which was laid down in 1861, after many Southern Senators and Representatives had left their seats in Congress and the secession movement became ominous of war; when it began to be admitted that perhaps, after all, for sufficient cause, brothers might shed the blood of brothers.

The steam-frigates were of too deep draught to be of much use in the shoal waters, to which the nature of the hostilities and the character of the Southern coast confined naval operations. Being extremely expensive in upkeep, with enormous crews, and not having speed under steam to make them effective chasers, they were of little avail against an enemy who had not, and could not have, any ships at sea heavy enough to compete with them. The *Wabash* of this class bore the flag of Admiral Dupont at the capture of Port Royal; and after the fight the negroes who had witnessed it on shore reported that when "that checker-sided ship," following the elliptical course prescribed to the squadron for the engagement, came abreast the enemy's works, the gunners, after one experience, took at once to cover. No barbette or merely embrasured battery of that day could stand up against the twenty or more heavy guns carried on each broadside by the steam-frigates, if these could get near enough. At New Orleans, even the less numerous pieces of the sloops beat down opposition so long as they remained in front of Fort St. Philip and close to; but when they passed on, so the first lieutenant of one of them told me, the enemy returned to his guns and hammered them severely. This showed that the fort was not seriously injured nor its armament decisively crippled, but that the personnel was completely dominated by the fire of many heavy guns during the critical period required for the smaller as well as larger vessels to pass. As most of the river work was, of this character, the broadsides of the sloops were determinative, and those of the frigates would have been more so, could they have been brought to the scene; but they could not. Much labor was expended in the attempt to drag the

Colorado, sister ship to the *Wabash*, across the bar of the Mississippi, but fruitlessly.

For the reason named, the screw-frigates built in the fifties had little active share in the Civil War. Were they then, from a national stand-point, uselessly built? Not unless preparation for war is to be rejected, and reliance placed upon extemporized means. To this resort our people have always been inclined to trust unduly, owing to a false or partial reading of history; but to it they were excusably compelled by the extensive demands of the War of Secession, which could scarcely have been anticipated. At the time these frigates were built, they were, by their dimensions and the character of their armaments, much the most formidable ships of their class afloat, or as yet designed. Though correctly styled frigates – having but one covered deck of guns – they were open to the charge, brought against our frigates in 1812 by the British, of being ships-of-the-line in disguise; and being homogeneous in qualities, they would, in acting together, have presented a line of battle extorting very serious consideration from any probable foreign enemy. It was for such purpose they were built; and it was no reproach to their designers that, being intended to meet a probable contingency, they were too big for one which very few men thought likely. At that moment, when the portentous evolution of naval material which my time has witnessed was but just beginning, they were thoroughly up-to-date, abreast and rather ahead of the conclusions as yet reached by contemporary opinion. The best of compliments was paid them by the imitation of other navies; for, when the first one was finished, we sent her abroad on exhibition, much like a hen cackling over its last performance, with the result that we had not long to congratulate ourselves on the newest and best thing. It is this place in a long series of development which gives them their historical interest.

But if the frigates were unfitted to the particular emergency of a civil contest, scarcely to be discerned as imminent in 1855, the advantage of preparation for general service is avouched by the history of the first year of hostilities, even so exceptional as those of 1861 and 1862. Within a year of the first Bull Run, Farragut's squadron had fought its way from the mouth of the Mississippi to Vicksburg. That the extreme position was not held was not the fault of the ships, but of backwardness in other undertakings of the nation. All the naval vessels that subdued New Orleans had been launched and ready before the war, except the *Oneida* and the gunboats; and to attribute any determinative effect in such operations to the gunboats, with their one heavy gun, is to misunderstand the conditions. Even a year later, at the very important passage of Port Hudson, the fighting work was done by the *Hartford*, *Richmond*, *Mississippi*, and *Monongahela*; of which only the last named, and least powerful, was built after the war began. It would be difficult to overrate the value, material and moral, of the early successes which led the way to the opening of the great river, due to having the ships and officers ready. So the important advantages obtained by the capture of Port Royal in South Carolina, and of Hatteras

Inlet in North Carolina, within the first six months, were the results of readiness, slight and inadequate as that was in reference to anything like a great naval war.

A brief analysis of the composition of the navy at the opening of the War of Secession, will bring out still more vividly how vitally important to the issue were the additions of the decade 1850-60. In March, 1861, when Lincoln was inaugurated, the available ships-of-war at sea, or in the yards, numbered sixty-one. Of these thirty-four were sailing vessels, substantially worthless; although, as the commerce of the world was still chiefly carried on by sailing ships, they could be of some slight service against these attempting to pass a blockade. For the most part, however, they were but scarecrows, if even respected as such. Of the twenty-seven steamers, only six dated from before 1850; the remainder were being built when I entered the Naval Academy in September, 1856. Their construction, with all that it meant, constituted a principal part of the environment into which I was then brought, of which the recasting of the list of officers was the other most important and significant feature. Both were revolutionary in character, and prophetic of further changes quite beyond the foresight of contemporaries. From this point of view, the period in question has the character of an epoch, initiated, made possible, by the invention of the screw-propeller; which, in addition to the better nautical qualities associated with it, permitted the defence of the machinery by submersion, and of the sides of the ship by the application of armor. In this lay the germ of the race between the armor and the gun, involving almost directly the attempt to reach the parts which armor cannot protect, the underwater body, by means of the torpedo. The increases of weight induced by the competition of gun and armor led necessarily to increase of size, which in turn lent itself to increases of speed that have been pushed beyond the strictly necessary, and at all events are neither militarily nor logically involved in the progress made. It has remained to me always a matter of interest and satisfaction that I first knew the navy, was in close personal contact and association with it, in this period of unconscious transition; and that to the fact of its being yet incomplete I have owed the experience of vessels, now wholly extinct, of which it would be no more than truth to say that in all essential details they were familiar to the men of two hundred years ago. Nay, in their predecessors of that date, as transmitted to us by contemporary prints, it is easy to trace the development, in form, of the ships I have known from the mediæval galley; and this, were the records equally complete, would doubtless find its rudimentary outlines in the triremes of the ancient world. Of this evolution of structure clear evidences remain also in terminology, even now current; survivals which, if the facts were unknown, would provoke curiosity and inquiry as to their origin, as physiologists seek to reconstruct the past of a race from scanty traces still extant.

I have said that the character of the ships then building constituted a chief part of my environment in entering the navy. The effect was inevitable, and amounted in fact simply to making me a man of my period. My most susceptible years were colored by the still lingering traditions of the sail period, and of the "marling-spike seaman;" not that I, always clumsy with my fingers, had any promise of ever distinguishing myself with the marling-spike. This expressive phrase, derived from its chief tool, characterized the whole professional equipment of the then mechanic of the sea, of the man who, given the necessary rope-yarns, and the spars shaped by a carpenter, could take a bare hull as she lay for the first time quietly at anchor from the impetus of her launch, and equip her for sea without other assistance; "parbuckle" on board her spars lying alongside her in the stream, fit her rigging, bend her sails, stow her hold, and present her all a-taunt-o to the men who were to sail her. The navigation of a ship thus equipped was a field of seamanship apart from that of the marling-spike; but the men who sailed her to all parts of the earth were expected to be able to do all the preliminary work themselves, often did do it, and considered it quite as truly a part of their business as the handling her at sea. Of course, in equipping ships, as in all other business, specialization had come in with progress; there were rope-makers, there were riggers who took the ropes ready-made and fitted them for the ship, and there were stevedores to stow holds, etc.; but the tradition ran that the seaman should be able on a pinch to do all this himself, and the tradition kept alive the practice, which derived from the days not yet wholly passed away when he might, and often did, have to refit his vessel in scenes far distant from any help other than his own, and without any resources save those which his ready wit could adapt from materials meant for quite different uses. How to make a jib-boom do the work of a topsail-yard, or to utilize spare spars in rigging a jury-rudder, were specimens of the problems then presented to the aspiring seaman. It was somewhere in the thirties, not so very long before my time, that a Captain Rous, of the British navy, achieved renown – I would say immortal, were I not afraid that most people have forgotten – by bringing his frigate home from Labrador to England after losing her rudder. It is said that he subsequently ran for Parliament, and when on the hustings some doubter asked about his political record, he answered, "I am Captain Rous who brought the *Pique* across the Atlantic without a rudder." Of course the reply was lustily cheered, and deservedly; for in such seas, with a ship dependent upon sails only, it was a splendid, if somewhat reckless achievement. Cooper, in his *Homeward Bound*, places the ship dismasted on the coast of Africa. Close at hand, but on the beach, lies a wrecked vessel with her spar standing; and there is no exaggeration in the words he puts into the mouth of Captain Truck, as he looked upon these resources: "The seaman who, with sticks, and ropes, and blocks enough, cannot rig his ship, might as well stay ashore and publish an hebdomadal."

Such was the marling-spike seaman of the days of Cooper and Marryat, and such was still the able seaman, the "A.B.," of 1855. It was not indeed necessary, nor expected, that most naval officers should do such things with their own hands; but it was justly required that they should know when a job of marling-spike seamanship was well or ill done, and be able to supervise, when necessary. Napoleon is reported to have said that he could judge personally whether the shoes furnished his soldiers were well or ill made; but he needed not to be a shoemaker. Marryat, commenting on one of his characters, says that he had seldom known an officer who prided himself on his "practical" knowledge who was at the same time a good navigator; and that such too often "lower the respect due to them by assuming the Jack Tar." Oddly enough, lunching once with an old and distinguished British admiral, who had been a midshipman while Marryat still lived, he told me that he remembered him well; his reputation, he added, was that of "an excellent seaman, but not much of an officer," an expressive phrase, current in our own service, and which doubtless has its equivalent in all maritime languages.

In my early naval life I came into curious accidental contact with just such a person as Marryat described. I was still at the Academy, within a year of graduation, and had been granted a few days' leave at Christmas. Returning by rail, there seated himself alongside me a gentleman who proved to be a lieutenant from the flag-ship of the Home Squadron, going to Washington with despatches. Becoming known to each other, he began to question me as to what new radicalisms were being fostered in Annapolis. "Are they still wasting the young men's time over French? I would not permit them to learn any other language than their own. And how about seamanship? What do they know about that? As far as I have observed they know nothing about marling-spike seamanship, strapping blocks, fitting rigging, etc. Now I can sit down alongside of any seaman doing a bit of work and show him how it ought to be done; yes, and do it myself." It was Marryat's lieutenant, Phillott, *ipsissimis verbis*. I listened, over-awed by the weight of authority and experience; and I fear somewhat in sympathy, for such talk was in the air, part of the environment of an old order slowly and reluctantly giving way to a new.

Of course I shared this; how should I not, at eighteen? In giving expression to it once, I drew down on my head a ringing buffet from my father, in which he embodied an anecdote of Decatur I never saw elsewhere, and fancy he owed to his boyhood passed near a navy-yard town – Portsmouth, Virginia – while Decatur was in his prime. I had written home with reference to some study, in which probably I did not shine, "What did Decatur know about such things?" A boy may be pardoned for laying himself open to the retort which so many of his superiors equally invited: "Depend upon it, if Decatur had been a student at the Academy, he would, so far as his abilities permitted, have got as far to the front as he always did in fighting. He always aimed to be first. It is told of him that he commanded one of two ships ordered on a common service, in which the other arrived first at a point on the way. Her captain, instead of pushing forward, waited for Decatur to come up; on hearing which the latter exclaimed in his energetic way, 'The d----d fool!'" Decatur, however, also shared, and shared inevitably, the prepossessions of his day. I was told by Mr. Charles King, when President of Columbia College, that he had been present in company with Decatur at one of the early experiments in steam navigation. Crude as the appliances still were, demonstration was conclusive; and Decatur, whatever his prejudices, was open to conviction. "Yes," he said, gloomily, to King, "it is the end of our business; hereafter any man who can boil a tea-kettle will be as good as the best of us." It is notable that in my day a tradition ran that Decatur himself was not thoroughly a seaman. The captain of the first ship in which I served after graduation, a man of much solid information, who had known the commodore's contemporaries, speaking about some occurrence, said to me, "The trouble with Decatur was, that he was not a seaman." I repeated the remark to one of our lieutenants, and he ejaculated, with emphasis, "Yes, that is true." I cannot tell how far these opinions were the result of prepossession in those from whom they derived. There had been hard and factious division in the navy of Decatur's day, culminating in the duel in which he fell; and the lieutenant, at least, was associated by family ties with Decatur's antagonist.

To deny that the methods of the Naval Academy were open to criticism would be to claim for them infallibility. Upon the whole, however, in my time they erred rather on the side of being over-conservative than unduly progressive. Twenty years later, recalling some of our Academy experiences to one of my contemporaries, himself more a man of action than a student, and who had meanwhile distinguished himself by extraordinary courage in the War of Secession – I mean Edward Terry – he said, "Oh yes, those were the days before the flood." The hold-back element was strong, though not sufficiently so to suit such as my friend of the railroad. Objectors laid great stress on the word "practical;" than which, with all its most respectable derivation and association, I know none more frequently – nor more effectually – used as a bludgeon for slaying ideas. Strictly, of course, it means knowing how to do things, and doing them; but colloquially it usually means doing them before learning how. Leap before you look. The practical part is bruising your shins for lack of previous reflection. Of course, no one denies the educational value of breaking your shins, and everything else your own – a burnt child dreads the fire; but the question remains whether an equally good result may not be reached at less cost, and so be more really practical. I recall the fine scorn with which one of our professors, Chauvenet, a man of great and acknowledged ability, practical and other, used to speak of "practical men." "Now, young gentlemen, in adjusting your theodolites in the field, remember not to bear too hard on the screws. Don't put them down with main force, as though the one object was never to unscrew them. If you do, you indent the plate, and it will soon be quite impossible to level the instrument properly. That," he would continue, "is the way with your practical men. There, for instance, is Mr. ----," naming an assistant in another department, known to the midshipmen as Bull-pup, who I suppose had been a practical surveyor; "that is what he does." I presume the denunciation was due to B. P. having at one time borrowed an instrument from the department, and returned it thus maltreated. But "practical," so misapplied – action without thought – was Chauvenet's red rag.

An amusing reminiscence, illustrative of the same common tendency, was told me by General Howard. I had the pleasure of meeting Howard, then in command of one wing of Sherman's army, at Savannah, just after the conclusion of the march to the sea, in 1864. He spoke pleasantly of his associations with my father, when a cadet at the Military Academy, and added, "I remember how he used to say, 'A little common-sense, Mr. Howard, a little common-sense.'" Howard did not say what particular occasions he then had in mind, but a student reciting, and confronted suddenly with some question, or step in a demonstration, which he has failed to master, or upon which he has not reflected, is apt to feel that the practical thing to do is not to admit ignorance; to trust to luck and answer at random. Such a one, explaining a drawing of a bridge to my father, was asked by him what was represented by certain lines, showing the up-stream part of a pier. Not knowing, he replied, "That is a hole to catch the ice in." "Imagine," said my father, in telling me the story, "catching all the ice from above in holes in the piers." A little common-sense – exercised first, not afterwards – is the prescription against leaping before you look, or jamming your screws too hard.

To substitute acquired common-sense – knowledge and reflection – for the cruder and tardier processes of learning by hard personal experience and mistakes, is, of course, the object of all education; and it was this which caused the foundation of the Naval Academy, behind which at its beginning lay the initiative of some of the most reputed and accomplished senior officers of the navy, conscious of the needless difficulties they themselves had had to surmount in reaching the level they had. It involved no detraction from their professional excellence, the excellence of men professionally self-made; but none comprehend the advantages of education better than candid men who have made their way without it. By the time I entered, however, there had been a decided, though not decisive, reaction in professional feeling. Ten years had elapsed since the founding of the school, and already development had gone so far that suspicion and antagonism were aroused. Up to 1850 midshipmen went at once to sea, and, after five years there, spent one at Annapolis; whereupon followed the final examination for a lieutenancy. This effected, the man became a "passed" midshipman. Beginning with 1851, the system was changed. Four years at the Academy were required, after which two at sea, and then examination. This, being a clean break with the past, outraged conservatism; it introduced such abominations as French and extended mathematics; much attention was paid to infantry drill – soldiering; the scheme was not "practical;" and it was doubtless true that the young graduate, despite six months of summer cruising interposed between academic terms, came comparatively green to shipboard. In that particular respect he could not but compare for the moment unfavorably with one who under the old plan would have spent four years on a ship's deck. Whether, that brief period of inexperience passed, he would not be permanently the better for the prior initiation into the *rationale* of his business, few inquired, and time had not yet had opportunity to show.

Perhaps, too, there was among the graduates something of the "freshness" which is attributed to the same age in leaving a university. I do not think it; the immediate contact with conditions but partly familiar to us, yet perfectly familiar to all about us, excited rather a wholesome feeling of inferiority or inadequacy. We had yet to find ourselves. But there remained undoubtedly some antagonism between the old and the new. Not that this ever showed itself offensively; nothing could have been kinder or more open-hearted than our reception by the lieutenants who had not known the Academy, and who probably depreciated it in their hearts. Whatever they thought, nothing was ever said that could reflect upon us, the outcome of the system. It was not even hinted that we might have been turned out in better shape under different conditions. From my personal experience, I hope we proved more satisfactory than may have been expected. When we returned home in 1861, just after the first battle of Bull Run, our third lieutenant said to me that he expected a command, and would be glad to have me as his first lieutenant; and upon my detachment one of the warrant officers expressed his regret that I was not remaining as one of the lieutenants of the ship. Both being men of mature years and long service, and with no obligation to speak, it is permissible to infer that they thought us fit at least to take the deck. As it was, in the uproar of those days, no questions were asked. The usual examinations were waived, and my class was hurried out of the midshipmen's mess into the first-lieutenant's berth. Without exception, I believe, we all had that duty at once – second to the captain – missing thereby the very valuable experience of the deck officer. In the face of considerable opposition, as I was told by Admiral Dupont, the leading officers of the day frustrated the attempt to introduce volunteer officers from the merchant service over our heads; another proof of confidence in us, as at least good raw material. The longer practice of the others at sea was alleged as a reason for thus preferring them, which was seriously contemplated; but the reply was that acquaintance with the organization of a ship-of-war, with her equipment and armament, the general military tone so quickly assimilated by the young and so hardly by the mature, outweighed completely any mere question of attainment in handling a ship. As drill officers, too, the general excellence of the graduates was admitted.

Within a fortnight of doing duty on the forecastle, as a midshipman, I thus found myself first lieutenant of a very respectable vessel. One of my shipmates, less quickly fortunate, was detailed to instruct a number of volunteer officers with the great guns and muskets. One of them said to him, "Yes, you can teach me this, but I expect I can teach you something in seamanship"; a freedom of speech which by itself showed imperfect military temper. At the same moment, I myself had a somewhat similar encounter, which illustrates why the old officers insisted on the superior value of military habit, and the necessarily unmilitary attitude, at first, of the volunteers. I had been sent momentarily to a paddle-wheel merchant-steamer, now purchased for a ship-of-war, the *James Adger*, which had plied between Charleston and New York. A day or two after joining, I saw two of the engineer force going ashore without my knowledge. I stopped them; and a few moments afterwards the chief engineer, who had long been in her when she was a packet, came to me with flaming eyes and angry voice to know by what right I interfered with his men. It had to be explained to him that, unlike the merchant-service, the engine-room was but a department of the military whole of the ship, and that other consent than his was necessary to their departure. A trivial incident, with a whole world of atmosphere behind it.

III
THE NAVAL ACADEMY IN ITS
RELATION TO THE NAVY AT LARGE

1850-1860

Probably there have been at all periods educational excesses in the outlook of some of the Naval Academy authorities; and I personally have sympathized in the main with those who would subordinate the technological element to the more strictly professional. I remember one superintendent – and he, unless rumor was in error, had been one of the early opposition – saying to me with marked elation, "I believe we carry the calculus farther here than they do at West Point." I myself had then long forgotten all the calculus I ever knew, and I fear that with him, too, it was a case of *omne ignotum pro magnifico*. A more curious extravagancy was uttered to me by a professor of applied mathematics. I had happened to say that, while it was well each student should have the opportunity to acquire all he could in that department, I did not think it necessary that every officer of the deck should be able to calculate mathematically the relation between a weight he had to hoist on board and the power of the purchase he was about to use; which I think a mild proposition, considering the centuries during which that knowledge had been dispensed with. "Oh, I differ with you," he replied; "I think it of the utmost importance they should all be able to do so." Nothing like sails, said my friend the sailmaker; nothing like leather, says the shoemaker. I mentioned this shortly afterwards to one of my colleagues, himself an officer of unusual mathematical and scientific attainment. "No!" he exclaimed; "did he *really* say that?"

This was to claim for this mere head knowledge a falsely "practical" value, as distinguished from the educational value of the mental training involved, and from the undoubted imperative need of such acquisitions in those who have to deal with problems of ship construction or other mechanical questions connected with naval material. His position was really as little practical as that of the men who opposed the Academy plan in general as unpractical; as little practical as it would be to maintain that it is essential that every naval officer to-day should be skilled to handle a ship under sail, because the habit of the sailing-ship educated, brought out, faculties and habits of the first value to the military man. Still, there is something not only excusable, but laudable, in a man magnifying his office; and it was well that my friend the professor should have a slightly exaggerated idea of the bearing of the calculus on the daily routine or occasional emergencies of a ship. What is needed is a counterpoise, to correct undue deflection of the like kind, to which an educational institution from its very character and object is always liable. That the Sabbath was made for man, and not man for the Sabbath, is a saying of wide application. The administrator tends to think more of his administrative machine than of the object for which it exists, and the educator to forget that while the foundation is essential, it yet exists only for the building, which is the "practical" end in view. The object of naval education is to make a naval officer. Too much as well as too little of one ingredient will mar the compound; and if exaggeration cannot be wholly avoided, it had better rest upon the professional side. This was the function discharged by the critical attitude of the outside service, such as my friend of the railroad; at times somewhat irrational, but still as a check effective after the manner of other public opinion, of which in fact it was an instance.

In September, 1856, when I entered, professional influence was perhaps in excess. The preceding June had seen the graduation of the last class of "oldsters" – of those who, after five years at sea, had spent the sixth at the Academy, subjected formally to its discipline and methods. I therefore just missed seeing that phase of the Academy's history; but I could not thereby escape the traces of its influence. However transient, this lasted my time. It may be imagined what an influential, yet incongruous, element in a crowd of boys was constituted by introducing among them twenty or thirty young men, too young for ripeness, yet who for five years had been bearing the not slight responsibility of the charge of seamen, often on duty away from their superiors, and permitted substantially all the powers and privileges conceded to their seniors, men of mature years. How could such be brought under the curb of the narrowly ordered life of the school, for the short eight months to which they knew the ordeal was restricted? Could this have been attempted seriously, there would probably have been an explosion; but in truth, as far as my observation went, most of the disciplinary officers, the lieutenants, rather sympathized with irregularities, within pretty wide limits. A midshipman was a being who traditionally had little but the exuberance of his spirits to make up for the discomforts of his lot. The comprehensive saying that what was nobody's business was a midshipman's business epitomized the harrying of his daily life, with its narrow quarters, hard fare, and constant hustling for poor pay. Like the seaman, above whom in earlier days he stood but little, the midshipman had then only his jollity – and his youth – to compensate; and also like the seaman a certain recklessness was conceded to his moments of enjoyment. The very name carried with it the privilege of frolicking.

The old times of license among seafaring men were still of recent memory, and, though practice had improved, opinion remained tolerant. The gunner of the first ship in which I served after graduation told me that in 1832, when he was a young seaman before the mast on board a sloop-of-war in the Mediterranean, on Christmas Eve, there being a two-knot breeze – that is, substantially, calm – at sundown the ship was put under two close-reefed topsails for the night – storm canvas – and then the jollity began. How far it was expected to go may be inferred from the precautions; and we gain here some inkling of the phrase "heavy weather" applied to such conditions. But of the same ship he told me that she stood into the harbor of Malta under all sail, royal and studding sails, to make a flying moor; which,

I must explain to the unprofessional, is to drop an anchor under sail, the cable running out under the force of the ship's way till the place is reached for letting go the second anchor, the ship finally being brought to lie midway between the two. An accurate eye, a close judgment as to the ship's speed, and absolute promptness of execution are needed; for all the sail that is on when the first anchor goes must be off before the second. In this case nothing was started before the first. Within fifteen minutes all was in, the ship moored, sails furled, and yards squared, awaiting doubtless the final touches of the boatswain. Whether the flag of the port was saluted within the same quarter-hour, I will not undertake to say; it would be quite in keeping to have attempted it. System, preparation, and various tricks of the trade go far to facilitate such rapidity. Now I dare say that some of my brother officers may cavil at this story; but I personally believe it, with perhaps two or three minutes' allowance for error in clocks. Much may be accepted of seamen who not uncommonly reefed topsails "in stays" – that is, while the ship was being tacked. Of the narrator's good faith I am certain. It was not with hint one of the stock stories told about "the last cruise;" nor was he a romancer. It came naturally in course of conversation, as one tells any experience; and he added, when the British admiral returned the commander's visit he complimented the ship on the smartest performance he had ever seen. But it is in the combination of license and smartness that the pith of these related stories lies; between them they embody much of the spirit of a time which in 1855 was remembered and influential. Midway in the War of Secession I met the first lieutenant who held the trumpet in that memorable manoeuvre – a man of 1813; now a quiet, elderly, slow-spoken old gentleman, retired, with little to suggest the smart officer, at the stamp of whose foot the ship's company jumped, to use the gunner's expression.

Such performances exemplify the ideals that still obtained – were in full force – in the navy as first I knew it. In the ship in which the gunner and I were then serving, it was our common performance to "Up topgallant-masts and yards, and loose sail to a bowline," in three minutes and a half from the time the topmen and the masts started aloft together from the deck. For this time I can vouch myself, and we did it fairly, too; though I dare say we would have hesitated to carry the sails in a stiff breeze without a few minutes more. It was a very dramatic and impressive performance. The band, with drum and fife, was part of it. When all was reported ready from the three masts – but not before – it was permitted to be eight o'clock. The drums gave three rolls, the order "Sway across, let fall," was given, the yards swung into their places, the sails dropped and were dragged out by their bowlines to facilitate their drying, the bell struck eight, the flag was hoisted, and close on the drums followed the band playing the "Star-Spangled Banner," while the ship's company went to breakfast. It was the transformation scene of a theatre; within five minutes the metamorphosis was complete. There was doubtless a flavor of the circus about it all, but it was a wholesome flavor and tonicked the

professional appetite. Yes, and the natural appetite, too; your breakfast tasted better, especially if
some other ship had got into trouble with one of
her yards or sails. "Did you see what a mess the
---- made of fore-topgallant-yard this morning?"
An old boatswain's mate of the ship used to tell
me one of his "last-cruise" stories, of when he "was
in the *Delaware*, seventy-four, up the Mediterranean, in 1842." Of course, the *Delaware* had beaten
the *Congress's* time; the last ship always did. Then
he would add: "I was in the foretop in those days,
and had the fore-topgallant-yard; and if one of us
fellows let his yard show on either side of the
mast before the order 'Sway across,' we could
count on a dozen when we got down just as sure
as we could count on our breakfast." Flogging was
not abolished until about 1849. No wonder men
were jolly when they could be, without worrying
about to-morrow's headache.

Part of the preparation was to let the captain
know beforehand that it was eight o'clock, and get
his authority that it might be so; subject always to
the yet higher authority that the yards and sails
were ready. If they were not, so much the worse
for eight o'clock. It had to wait quite as imperatively as the sun did for Joshua. Sunset, when the
masts and yards came down, was equally under
bonds; it awaited the pleasure of the captain or
admiral. Indeed, in my time a story ran of a
court-martial at a much earlier day, sitting in a
capital case. By law, each day's session must end
by sundown. On the occasion in question, sundown was reported to the admiral – or, rather,
commodore; we had no admirals then. He sent to

know how soon the court could finish. The reply was, in about fifteen minutes. "Tell the officer of the deck not to make it sundown until he hears from me;" and, in defiance of the earth's movement, the colors were kept flying in attestation that the sun was up. One other hour of the twenty-four, noon, was brought in like manner to the captain's attention, and required his action, but it was treated with more deference; recognition rather than authority was meted to it, and it was never known to be tampered with. The circumstance of the sun's crossing the ship's meridian was unique in the day; and the observation of the fact, which drew on deck all the navigating group with their instruments, establishing the latitude immediately and precisely, was of itself a principal institution of the ship's economy. Such claims were not open to trifling; and were there not also certain established customs, almost vested interests, such as the seven-bell nip, cocktail or otherwise, connected with the half-hour before, when "the sun was over the fore-yard"? I admit I never knew whence the latter phrase originated, nor just what it meant, but it has associations. Like sign language, it can be understood.

I was myself shipmate, as they say, with most of this sort of thing; for with its good points and its bad it did not disappear until the War of Secession, the exigencies of which drove out alike the sails and the sailor. The abolition of the grog ration in 1862 may be looked upon as a chronological farewell to a picturesque past. We did not so understand it. Contemporaries are apt to be blind to bloodless revolutions. Had we seen the full bearing, perhaps there might have been observed a professional sundown, in recognition of the fact that the topgallant-yards had come down for the last time, ending one professional era. A protest was recorded by one eccentric character, a survival whom Cooper unfortunately never knew, who hoisted a whiskey demijohn at the peak of his gunboat – the ensign's allotted place. To the admiral's immediate demand for an explanation, he replied that that was the flag he served under; but he was one of those to whom all things are forgiven. The seaman remains, and must always remain while there are seas to cross and to rule; but the sailor, in his accomplishments and in his defects, began then to depart, or to be evolutionized into something entirely different. I am bound to admit that in the main the better has survived, but, now that such hairs as I have are gray, I may be permitted to look back somewhat wistfully and affectionately on that which I remember a half-century ago; perhaps to sympathize with the seamen of the period, who saw themselves swamped out of sight and influence among the vast numbers required by the sudden seven or eight fold expansion of the navy for that momentous conflict. Occasionally one of these old salts, mournful amid his new environment, would meet me, and say, "Ah! Mr. Mahan, the navy isn't what it was!" True, in 1823, Lord St. Vincent, then verging on ninety, had made the same remark to George IV.; and I am quite sure, if the aged admiral had searched his memory, he could have recalled it in the mouth of some veteran of 1750. The worst of it is, this is perennially true. From period to period the gain exceeds, but still there has been loss as well; and to sentiment, ranging over the past, the loss stands more conspicuous. "Memory reveals every rose, but secreteth its thorn."

This is the more apparent when the change has been sudden, or on such a scale as to overwhelm, by mere bulk, that subtle influence for which we owe to the French the name of *esprit de corps*. It is the breath of the body, the breath of life. Before the War of Secession our old friends the marines had a deserved reputation for fidelity, which could not survive the big introduction of alien matter into the "corps." I remember hearing an officer of long service say that he had known but a single instance of a marine deserting; and as to the general fact there was no dissent among the by-standers. The same could scarcely be said now, nor of seamen then. The sentiment of particular faithfulness had been nurtured in the British marines under times and conditions which made them at a critical moment the saviors of discipline, and thereby the saviors of the state. It is needless to philosophize the strength of such a tradition, so established, nor its effect on each member of the body; and from thence, not improbably, it was transmitted to our younger navy. Whencever coming, there it was. One marine private, in the ship to which I belonged, returning from liberty on shore, was heard saying to another with drunken impressiveness, "Remember, our motto is, 'Patriotism and laziness.'" Of course, this went round the ship, greatly delighting on both counts our marine officers, and became embodied in the chaff that passed to and fro between the two corps; of which one saying, "The two most useless things in a ship were the captain of marines and the mizzen-royal," deserves for its drollery to be committed to writing, now that mizzen-royals have ceased to be. May it be long before the like extinction awaits the captains of marines! Our own, however, an eccentric man, who had accomplished the then rare feat of working his way up from the ranks, used to claim that marines were an absurdity. "It is having one army to keep another army in order," he would say. This was once true, and might with equal truth be said of a city police force – one set of citizens to keep the other citizens orderly. In the olden time it had been the application of the sound statesmanship dogma, "*Divide et impera.*" For this, in the navy, happily, the need no longer exists; but I can see no reason to believe the time at hand when we can dispense with a corps of seamen, the specialty of which is infantry – and shore expedition when necessary. Patriotism, as our marine understood it, was sticking by your colors and your corps, and doing your duty through thick and thin; no bad ideal.

In like mingling of good and evil, the oldsters at the Naval Academy, along with some things objectionable, including a liberty that under the conditions too often resembled license, brought with them sound traditions, which throughout my stay there constituted a real *esprit de corps*. In nothing was this more conspicuous than in the attitude towards hazing. Owing to circumstances I will mention later, I entered at once the class which, as I understand, most usually perpetrated the outrageous practices that became a scandal in the country – the class, that is, which is entering on its second year at the Academy. My home having always been at the Military Academy, I, without much thinking, expected to find rife the same proceedings which had prevailed there from time to me immemorial. Such anticipations made deeper and more lasting the impression produced by the contrary state of things, and yet more by the wholly different tone prevalent at Annapolis. Not only was hazing not practised, but it scarcely obtained even the recognition of mention; it was not so much reprobated as ignored; and, if it came under discussion at all, it was dismissed with a turn of the nose, as something altogether beneath us. That is not the sort of thing we do here. It may be all very well at West Point – much as "what would do for a marine could not be thought of for a seaman" – but we were "officers and gentlemen," and thought no small beans of ourselves as such. There were at times absurd manifestations of this same precocious dignity, of which I may speak later; still, as O'Brien said of Boatswain Chucks, "You may laugh at such assumptions of gentility, but did any one of his shipmates ever know Mr. Chucks to do an unhandsome or a mean action? – and why? Because he aspired to be a gentleman."

While I can vouch for this general state of feeling, I cannot be sure of its derivation; but I have always thought it due to the presence during the previous five years of the "oldsters," nominally under the same discipline as ourselves, but looked up to with the respect and observance which at that age are naturally given to those two or three seasons older. And these men were not merely more advanced in years. They were matured beyond their age by early habits of responsibility and command, and themselves imbued by constant contact with the spirit of the phrase "an officer and a gentleman," which constitutes the norm of military conduct. Their intercourse with their seniors on board ship had been much closer than that which was possible at the school. This atmosphere they brought with them to a position from which they could not but most powerfully influence us. How far the tradition might have been carried on, in smooth seas, I do not know; but along with many other things, good and bad, it was shattered by the War of Secession. The school was precipitately removed to Newport, where it was established in extemporized and temporary surroundings; the older undergraduates were hurried to sea, while the new entries were huddled together on two sailing frigates moored in the harbor, dissociated from the influence of those above them. The whole anatomy and, so to say, nervous system of the organization were dislocated. For better or for worse, perhaps for better and for worse, the change was more like death and resurrection than life and growth. The potent element which the oldster had contributed, and the upper classes absorbed and perpetuated, was eliminated at once and entirely by the detachment of the senior cadets and the segregation of the new-corners. New ideals were evolved by a mass of school-boys, severed from those elder associates with the influence of whom no professors nor officers can vie. How hazing came up I do not know, and am not writing its history. I presume it is one of the inevitable weeds that school-boy nature brings forth of itself, unless checked by unfavorable environment. I merely note its almost total absence in my time; its subsequent existence was unhappily notorious.

A general good-humored tolerance, easy-going, and depending upon a mutual understanding, none the less clear because informal, characterized the relations of the officers and students. Primarily, each were in the appreciation of the other officers and gentlemen. So far there was implicit equality; and while the ones were in duty bound to enforce academic regulations, which the others felt an equal obligation to disregard, it was a kind of game in which they did not much mind being losers, provided we did not trespass on the standards of the gentleman, and of the officer liberally construed. They, I think, had an unacknowledged feeling that while under school-boy, or collegiate, discipline as to times or manners, some relaxation of strict official correctness must be endured. Larking, sometimes uproarious, met with personal sympathy, if official condemnation. Nor did we resent being detected by what we regarded as fair means; to which we perhaps gave a pretty wide interpretation. The exceptional man, who inspected at unaccustomed hours, which we considered our own prescriptive right – though not by rules – who came upon us unawares, was apt to be credited with rather unofficer-like ideas of what was becoming, and suspected of the not very gentlemanly practice of wearing noiseless rubber shoes. That intimation of his approach was conveyed by us from room to room by concerted taps on the gas-pipes was fair war; nor did our opponents seem to mind what they could not but clearly hear. Indeed, I think most of them were rather glad to find evidences of order and propriety prevailing, where possibly but for those kindly signals they might have detected matter for report.

There was one lieutenant, however, the memory of whom was still green as a bay-tree in my day, though it would have been blasted indeed could cursing have blighted it, to whom the game of detective seemed to possess the fascination of the chase; and so successful was he that his baffled opponents could not view the matter dispassionately, nor accept their defeat in sportsman-like spirit. I knew him later; he had a saturnine appearance, not calculated to conciliate a victim, but he liked a joke, especially of the practical kind, and for the sake of one successfully achieved could forgive an offender. Night surprises, inroads on the enemy's country, at the hours when we were mistakenly supposed to be safe in bed, and regulations so required, were favorite stratagems with him. On one occasion, so tradition ran, some half-dozen midshipmen had congregated in a room "after taps," and, with windows carefully darkened, had contrived an extempore kitchen to fry themselves a mess of oysters. The process was slow, owing to the number of oysters the pan could take at once and the largeness of the expectant appetites; but it had progressed nearly to completion, when without premonition the door opened and ---- appeared. He asked no questions and offered no comments, but, walking to the platter, seized it and threw out of the window the accumulated results of an hour's weary work. No further notice of the delinquency followed; the discomfiture of the sufferers sufficiently repaid his sense of humor. At another midnight hour a midshipman visiting in a room not his, lured thither, let us hope, by the charms of intellectual conversation, was warned by the gas-pipes that the enemy was on the war-path. Retreat being cut off, he took refuge under a bed, but unwittingly left a hand visible. ---- caught sight of it, walked to the bed, flashed his lantern in the eyes of its occupant, who naturally was sleeping as never before, and at the same time trod hard on the exposed fingers. A squeal followed this unexpected attention, and the culprit had to drag himself out; but the lieutenant was satisfied, and let him go at that.

I have said that larking met with more than toleration – with sympathy. The once magic word "midshipman" seemed to cloak any outburst of frolicking; otherwise some exhibitions I witnessed could scarcely have passed unscathed. They were felt to be in character by the older officers; and, while obliged to reprehend, I doubt whether some of them would not have more enjoyed taking a share. They knew, too, that we were just as proud as they of the service, and that under all lay an entire readiness to do or to submit to that which we and they alike recognized as duty. Sometimes rioting went rather too far, but for the most part it was harmless. One rather grave incident, shortly before my entry, derived its humor mainly from the way in which it was treated by the superintendent. One of the out-buildings of the Academy, either because offensive or out of sheer deviltry, was set on fire and destroyed. The perpetrator of this startling practical joke was Alexander F. Crosman, of the '51 Date, whom many of us yet living remember well. Small in stature, with something of the "chip-on-the-shoulder" characteristic, often seen in such, he was conspicuous for a certain chivalrous gallantry of thought and mien, the reflection of a native brilliant courage; a trait which in the end caused his death, about 1870, by drowning, in the effort to save an imperilled boat's crew. The superintendent, a man of ponderous dimensions, and equally ponderous but rapid speech – though it is due to say also unusually accomplished, both professionally and personally – was greatly outraged and excited at this defiance of discipline. The day following he went out to meet the corps, when it had just left some formation, and, calling a halt, delivered a speech on the basis of the *Articles of War*, a copy of which he brandished before his audience. These ancient ordinances, among many other denunciations of naval crimes and misdemeanors, pronounced the punishment of death, or "such other worse" as a court-martial might adjudge, upon "any person in the Navy who shall maliciously set on fire, or otherwise destroy, any government property not then in the possession of an *enemy, pirate, or rebel*." The gem of oratory hereupon erected was paraphrased as follows by the culprit himself, aided and abetted in his lyrical flight by his room-mate, John S. Barnes, who, after graduating left the service, returned for the War of Secession, and subsequently resigned finally. To this survivor of the two collaborators I owe the particulars of the affair. How many more "traitors" there were I know not. Those who recall the speaker will recognize that the parody must have followed closely the real words of the address:

"Young gentlemen assembled! – It makes no matter where – I only want to speak to you, So hear me where you are.

"Some vile incendiary Last night was prowling round, Who set fire to our round-house And burned it to the ground.

"I'll read the Naval Law; The man who dares to burn A round-house, – not the Enemy's, – A traitor's fate shall learn.

"And if a man there be, Who does this traitor know, And keeps it to himself, He shall suffer death also!

"'Tis well, then, to tell, then, Who did this grievous ill; And, d--n him, I will hang him, So help me God! I will!"

If anything could have added to the gayety of the fire, such an outburst would.

In after years I sailed under the command of this speechmaker. At monthly musters he reserved to himself the prerogative of reading the *Articles*, probably thinking that he did it more effectively than the first lieutenant; in which he was quite right. It so happened that, owing to doubt whether a certain paragraph applied to the Marine Corps, Congress had been pleased to make a special enactment that the word "persons" in such and such a clause "should be construed to include marines." Coming as this did near the end, some humorist was moved to remark that the first Sunday in the month muster was for the purpose of informing us authoritatively that a marine was a person. As the captain read this interesting announcement, his voice assumed a gradual *crescendo*, concluding with a profound emphasis on the word "marines," which he accompanied with a half turn and a flourish of the book towards that honorable body, drawn up in full uniform, at parade rest, its venerable captain, whose sandy hair was fast streaking with gray, standing at its head, his hands meekly crossed over his sword-hilt, the blade hanging down before him; all doubtless suitably impressed with this definition of their status, which for greater certainty they heard every month. It was very fine, very fine indeed; appealing to more senses than one.

The shore drills – infantry and field artillery – furnished special occasions for organized – or disorganized – upheavals of animal spirits. For these exercises we then had scant respect. They were "soldiering;" and from time immemorial soldier had been an adjective to express uselessness, or that which was so easy as to pass no man's ability. A soldier's wind, for example, was a wind fair both ways – to go and to return; no demands on brains there, much less on seamanship. The curious irrelevancy of such applications never strikes persons; unless, indeed, a perception of incongruity is the soul of wit, a definition which I think I have heard. To depart without the ceremony of saying good-bye takes its name from the most elaborately civil of people – French leave; while the least perturbable of nations has been made to contribute an epithet, Dutch, to the courage derived from the whiskey-bottle. In the latter case, however, I fancy that, besides the tradition of long-ago national rivalries, there may have been the idea that to excite a Dutchman you must, as they say, light a fire under him; or as was forcibly remarked by a midshipman of my time of his phlegmatic room-mate, he had to kick him in the morning to get him started for the day.

To return to the shore drills: these were then committed to one of the civil professors of the Academy, a fact which itself spoke for the familiarity with them of the sea lieutenants. As these always exercised us at ships' guns, the different estimation which the two obtained in the outside service was too obvious to escape quick-witted young fellows, and it was difficult to overcome the resultant disrespect. The professor was not one to effect the impossible. He was a graduate of West Point, a man of ability, not lacking in dignity, and personally worthy of all respect; but he stuttered badly, and this impediment not only received no mercy from youth, but interfered with the accuracy of manoeuvres where the word of command needed to be timely in utterance. Report ran that on one occasion, advancing by column of companies, while the professor was struggling with "H-H-H-Halt!" the leading company, composed martyrs to discipline, marched over the sea-wall into three feet of water. Had the water been deeper, they might have been less literal. Despite his military training, his bearing and carriage had not the strong soldierly stamp which might redeem his infirmity, and even in the class-room a certain whimsical atmosphere seemed borne from the drill-ground. He, I believe, was the central figure of one of the most humorous scenes in Herman Melville's *White Jacket*, a book which, despite its prejudiced tone, has preserved many amusing and interesting inside recollections of a ship-of-war of the olden time. The naval instructor on board the frigate is using Rodney's battle of 1782 to illustrate on the blackboard the principles of naval tactics to the class of midshipmen. "Now, young gentlemen, you see this disabled French ship in the corner, far to windward of her fleet, between it and the enemy. She has lost all three masts, and the greater part of the ship's company are killed and wounded; what will you do to save her?" To this knotty problem many extemporized "practical" answers are given, of which the most plausible is by Mr. Dash, of Virginia – "I should nail my colors to the mast and let her sink under me." As this could scarcely be called saving her, Mr. Dash is rebuked for irrelevance; but, after the gamut of possible solutions has been well guessed over, the instructor announces impressively, "That ship, young gentlemen, cannot be saved."

I cannot say that he dealt with us thus tantalizingly; but one of my contemporaries used to tell a story of his personal experience which was generically allied to the above. At the conclusion of some faulty manoeuvre, the instructor remarked aloud: "This all went wrong, owing to Mr. P.'s not standing fast in his own person. We will now repeat it, for the particular benefit of Mr. P." The repetition ensued, and in its course the instructor called out, "Be careful, Mr. P., and stand fast where you are." "I am standing fast," replied P., incautiously. "R-R-Report Mr. P. for talking in ranks." At the Academy, naval tactics were not within his purview; and of all our experiences with him in the class-room, one ludicrous incident alone remains with me. One of my class, though in most ways well at head, was a little alarmed about his standing in infantry tactics. He therefore at a critical occasion attempted to carry the text-book with him to the blackboard. This surreptitious deed, being not to get advantage over a fellow, but to save himself, was condoned by public opinion; but, being unused to such deceits, in his agitation he copied his figure upside down and became hopelessly involved in the demonstration. The professor next day took occasion to comment slightingly on our general performance, but "as to Mr. ----," he added, derisively, "he did r-r-r-wretchedly."

I sometimes wonder that we learned anything about "soldiering," but we did in a way. The principles and theory were mastered, if performance was slovenly; and in execution, as company officers, we got our companies "there," although just how we did it might be open to criticism. In our last year the adjutant in my class, who graduated at its head, on the first occasion of forming the battalion, after some moments of visible embarrassment could think of no order more appropriate than "Form your companies fore and aft the pavement." Fore and aft is "lengthwise" of a ship. No humiliation attended such a confession of ignorance – on that subject; but had the same man "missed stays" when in charge of the deck, he would have been sorely mortified. His successor of to-day probably never will have a chance to miss stays. There thus ran through our drills an undercurrent of levity, which on provocation would burst out almost spontaneously into absurdity. On one occasion the battalion was drawn up in line, fronting at some distance the five buildings which then constituted the midshipmen's quarters. The intimation was given that we were to advance and then charge. Once put in motion, I know not whether stuttering lost the opportunity of stopping us, but the pace became quicker and quicker till the whole body broke into a run, rushed cheering tumultuously through the passages between the houses, and reformed, peaceably enough, on the other side. The captains all got a wigging for failing to keep us in hand; but they were powerless. The whole thing was without preconcertment or warning. It could hardly have happened, however, had the instinct of discipline been as strong in these drills as in others.

A more deliberate prank was played with the field artillery. These light pieces, being of the nature of cannon rather than muskets, obtained more deference, being recognized as of the same genus with the great guns which then constituted a ship's broadside. On one occasion they were incautiously left out overnight on the drill-ground. Between tattoo and taps, 9.30 to 10 P.M., was always a half-hour of release from quarters. There was mischief ready-made for idle hands to do. The guns were taken in possession, rushed violently to and fro in mock drill performance, and finally taken to pieces, the parts being scattered promiscuously in all directions. Dawn revealed an appearance of havoc resembling a popular impressionist representation of a battle-field. Here a caisson with its boxes, severed from their belongings, stretched its long pole appealingly towards heaven; the wheels had been dispersed to distant quarters of the ground and lay on their sides; elsewhere were the guns, sometimes reversed and solitary, at others not wholly dismounted, canted at an angle, with one wheel in place. As there were six of them, complete in equipments, the scene was extensive and of most admired confusion; ingenuity had exhausted itself in variety, to enhance picturesqueness of effect. How the lieutenant in charge accounted for all this happening without his interference, I do not know. Certainly there was noise enough, but then that half-hour always was noisy. The superintendent of that time had, when walking, a trick of grasping the lapel of his coat with his right hand, and twitching it when preoccupied. The following day, as he surveyed conditions, it seemed as if the lapel might come away; but he made us no speech, nor, as far as I know, was any notice taken of the affair. No real damage had been done, and the man would indeed have been hard-heartedly conscientious who would grudge the action which showed him so comical a sight.

I once heard an excellent first lieutenant – Farragut's own through the principal actions of the War of Secession – say that where there was obvious inattention to uniform there would always be found slackness in discipline. It may be, therefore, that our habits as to uniform were symptomatic of the same easy tolerance which bore with such extravagances as I have mentioned; the like of which, in overt act, was not known to me in my later association with the Academy as an officer. We had a prescribed uniform, certainly; but regulations, like legislative acts, admit of much variety of interpretation and latitude in practice, unless there is behind them a strong public sentiment. In my earlier days there was no public sentiment of the somewhat martinet kind; such as would compel all alike to wear an overcoat because the captain felt cold. In practice, there was great laxity in details. I remember, in later days and later manners, when we were all compelled to be well buttoned up to the throat, a young officer remarked to me disparagingly of another, "He's the sort of man, you know, who would wear a frock-coat unbuttoned." There's nothing like classification. My friend had achieved a feat in natural history; in ten words he had defined a species. On another occasion the same man remorselessly wiped out of existence another species, consecrated by generations of blue-books and *Naval Regulations*. "I know nothing of superior officers," he said; "senior officers, if you choose; but superior, no!" Whether the *Naval Regulations* have yet recognized this obvious distinction, whether it is no longer "superior officers," but only senior officers, who are not to be "treated with contempt," etc., I have not inquired. Apart from such amusing criticism of the times past, it is undoubtedly true that attention to minutiæ is symptomatic of a much more important underlying spirit, one of exactness and precision running through all the management of a ship and affecting her efficiency. I concede that a thing so trifling as the buttoning of a frock-coat may indicate a development and survival of the fittest; but in 1855-60 frock-coats had not been disciplined, and in accordance with the tone of the general service we midshipmen were tacitly indulged in a similar freedom. This tolerance may have been in part a reaction from the vexatious and absurd interference of a decade before with such natural rights as the cut of the beard – not as matter of neatness, but of pattern. Even for some time after I graduated, unless I misunderstood my informants, officers in the British navy were not permitted to wear a full beard, nor a mustache; and we had out-breaks of similar regulative annoyance in our own service, one of which furnished Melville with a striking chapter. Discussing the matter in my presence once, the captain of a frigate said, "There is one reply to objectors; if they do not wish to conform, they can leave the service." Clearly, however, a middle-aged man cannot throw up his profession thus easily.

Another circumstance that may have contributed to indifference to details of dress was the carefulness with which the old-time sea officers had constantly to look after the set and trim of the canvas. Every variation of the wind, every change of course, every considerable manoeuvre, involved corresponding changes in the disposition of the sails, which must be effected not only correctly, but with a minute exactness extending to half a hundred seemingly trivial details, upon precision in which depended – and justly – an officer's general reputation for officer-like character. Not only so, but the mere weight of rigging and sails, and the stretching resultant on such strain, caused recurring derangements, which, permitted, became slovenliness. Yards accurately braced, sheets home alike, weather leaches and braces taut, with all the other and sundry indications which a well-trained eye instinctively sought and noted, were less the dandyism than the self-respecting neatness of a well-dressed ship, and were no bad substitute, as tests, for buttoned frock-coats. The man without fault in the one might well be pardoned, by others as well as himself, for neglects which had never occurred to him to be such. His attention was centred elsewhere, as a man may think more of his wife's dress than his own. After all, one cannot be always stretched with four pins, as the French say; there must be some give somewhere.

The frock was then the working coat of the navy. There was fuller dress for exceptional occasions, in which, at one festive muster early in the cruise, we all had to appear, to show that we had it; but otherwise it was generally done up in camphor. The jacket, which was prescribed to the midshipmen of the Academy, had informal recognition in the service, and we took our surviving garments of that order with us to sea, to wear them out. But, while here and there some officer would sport one, they could scarcely be called popular. One of our lieutenants, indeed, took a somewhat sentimental view of the jacket. "There was Mr. S.," he said to me, speaking of a brother midshipman, "on deck yesterday with a jacket. It looked so tidy and becoming. If there had been anything aloft out of the way, I could say to him, 'Mr. S., just jump up there, will you, and see what is the matter?'" War, which soon afterwards followed with its stern preoccupations and incidental deprivations, induced inevitably deterioration in matters of dress. With it the sack-coat, or pilot-jacket, burrowed its way in, the cut and insignia of these showing many variations. The undergraduates at the Academy in my day had for all uses a double-breasted jacket; but it was worn buttoned, or not, at choice. On the rolling collar a gold foul anchor – an anchor with a rope cable twined round it – was prescribed; but, while a standard embroidered pattern was supplied at the Academy store, those who wished procured for themselves metal anchors, and these not only were of many shapes and sizes, but for symmetrical pinning in place demanded an accuracy of eye and hand which not every one had. The result was variegated and fanciful to a degree; but I doubt if any of the officers thought aught amiss. So the regulation vest buttoned up to the chin, but very many had theirs made with rolling collar, to show the shirt. I had a handsome, very dandy, creole classmate, whom an admiring family kept always well supplied with fancy shirts; and I am sure, if precisians of the present day could have seen him starting out on a Saturday afternoon to pay his visits, with everything just so – except in a regulation sense – and not a back hair out of place, they must have accepted the results as a testimony to the value of the personal factor in uniform. Respect for individual tastes was rather a mark of that time in the navy. Seamen handy with their needle were permitted, if not encouraged, to embroider elaborate patterns, in divers colors, on the fronts of their shirts, and turned many honest pennies by doing the like for less skillful shipmates. Pride in personal appearance, dandyism, is quite consonant with military feeling, as history has abundantly shown; and it may be that something has been lost as well as gained in the suppression of individual action, now when an inspecting officer may almost be said to carry with him a yard-stick and micrometer to detect deviations.

A very curious manifestation of this disposition to bedeck the body was the prevalence of tattooing. If not universal, it was very nearly so among seamen of that day. Elaborate designs covering the chest, or back, or arms, were seen everywhere, when the men were stripped on deck for washing. There was no possible inducement to this except a crude love of ornament, or a mere imitation of a prevailing fashion, which is another manifestation of the same propensity. The inconvenience of being branded for life should have been felt by men prone to desertion; but the descriptive lists which accompany every crew were crowded with such remarks as, "Goddess of Liberty, r. f. a." – right forearm – the which, if a man ran away, helped the police of the port to identify him. My memory does not retain the various emblems thus perpetuated in men's skins; they were largely patriotic and extremely conventional, each practised tattooer having doubtless his own particular style. Many midshipmen of my time acquired these embellishments. I wonder if they have not since been sorry.

IV
THE NAVAL ACADEMY IN
ITS INTERIOR WORKINGS

PRACTICE CRUISES
1855-60

In the preceding pages my effort has been to re-constitute for the reader the navy, in body and in spirit, as it was when I entered in 1856 and had been during the period immediately preceding. There was no marked change up to 1861, when the War of Secession began. The atmosphere and environment which I at first encountered upon my entrance to the Naval Academy, in 1856, had nothing strange, or even unfamiliar, to a boy who had devoured Cooper and Marryat – not as mere tales of adventure, but with some real apprecia-tion and understanding of conditions as by them depicted. I had studied, as well as been absorbed by them. Cooper is much more of an idealist and romancer than is Marryat, who belongs essentially to the realistic school. Some of the Englishman's presentations may be exaggerated, though not beyond probability – elaborated would perhaps be a juster word – and in one passage he expressly abjures all willingness to present a caricature of the seaman he had known. Cooper, on the other hand, while his sea scenes are well worked up, has given us personalities which, tested by Mar-ryat's, are made out of the whole cloth; creations, if you will, but not resemblances. Marryat entered the navy earlier than his rival, and followed the sea longer; his experience was in every way wider.

Even in my time could be seen justifications of his portrayal; but who ever saw the like of Tom Coffin, Trysail, or Boltrope?

The interested curiosity concerning all things naval which possessed me, and held me enthralled by the mere sight of an occasional square-rigged vessel, such as at rare intervals passed our home on the Hudson, fifty miles from the sea, led me also to pore over a copy of the *Academy Regulations* which the then superintendent, Captain Louis Goldsborough, (afterwards Admiral), had sent my father. The two had been acquaintances in Paris, in the twenties of the century and of their own ages. I have always had a morbid fondness for registers and time-tables, and over them have wasted precious hours; but on this occasion the practice saved me a year. I discovered that, contrary to the established rule at the Military Academy, an appointee to the Naval might enter any class for which he could pass the examinations. Further inquiry confirmed this, and I set about fitting myself. At that date, even more than at present, the standard of admission to the two academies had to take into account the very differing facilities for education in different parts of the country, as well as the strictly democratic method of appointment. This being in the gift of the representative of the congressional district, the candidates came from every section; and, being selected by the various considerations which influence such patronage, the mass of lads who presented themselves necessarily differed greatly in acquirements. Hence, to enter either Annapolis or West Point only very rudimentary knowledge was demanded. Having grown up myself so far amid abundant opportunity, and been carefully looked after, I found that I was quite prepared to enter the class above the lowest, except in one or two minor matters, easily picked up. Thus forewarned, I came forearmed. There were probably in every class a dozen who could have done the same, but they accepted the prevailing custom without question. I believe I was the only one fortunate enough to make this gain. In some instances before, and in many after, the academic work was for certain classes compressed within three years, but I was singular in entering a class already of a twelvemonth's standing.

About my own examination I remember nothing except that it was successful; but one incident occurred in my hearing which has stuck by me for a half-century. One other youth underwent the same tests. He had already once entered, two or three years before, and afterwards had failed to pass one of the semi-annual tests. Such cases frequently were dropped into the next lower class, but the rule then was that a second similar lapse was final. This had befallen my present associate; but he had "influence," which obtained for him another appointment, conditional upon passing the requirements for the third class, fourth being the lowest. Examinations then were oral, not written; and, preoccupied though I was with my own difficulties, I could not but catch at times sounds of his. He was being questioned in grammar and in parsing, which I have heard – I do not know whether truly – are now looked upon as archaic methods of teaching; and the sentence propounded to him was, "Mahomet was driven from Mecca, but he returned in triumph." His rendering of the first words I did not hear, my attention not being arrested until "but," which proved to him a truly disjunctive conjunction. "But!" he ejaculated – "but!" and paused. Then came the "practical" leap into the unknown. "'But' is an adverb, qualifying 'he,' showing what he is doing." Poor fellow, it was no joke to him, nor probably his fault, but that of circumstances. When released from the ordeal, we stood round together, awaiting sentence. He was in despair, nor could I honestly encourage him. "Look at you," he said, "as quiet as if nothing had happened" – I was by no means confident that I had cause for elation. "If I were as sure that I had passed as that you have, I should be skipping all over the place." I never heard of him again; but suppose from his name, which I remember, and his State, of which I am less sure, that he took, and in any event would have taken, the Confederate side in the coming troubles. His loss by this failure was therefore probably less than it then seemed.

An intruder, in breach of well-settled precedent, might have expected to be looked on askance by the class which I thus unusually entered. Not the faintest indication of discontent was ever shown, nor I believe felt, even by those over whom I subsequently passed by such standing as I established, although the fact meant promotion over them. The spirit of the officer and the gentleman, which disdained hazing, disdained discourtesy equally, and thrust aside with the generosity of youth the jealousy that mature years more readily cherishes towards competitors. The habit in those days was to distinguish classes, not by the year of graduation, but by that of entry – colloquially, the so-and-so "Date" – a manner derived from an earlier period, when there was no other chronological point of departure for the career; and in those "days before the flood" nothing would have tempted us to depart from a time-honored custom. "Dates" frequently established among their contemporaries reputations analogous to those of individuals. At that time the "'41 Date," then in the prime of life, was obnoxious to those below it; not for its own fault, but because of its numbers, which, with promotion strictly by seniority, constituted a superincumbent mass that could not but be regarded bitterly by those who followed. At present there would be the consolation that retirement, though distant, would ultimately sweep them all away nearly simultaneously; but there was then no retired list. Whatever the motive, the Secretary of the Navy had been moved to introduce, in 1841, over two hundred midshipmen,[4] which put an almost total stop to appointments for several subsequent years, and gave the "Date" the invidious distinction it enjoyed. The well-known character in the service whose hoisting a demijohn for a flag I have before mentioned, and who found this great overplus above him, was credited with saying that those of them who did not drink themselves to death would strut themselves to death – a comment which testified rather to the warmth of his feelings than to the merits of the case. Of course, the greater the total, the more numerous the unworthy; and the unfortunate natural bias of mankind notices these more readily than it does the capable.

The class to which I now found myself admitted was the "'55 Date," and whatever their reputation in the service, then or thereafter, they thought themselves uncommonly fine fellows, distinctly above the average – not perhaps in attainments, which was a subsidiary matter, but in tone and fellowship. One among them, a turn-back from the previous Date, and for two years my room-mate, used to declare enthusiastically that he was glad of his misfortune, finding himself in so much better a crowd. I doubt if I could have gone as far as this, but in the general estimate I agreed fully. We numbered then twenty-eight, having started with forty-nine a twelvemonth before. Three years later we were graduated, twenty. The dwindling numbers testifies rather to the imperfection of educational processes throughout the country than to the severity of the tests, which were very far below those of to-day. I have often heard it said, and believe it true, that the difficulty was less with the knowledge – that is, the nominal acquirements – of the appointees than with the then prevalent methods of study and instruction, which had debauched the powers of application. My father, after a long experience, used to think that upon the whole there was better promise in a youth who came with nothing more than the three R's, which then constituted substantially the demands of the Military Academy, than in one with a more pretentious showing. The first had not to unlearn bad habits. An illustration that the courses were not too severe, for an average man beginning with the very smallest equipment, is afforded by a true story of the time. A lad from one of the Southern States, – Tennessee, I think, – having obtained an appointment, and being too poor to travel otherwise, walked his way to West Point, and then failed of admission. The affecting circumstances becoming known, a number of officers dubbed together and supported him for a year at a neighboring excellent school. He then entered, passed his course successfully, and proved a very respectable officer. There was, I believe, nothing brilliant in his record, except the earnestness and resolution shown; the absence of these, under demands which, though not excessive, were rigid, was the principal cause of failures.

The requirements were certainly moderate, and our healths needed not to suffer from over-application. The marking system of that time gave the numeral 4 as a maximum, with which standard 2.5 was a "passing average." He who reached that figure, as the combined result of his course of recitations and stated examinations, passed the test, and went on, or was graduated. The recitation marks being posted weekly, we had constant knowledge of our chances; and of the necessity of greater effort, if in danger, whether of failure or of being outstripped by a competitor. The latter motive was rarely evidenced, although I have seen the anxious and worried looks of one struggling for pre-eminence over a rival who amused himself by merely prodding where he might have surpassed. It is only fair to add, as I also witnessed, that no congratulations were more warmly received by the victor than those of the man who had so constantly trod on his heels. It is needless to say, to those who know the world in any sphere of life, that a certain proportion were satisfied with merely scraping through. The authorities leaned to mercy's side, where there was reasonable promise of a man's making a good sea officer. In the later period of written examinations an instructor of much experience said to me, "If a man's paper comes near 2.5, I always read it over again with a leaning towards a more favorable judgment on points;" and he accompanied the words with a gesture which dramatically suggested a leaning so pronounced that, it would certainly topple over the right way. Not strictly judicial, I fear, but perhaps practical. There were rare instances who played with 2.5, enticed perhaps by the mysterious charms of danger. Such a case I heard of, a man of unquestioned ability, who it was rumored boasted that he would get just above 2.5, and as near as he could. He was read dispassionately, and in the event came out 2.47. As an effort at approximation, this may be considered a success; but for passing it was inadequate, and his general character did not bias the final appeal in his favor. He was not dropped, indeed, but had to undergo a second examination three weeks later: a circumstance calculated to cloud his summer. A more amusing instance came directly under my observation. He was a candidate for entrance, and I then head of one of the departments of the Academy. Although I had nothing to do with admissions, his father came in to see me immediately after the results were known. He had a marked brogue, and was slightly "elevated," by success and by liquor. Placing his hand confidentially on my arm, he whispered: "He's got in; he's got in." I expressed my sympathy. He drew himself up with a smile of exultation, and said: "He only got a 2.7. I said to him, '----, why didn't you do better than that? – sure you could.' 'Whisht, father,' he replied, 'why should I do better, when all I need's a 2.5?' Just fancy his thinking of that!" cried the proud parent. "The 'cuteness of him?" I forget this lad's further career, if I ever knew it.

One of the distinguishing features of the two academies then, and I believe now, was the division of the classes into small sections, under several instructors. This gave the advantage of very frequent recitations for each student. None was safe in counting upon being overlooked on any day, and the teacher was kept familiar with the progress and promise of every one under his charge. It admitted also of a more extensive course for those who could stick in the higher sections – a kind of elective, in which the election depended on the teacher, not the taught. Thoroughness of acquisition was favored by this steady pressure, the virtue of which lay less in its weight than in its constancy; but it is practicable only where large resources permit many tutors to be employed. The Naval Academy has had frequent difficulty, not chiefly of a money kind, but because the needed naval officers cannot always be spared from general service. A sound policy has continuously favored the employment of sea officers, where possible; not because they can often be equal in acquirement to chosen men from the special fields in question, but because through them the spirit and authority of the profession pervades the class-room as well as the drill-ground, and so forwards the highly specialized product in view. Besides, as I have heard observed with admiration by a very able civilian, head of one of the departments, who had several officers under him, the habit of turning the hand to many different occupations, and of doing in each just what was ordered, following directions explicitly, gives naval officers as a class an adaptability and a facility which become professional characteristics. It may be interesting to note that the same was commonly remarked of the old-time seaman. His specialty was everything – versatility; and he was handy under the least expected circumstances, on shore as well as afloat. Burgoyne used chaffingly to attribute his misfortunes at Saratoga to the aptitude with which a British midshipman and seamen threw a bridge over the upper Hudson. "If it had not been for you," he said to the culprit, "we should never have got as far as this."

In my day the proportion of officers was less than afterwards, when the graduates themselves took up the task of instruction. There were two who taught us mathematics, one of whom remains in my memory as the very best teacher, to the extent of his knowledge, that I ever knew. The professional branches, seamanship and gunnery, fell naturally to the sea officers who conducted the drills. These studies, as pursued, reflected the transition condition of the period which I have before depicted; the grasp on the old still was more tenacious than that on the new. The preparation of text-books for young seamen far antedated the establishment of naval schools. There was one, *The Sheet Anchor*, by Darcy Lever, a British seaman, published before 1820, which had great vogue among us. Among other virtues, it was illustrated with very taking pictures of ships performing manoeuvres in the midst of highly conventional waves. As far as memory serves me, I think we were justified in regarding it as more instructive than the American work assigned to us by the course, *The Kedge Anchor*, by a master in our navy named Brady. A kedge, the unprofessional must know, is a light anchor, dropped for a momentary stop, or to haul a ship ahead, the title being in so far very consonant to the object of instruction; whereas the sheet-anchor is the great and last stand-by of a vessel, let go as a final resource after the two big "bowers," which constitute the usual reliance. The rareness with which the sheet anchor touched ground (the bottom) gave rise to the proverb, "To go ashore with the sheet anchor," as the ultimate expression of attention to duty; and the story ran of a British captain, a devoted ship-keeper, who, to a lieutenant remonstrating on the little privilege of leave enjoyed by the junior officers, replied: "Sir, when I and the sheet anchor go ashore, you may go with us." By the prescription of our seniors we had to tie to *The Kedge Anchor*, let us hope in the cause of progress, to haul us ahead; but in a tight place *The Sheet Anchor* was our recourse, and by it think I may say we – swore. I always mistrusted *The Kedge Anchor* after my researches into a mysterious sentence –"A celebrated master, now a commander, in the navy never served the bowsprit rigging all over." In the old-time frigates, of the days of Nelson and Hull, the master was at the head of the marling-spike division of the ship's economy, being, in fact, the descendant of the master (captain) of more than a century earlier, who managed the ship while soldiers commanded and fought her. But the masters were not in the line of promotion; in the British navy they rarely rose, in our own much more rarely. Who, then, was this celebrated master, now a commander? Eventually I found the sentence in a British book, and my faith in the pure product of American home industry was suddenly shaken. It is only fair to say that books on seamanship, being essentially an accumulation of facts, must be more or less compilations. Methods were too well established to allow much originality, even of treatment.

There were many other works of like character, the enumeration of which would be tedious. *The Young Officer's Assistant* was less a specific title than a generic description. Several of them were contemporary; and one, by a Captain Boyd of the British navy, summed up the convictions of us all, teachers as well as pupils, in the sententious aphorism: "It is by no means certain that coal whips will outlive tacks and sheets." It is scarcely kind to resurrect a prophecy, even when so guarded in expression and safely distant in prediction as was this; but I fear that for navies tacks and sheets are dead, and coal whips very much alive. The wish in those days fathered the thought. Who to dumb forgetfulness a prey could voluntarily relinquish all that had been so identified with life and thought, nor cast a longing, lingering

110

look behind? So we plodded on, acquiring laboriously, yet lovingly, knowledge that would have fitted us to pass the examinations of Basil Hall and Peter Simple. To mention the details of cutting and fitting rigging, getting over whole and half tops, and other operations yet more recondite, would be to involve the unprofessional reader in a maze of incomprehensible terms, and the professional – of that period – in familiar recollections. Let me, however, linger lovingly for ten lines on the knotting – "knotting and splicing," as the never-divorced terms ran in the days when rigging a topgallant-yard was a constituent part of our curriculum. The man who has never viewed the realm of a seaman's knots from the outside, and tried to get in, must not flatter himself that he fully appreciates the phrase "knotty problem." I never got in; a few elementary "bends," a square knot, and a bowline, were very near the extent of my manual acquirements. The last I still retain, and use whenever I make up a bundle for the express; but before such mysteries – to me – as a Turk's-head and a double-wall, I merely bowed in reverence. When handsomely turned out, I could recognize the fact; but do them myself, no. I remember with humiliation that in 1862, being then a young lieutenant, I was called without warning to hear a section, one hour, in seamanship. As bad luck would have it, the subject happened to be knotting, and there was one of the midshipmen who had made a cruise in a merchant-ship. The knots I had to ask about – to which that diabolical youngster invariably replied, "I can't describe it, sir, but I will make it for you" – the convolutions through which the strands went in his ready fingers, and my eyes vainly strove to follow, are a poignant subject. There was no room for the time-honored refuge of a puzzled instructor – "We will take up that subject next recitation;" the confounded boy was ready right along, and I had only to be thankful that there were "no questions asked."

There was one professional subject, "Naval Fleet Tactics" under sail, which at the end of my time shone forth with a kind of sunset splendor, the dying dolphin effect curiously characteristic of the passing period in which we were. This had always had a recognition – *d'estime*, as the French say; but in my final year it fell into the hands of a new instructor, who proceeded to glorify it by amplification. He was a very accomplished man in his profession, a student of it in all its branches, though there was among us a certain understanding that he was not an eminently practical seaman; and he eventually lost his life in what appeared to me a very unpractical manner, being where it did not seem his business to be, and doing work which a junior would probably have done better. We remember William III. at the battle of the Boyne. "Your majesty, the Bishop of Derry has been killed at the ford." "What business had he to be at the ford?" was the unsympathetic answer. The text-book used by our new instructor was by a French lieutenant, written in the thirties of the century, and characterized by something of the peculiar French naval genius. The simpler changes of formation were so simple that complication could not be got into them; but, that happy stage past, we went on to evolutions of huge masses of ships in three columns, in which the changes of dispositions, from one order to another, became subjects of trigonometrical demonstration, quite as troublesome as Euclid. Sines, cosines, and tangents, of fractional angles figured profusely in the processes; and in the result courses to be steered would be laid down to an eighth of a point, when to keep a single vessel, let alone a column, steady within half a point[5] was considered good helmsmanship. There being no translation of the book, our text was provided by copying, individually, from a manuscript prepared by our teacher, which increased our labor; but, curiously enough, the effect of the whole procedure was so to magnify the subject as materially to increase the impression upon our minds.

This is really an interesting matter for speculation, as to what in effect is practical. The mastery of conclusions, to which practical effect never could have been given, served to drive home principles which would have come usefully into play, had the sail era continued and the United States maintained fleets of sailing battle-ships to handle. For myself personally, when I came to write naval history, long years after, I derived invaluable aid from the principles and the simpler evolutions, thus assimilated and remembered. But for them I should often have found it difficult to understand what with them was obvious. A singular circumstance thus brought out was the want of exactness and precision in English terminology in this field. The most notable instance that occurs to me was in Nelson's journal on Trafalgar morning, "The enemy wearing in succession," when, in fact, as a matter of manoeuvre, the hostile fleet "wore together," though the several vessels wore "in succession;" a paradox only to be understood at a glance by those familiar with fleet tactics under sail. The usual version of the attack at Trafalgar has of late been elaborately disputed by capable critics. I myself have no doubt that they are quite mistaken; but it would be curious to investigate how far their argument derives from inexact phraseology – as, for example, the definition of "column" and "line" applied to ships.

These mathematical demonstrations of naval evolutions might be considered a lapse from practicalness characteristic of the particular officer. They took up a good deal of valuable time, and on any drill-ground manoeuvres are less a matter of geometric precision than of professional aptitude and eye judgment. The same mistake could scarcely be addressed at that time to the other parts of the Academy curriculum. Either as foundation, or as a super-structure in which it was sought to develop professional intelligence, to inform and improve professional action, there was little to find fault with in detail, and less still in general principle. The previous reasonable professional prejudice had been in favor of the practical man, the man who can do things – who knows *how* to do them; the new effort was to give the "why" of the "how," and to save time in the process by giving it systematically. In this sense – that all we learned ministered to professional intelligence – the scholastic part was thoroughly professional in tone; and I think I have shown that the outside professional sentiment was also strongly felt among us. There is always, of course, a disposition latent in educators to deny that practical work may be sufficiently accomplished by cruder processes – by what we call the rule of thumb – and a corresponding inclination to represent that to be absolutely necessary which is only an advantage; to exaggerate the necessity of mastering the "why" in order to put the "how" into execution. An instance in point, already quoted, is that of the professor who maintained that every officer should be able to calculate mathematically the relation between weights and purchases. But between 1855 and 1860, if such a tendency existed in germ, it had no effect in practice. As I look back, the relation between what we were taught and what we were to do was neither remote nor indirect. In its own sphere, in both its merits and its faults, the Academy was in aspiration as professional as the outside service.

This means that the Academy constituted for us an atmosphere perfectly accordant with the life for which we were intended; and an educational institution has no educative function to discharge higher than this. This influence was enhanced by the social customs, in favor of which disciplinary exactions were relaxed to the utmost possible; herein departing from the practice at the Military Academy, as then known to me. Not only on Saturdays and holidays, but every day, and at all hours not positively allotted to study or drills, the midshipmen might visit the houses of officers or professors to which they had the entrance. As a rule, very properly, no one was allowed to be absent from mess; but permission could always be obtained to accept an invitation to the evening meal with any of the families. This freedom of intercourse contributed its share to the formation of professional tone, for the heads of the families were selected professional men, who were thus met on terms of intimacy, precluded elsewhere by the official relations of the parties. More training is imparted by such association than by teaching – the familiar contrast of example and precept. An even greater gain, however – and a strictly professional gain, too – was the social facility thus acquired. In all callings probably, certainly in the navy, social aptitude is professionally valuable. Nelson's dictum that naval officers should know how to dance was only one way of saying that they should be men of affairs, at home in all conditions where men – or women – gather for business or amusement. The phrase "all sorts and conditions of men" never had wider or juster application than to the assembly of green lads, from every variety of parentage and previous surroundings, pitchforked into Annapolis once every year; and, of all the humanizing and harmonizing influences under which they came, none exceeded that of the quiet gentlefolk, of modest means, with whom they mingled thus freely. Indeed, one of the most astute of our superintendents took into account the family of an officer before asking that he be ordered.

An element in our social environment which should not be omitted was the prevalence of a Southern flavor. In our microcosm, this reflected the general sentiment of the world outside, then slowly freeing itself from the spirit of compromise which had dominated the statesmanship of two generations in their efforts to reconcile the incompatible. There were certainly strong Northern men in plenty, as well as strong Southerners; but every Southerner was convinced that the justice was all on their side, that their rights as well as interests were being attacked, whereas the Northerners were divided in feeling. There were some pronounced abolitionists, here and there, prepared to go all party lengths; but in the majority from the North, the devotion to the Union, which rose so instantaneously to the warlike pitch when fairly challenged, for the present counselled concession to the utmost limit, if only thereby the Union might endure. In this the membership of the school reproduced the political character of the House of Representatives, with whom appointment rested; and at our age, of course, we simply re-echoed the tones of our homes. Never in my now long life have I seen so evident the power of conviction as in the Southern men I then knew. They simply had no hesitations; whereas we others were perplexed. Yet I now doubt whether the Southern conviction was not really, if unconsciously, the resolution of despair; of doom felt, though unacknowledged; not before the attacks of the North, but before the resistless progress of the world, of which the North was to be the instrument. So also the patience of the North, if so noble a word can be conceded to our long temporizing, was an unconscious manifestation of latent power. To those who knew what the Union meant to those who exalted it – should I not rather say her? – in passionate adoration, need never have doubted what the response would be, if threat passed into act and hands were lifted against her. Conviction was absolute and deep-rooted on that side as on the other; but it was less on the surface, and sought ever a solution of peace.

The Muse of History of late years has become so analytic, and withal so embarrassed with the accumulations of new material, revealing still more the complication of causes which undoubtedly concur to any general result, that she is prone to overlook the overpowering influence of the simple elemental passions of human nature. "Our country, right or wrong," may be very bad morality, but it is a tremendous force to reckon with. One is wise overmuch who thinks that interest can restrain or statesmen control; wise unto folly who ignores that disinterested emotion, even unreasoning, may be just the one factor which diplomacy cannot master. I was in Rome when our late troubles with Spain came on, and dined with a number of the diplomatic body. "Oh yes," said to me one of these illuminati, "it is all very well to talk about humanity. The truth is, the United States wants Cuba." More profound was the remark of an American politician, who had recently visited the island. "I did not dare to tell all I saw; for, if I had, there would be no holding our people back." Personally, I believed that the interests of the United States made expedient the acquisition of Cuba, if righteously accomplished, and prior to the war I knew little of the conditions on the island; but Cuba would be Spanish now, if interests chiefly had power to move us. So in the War of

Secession. Innumerable precedent occurrences had produced a condition, but it was the passion for the Union, the strong loyalty to that sovereign, which dominated the situation, and in truth had been dominating it silently for years; a passion as profound and, though justifiable to reason, as un-reasoning as any simple love that ever bound man to woman. Could this have been appreciated, what reams of demonstration might have been spared to foreign pens – demonstration of the fol-ly, the hopelessness, the lust of conquest, the self-interest in myriad forms, which were sup-posed to be the actuating causes.

Effectively, the South had lost this love of the Union. In this respect the two sections, I fancy, had parted company, unwittingly, soon after the War of 1812; through which, as we all well know, in many quarters sectional feeling had still pre-vailed over national. The North had since moved towards national consciousness, the South to-wards sectional, on paths steadily and rapidly diverging. As I recall those days, when I first awoke to political observation, I should say that the feeling of my Southern associates towards the Union was that which men have towards a friend lately buried. Affection had not wholly disap-peared; but life called. Let the dead bury their dead. I remember on my first practice cruise, in 1857, standing in the main-top of the ship with a member of the class immediately before mine, the son of a North Carolina member of Congress. "Yes," he said to me, "Buchanan [inaugurated four months before] will be the last President of the United States." He was entirely unmoved, simply repeating certitudes to which familiarity had reconciled him; I, to whom such talk was new, as much aghast as though I had been told my mother would die within the like term. This outlook was common to them all. The Union still was, and they continued in it; but to them the warning had sounded, they were ready and acquiescent in its fall; regretful, but resigned – very much resigned. This attitude was more marked among the younger men, those at the school. In the service outside I found somewhat the same point of view, but repulsion was keener. The navy then, even more than now, symbolized the exterior activities of the country, which are committed by the Constitution to the Union. Hence, the life of the profession naturally nurtured pride in the nation; and while States'-Rights had undermined the principle of loyalty to the Union, it had been less successful in destroying love for it. But to most the prospect was gloomy. That Massachusetts and South Carolina should be put into a pen together, and left to fight it out, was the solution expressed to me by a lieutenant who afterwards fell nobly, in command, on a Union deck in the war; the gallant Joe Smith, concerning whom runs a story that cannot be too widely known, even though often repeated. When it was reported to his father that the *Congress* had surrendered, he said, simply, "Then Joe's dead." Joe was dead; but it is only fair to the survivors to say that ninety out of her crew of four hundred were also dead, the ship aground, helpless, and in flames.

In Annapolis, the capital of a border slave state, the general sentiment was, as might be expected, a blending of North and South; a desire to maintain the Union, but, distinctly superior in motive, sympathy with the Southern view of the case. In all my fairly intimate acquaintance with the small society of the town outside the Academy walls, there was but one family the heads of which were decisively Union – not Northern; and of it two sons fought in the Southern armies. Between this influence and that of my comrades I remained as I had been brought up – the Union first and above all, but with the conviction that the great danger to the Union lay in the abolition propaganda. My father was by upbringing a Virginian; by life-long occupation an officer of the general government, imbued to the marrow with the principles of military loyalty. Having married and continuously lived in the North, he had escaped all taint of the extreme States'-Rights school; but the memories of his youth kept him broadly Southern in feeling, less by local attachment than by affection for friends. More than twenty years after his death, when I was on court-martial duty in Richmond, an old Confederate general, whom I had never seen, sought me out in memory of the ties that had bound both himself and his wife's family to my father. With these clinging sympathies, the abolition agitation was an attack upon his friends, and, still worse, a wanton endangering of the Union. To save me from being carried away by the swelling tide was one of his chief aims.

Regarded by themselves, nothing can well be less important than the political opinions of one boy of eighteen to twenty; but few things are more important, if they are those of the mass of his generation, for then they are the echo from many homes. I believe, from what I saw at the Naval Academy, that mine were those of the large majority of the Northern youth, and that the very greatness of the concession which such were ready to make for the sake of the Union should have warned the disunionists that the same love was capable of equally great sacrifices in the other direction. They failed so to understand; chiefly, perhaps, because they could not appreciate the living force of the simple sentiment. Never in their lifetimes, if ever before, had the Union held the first place in the hearts of men of their section; and such love as had been felt was already moribund, overcome by supposed interest and local pride. Thus misled, it was easy to believe that in the North, controlled by considerations of advantage, yielding would follow yielding, even to permitting a disruption of the Union – a miscalculation of forces more fatal even than that of "Cotton is King." But forces will often be miscalculated by those who reckon interest as more powerful than principle or than sentiment.

Singularly enough, considering the exodus of States'-Rights officers from the navy at the outbreak of the War of Secession, my first service during it brought me into close relations with two captains, both Southerners, whose differing points of view shed interesting light upon the varying motives which in times of stress determined men into a common path. The first, Percival Drayton, a South-Carolinian, had a strength of conviction on the question of slavery, in itself, and the wrong-headed course of the slave power, as well as a strong devotion to the Union, all which were needed to keep a son of that extreme state firm in his allegiance. I question, however, whether any other one of the seceding communities furnished as large a proportion of officers who stuck to the national flag, chiefly among the older men; a result scarcely surprising, for the intensity of affection for the Union necessary to withstand nearest relatives and the headlong sweep of separatist impulse, where fiercest, naturally throve upon the opposition which it met, eliciting a corresponding tenacity of adherence to the cause it had embraced. No more than that other Southerner, Farragut, did Drayton feel doubt as to where he belonged in the coming struggle. "I cannot exactly see the difference between my relations fighting against me and I against them, except that their cause is as unholy a one as the world has ever seen, and mine just the reverse." "Were the sword in the one hand powerful enough, the secessionists would carry slavery with the other to the uttermost parts of the Union, and I do not think the North has been at all too quick in stopping the movement." "I do not think there will ever be peace between the two sections until slavery is so completely scotched as to make extension a hopeless matter."[6]

Drayton stayed with us but a brief time. His successor, George B. Balch, who still survives, now the senior rear-admiral on the retired list of the navy, a man beloved by all who have known him for his gallantry, benevolence, and piety, was equally pronounced and equally firm; but his position illustrated and carried on my experiences at the Academy, and afterwards in the service, and for the time confirmed my old prepossessions. He was fighting for the Union, assailed without just cause; not against slavery, nor for its abolition. Were the latter the motive of the war, he would not be in arms. This, of course, was then the attitude of the government and of the people at large. Abolition, which came not long after, was a war measure simply; received with doubt by many, but which a few months of hostilities had prepared us all to accept. My own conversion was early and sudden. The ship had made an expedition of some fifty miles up a South Carolina river, in the course of which numerous negroes fled to her. Unlike Drayton, our captain was rather disconcerted, I think, at having forced upon him a kind of practical abolition, in carrying off slaves; but his duty was clear. As for me, it was my first meeting with slavery; except in the house-servants of Maryland, superficially a very different condition; and as I looked at the cowed, imbruted faces of the field-hands, my early training fell away like a cloak. The process was not logical; I was generalizing from a few instances, but I was convinced. Knowing how strongly my father had felt, I wondered how I should break to him my instability; but when we met I found that he, too, had gone over. Youngster as I still was, I should have divined the truth, that in assailing the Union his best friend became his enemy, to down whom abolition was good and fit as any other club. "My son," he said, "I did not think I could ever again be happy should our country fall into her present state; but now I am so absorbed in seeing those fellows beaten that I lose sight of the rest." Peculiar and personal association enhanced his interest; for, having been then over thirty years at the Military Academy, there were very few of the prominent generals on either side who had not been his pupils. The successful leaders were almost all from that school: Grant, Sherman, Thomas, Schofield, on the Union side; Lee, Jackson, and the two Johnstons on the Confederate, were all graduates, not to mention a host of others only less conspicuous.

In last analysis slavery may have been, probably was, the cause of the war; but, historically, it was not the motive. Lincoln's words – "I will save the Union with slavery, or I will save it without slavery, as the case may demand" – voiced the feeling prevalent in the military services, and also the will of the great body of the Northern people, whom he profoundly understood and in his own mental advance illustrated. I cannot but think that such an aim was more statesmanlike than would have been the attempt to overturn immediately and violently an entire social and economical system, for the establishment of which the current generation was not responsible. In the long run, to allow the tares of bondage to stand with the wheat of freedom was wiser than the wish prematurely to uproot. It had become the definite policy of the enemies of slavery to girdle the tree, by strict encompassing lines, leaving it to consequent sure process of decay. Its friends forced the issue. To the ones and to the others the harvest of generations, in the form it took, came unexpected and suddenly – a day of judgment, a crisis, like a thief in the night. It is a consummate proof of the accuracy of popular instinct, given time to work, that the uprising of 1861 rested upon recognition of the fact that the cause of the nation and of the world depended more upon the preservation of a single authority over all the territory involved, upon the consequent avoidance of future permanent oppositions, than it did upon the destruction of a particular institution, the life of which might be protracted, but under conditions of union must wane and ultimately expire. The gradual progress of decision by the American people was wiser than the abrupt action asked by foreign impatience; and abolition came with less shock and more finality as a military measure than it could as a political. Its advisability was more evident. If statesmanship is shown in bringing popular will to accord with national necessity, Lincoln was in this most sagacious; but not the least element in the tribute due him is that he was the barometer of popular impulse, measuring accurately the invisible force upon which depended the energy of that stormy period.

Before taking final leave of my shore experiences at the Naval Academy, I will recall, as among them, the superb comet of the autumn of 1858, which we at the school witnessed evening after evening in October of that year, during the release from quarters following supper. After the lapse of so nearly a half-century, the survivors of those who saw that magnificent spectacle must be in a minority among their contemporaries, whether of that day or this. Since its disappearance there has been visible one other notable comet, which I remember waking my children after midnight to see; but compared with that of 1858, whether in size or in splendor, it was literally as moonlight unto sunlight, or, in impression, as water unto wine. As the astronomers compute the period of return for the earlier at two thousand years, more or less, we of that generation were truly singular in our opportunity of viewing this, among the very few "most magnificent of modern times." The tail, broadening towards the end, with a curve like that of a scimitar, was in length nearly a fourth of the span of the heavens, and its brightness that of a full moon. My memory retains the image with all the tenacity of eighteen.

* * * * *

Corresponding in some measure to the summer encampment at the Military Academy, the Naval gave the three months from July to September, inclusive, to shipboard and the sea. In both institutions the period was one of study interrupted, in favor of out-door work; but at West Point it was accompanied by a degree of social entertainment impossible to ship conditions. There were two theories as to the conduct of the practice cruises. One was that they should be confined to home waters, where regular hours and systematized instruction in "doing things" would suffer little interference from weather; the other was to make long voyages, preferably to Europe, leaving to the normal variability of the ocean and the watchful improvement of occasions the burden of initiating a youth into practical acquaintance with the exigencies of his intended profession. Personally I have always favored the latter, being somewhat of the opinion of the old practical politician – "Never contrive an opportunity." Naturally an opportunist, the experience of life has justified me in rather awaiting than contriving occasions. One learns more widely and more thoroughly by reefing topsails when it has to be done, than by doing it at a routine hour, without the accompaniments of the wind, the wet, and the lurching, which give the operation a tone and a tonic – the real thing, in short. Doubtless we may wait too long, like Micawber, even for a reef-topsail gale to turn up, though the ocean can usually be trusted to be nasty often enough; but, on the other hand, one over sedulously bent on making opportunity is apt to be too preoccupied to see that which makes itself. Truth, doubtless, lies between the extremes.

In my day long cruises had unquestioned preference; and, whatever their demerits otherwise, they were certainly eye-openers, even to those who, like myself, had obtained some intelligent impression of ships at sea. As instruction in seamanship was then never attempted, neither by work nor book, until after the second year, we went on board not knowing one mast from another, so far as teaching went. How far initial ignorance could go may be illustrated by an incident, to be appreciated, unluckily, only by seamen, which happened in my hearing. We had then been nearly two months on board, when one who had improved his opportunities was displaying his acquirements by the pleasing method of catechising another. He asked: "Do you know what the topsail-tie is?" The rejoinder, perfectly serious, was: "Do you mean the cross-tie?" The topsail-tie being one of the principal "ropes" in a ship, the ignorance was really symptomatic of character; and had not the hero of it been long dead, I would not have preserved it, even incog. I fear it may be cited against my view of practice cruises, as proving that systematic training is better than picking-up; to which my reply would be that the picking-up showed aptitude – or the reverse – if only some means could be devised of making it tell in selection, as it assuredly did in character. But at the beginning, despite any little previous inklings, we were all quite green. I still recall the innocent astonishment when we anchored in Hampton Roads, after the run down the Chesapeake, and the boatswain, as by custom, pulled round the ship to see the yards square and rigging taut. Semaphore signalling was not then used, as later; and his stentorian lungs conveyed to us distinct sounds, bearing meanings we felt could never be compassed by us. "Haul taut the main-top bowlines!" "Haul taut the starboard fore-topgallant-sheet." "Maintop, there! Send a hand up and square the bunt gaskets of the top-gallant-sail!" "By Jove!" said one of the admiring listeners, "there's seamanship for you!" We all silently agreed, and I dare say many thought we might as well give it up and go home. Such excellence was not for us.

The subsequent process of picking-up was attended sometimes by comical, as well as painful, incidents. Peter Simple's experiences, as told by Marryat, were not yet quite obsolete in practice. A story ran of one, not long before my "date," who, having been sent on two or three bootless errands by unauthorized jesters, finally received from a person in due authority the absurd-sounding, but legitimate, message to have the jackasses put in the hawse-holes.[7] "Oh no," he replied, resentfully, "I have been fooled often enough! That I will not do." I can better vouch for another, which happened on my first practice cruise. In a sailing-ship properly planned, the balance of the sails is such that to steer her on her course the rudder need not be kept more to one side than the other; the helm is then amidships. But error of design, or circumstances, such as a faulty trim of the sails or the ship inclining in a strong side-wind, will sometimes so alter the influencing forces that the helm has to be carried steadily on one side, to correct the ship's disposition to turn to that side. She is then said to carry weather helm or lee helm, as the case may be; and the knowing ones used to assert noticeable differences of sailing in certain conditions. In many ships to carry a little weather helm was thought advantageous, and it was told of a certain deck-officer – he who repeated the story to me made the late Admiral Porter the hero – that the ship being found to sail faster in his watch than in any other, the commander sent for him and asked the reason. "Well, sir," replied the lieutenant, "I will tell you my secret. As soon as the officer I relieve is gone below and out of sight, while the watch is mustering, I walk forward, look round at things generally, and say casually to the captain of the forecastle: 'Just slack off a little of this jib-sheet.' Then about ten minutes before eight bells, after the last log of the watch has been hove, while the men are rousing to go below, I go forward again and say, 'Come here, half a dozen of us, and get a pull of the jib-sheet;' and I turn the deck over to my relief with the jib well flattened in." In result, the frigate during his watch, and his only, carried a weather helm. My own experience of sailing ships was neither prolonged enough nor responsible enough to estimate just what weight to attach to these impressions, but they existed; and in any case, as the helm varying far from amidships showed something wrong, the question was frequent to the helmsman, "How does she carry her helm?" varied sometimes to, "What sort of helm does she carry?" Now we had among our green midshipmen one from the West, tall, angular, swarthy, with a coal-black eye which had a trick of cocking up and out, giving a queer, perplexed, yet defiant cast to his countenance; moreover, he stuttered a little, not from imperfection of organs, but from nervous excitability. We had also a lieutenant from far down East, red-haired, sanguine of complexion, bony of structure, who had a gesture of tossing his hair and head back, and looking tremendously leonine and master of the situation – monarch of all he surveyed. The two were naturally antagonistic, as was amusingly shown more than once; but on this occasion the midshipman was at the "lee wheel," not himself steering, but helping the steersman in the manual labor. To him the lieutenant, pausing in his stride and tilting his chin in the air, says: "Mr. ----, what sort of helm does she carry?" ----, who had never heard of weather or lee helms, and probably was not yet recovered from the effects of the boatswain's seamanship, twisted his eye and his head, looking more than ever confounded and saucy, and stammered: "I – I – I'm not sure, sir, but I think it's a wooden one." Tableau! – as the French say.

In position on board we were midshipmen indeed, in a sense probably somewhat different from that which first gave birth to the title. We were not seamen; and it could scarcely be claimed that we were in any full sense officers, much as we stuck to that designation. We stood midway. There was a tradition in the British service that a midshipman, though in training for promotion, did not, while in the grade, rank with the boatswain or gunner, who had no future prospects, and who, with the carpenter, stood in a class by themselves. Marryat, who doubtless drew his characters from life, tells us that the gunner who sailed with Mr. Midshipman Easy was strong on the necessity for the gunner mastering navigation, and had many instances in point where all the officers had been killed down to the gunner, who in such case would have been sadly handicapped by ignorance of navigation. I fancy the doubt seldom needed to be settled in service; the duties of midshipman and boatswain could rarely come into collision, if each minded his own business. By luck, just after writing these words, I for the first time in my life have found a plausible derivation for midshipman.[8] It would appear that in the days immediately after the flood the vessels were very high at the two ends, between which there was a deep "waist," giving no ready means of passing from one to the other. To meet this difficulty there were employed a class of men, usually young and alert, who from their station were called midshipmen, to carry messages which were not subject for the trumpet shout. If this holds water, it, like forecastle, and after-guard, and knightheads, gives another instance of survival from conditions which have long ceased.

Whatever the origin of his title, it well expressed the anomalous and undefined position of the midshipman. He belonged, so to say, to both ends of the ship, as well as to the middle, and his duties and privileges alike fell within the broad saying, already quoted, that what was nobody's business was a midshipman's. When appointed as such, in later days, he came in "with the hay-seed in his hair," and went out fit for a lieutenant's charge; but from first to last, whatever his personal progress, he remained, as a midshipman, a handy-billy. He might be told, as Basil Hall's first captain did his midshipmen, that they might keep watch or not, as they pleased – that is, that the ship had no use for them; or he might be sent in charge of a prize, as was Farragut, when twelve years old, doubtless with an old seaman as nurse, but still in full command. Anywhere from the bottom of the hold to the truck – top of the masts – he could be sent, and was sent; every boat, that went ashore had a midshipman, who must answer for her safety and see that none got away of a dozen men, whose one thought was to jump the boat and have a run on shore. Between times he passed hours at the mast-head in expiation of faults which he had committed – or ought to have committed, to afford a just scapegoat for his senior's wrath. As Marryat said, it made little difference: if he did not think of something he had not been told, he was asked what his head was for; if he did something off his own bat, the question arose what business he had to think. In either case he went to the mast-head. Of course, at a certain age one "turns to mirth all things of earth, as only boyhood can;" and the contemporary records of the steerage brim over with unforced jollity, like that notable hero of Marryat's "who was never quite happy except when he was d----d miserable."

Such undefined standing and employments taught men their business, but provided no remedy for the miscellaneous social origin of midshipmen. In the beginning of things they were probably selected from the smart young men of the crew; often also from the more middle-aged – in any event, from before the mast. Even in much later days men passed backward and forward from midshipman to lower ratings; Nelson is an instance in point. When a man became a lieutenant, he was something fixed and recognized, professionally and socially. He might fall below his station, but he had had his chance. In the British navy many most distinguished officers came from anywhere – through the hawse-holes, as the expression ran; and a proud boast it should have been at a time when every Frenchman in his position had to be of noble blood. What was all very well for captains and lieutenants, once those ranks were reached, was not so easy for midshipmen. We know in every walk of life the woes of those whose position is doubtful or challenged; and what was said to his crew by Sir Peter Parker, an active frigate captain who was killed in Chesapeake Bay in 1814, "I'll have you touch your hat to a midshipman's jacket hung up to dry" (curiously reminiscent of William Tell and Gessler's cap), not improbably testifies to equivocalness even at that late date. The social instinct of seamen is singularly observant and tenacious of their officers' manners and bearing. I have known one, reproved for a disrespect, say, sullenly: "I have always been accustomed to sail with gentlemen." In the instance the comment was just, though not permissible. Deference might be conceded to the midshipman's jacket, but it could not cover defects of a certain order.

The midshipman's berth, as attested by contemporary sketches, was peopled by all sorts in age, fitness, and manners. In one of the many tales I devoured in youth, a middle-aged shellback of a master's mate, come in from before the mast, says with an oath to an aristocratic midshipman: "Isn't my blood as red as yours?" Still, even in the British navy, with its fine democratic record, the social rank was more regarded than the military. His Majesty's ship *So-and-So* was commanded by John Smith, Esquire; and I have heard this point of view stated by competent authority as accounting for the address – George Washington, Esquire – placed by Howe on the letter which Washington refused to accept because not carrying the rank conferred on him by Congress. This does not, however, explain away the "etc., etc.," which followed on the cover. John Byng, Esquire, Admiral of the Blue, would thus be of higher consideration as Esquire than as Admiral. Even in our own service I remember an old log, the pages of which were headed, "Cruise of the U. S. Ship *Preble*, commanded by J. B. M----, Esquire."

In the practice cruises the social question did not arise. Independent of the democratic tendency of all boys' schools, where each individual finds his level by natural gravitation, the Naval Academy, for reasons before alluded to, has been remarkably successful in assimilating its heterogeneous raw material and turning out a finished product of a good average social quality. Beyond this, social success or failure depends everywhere upon personal aptitudes which no training can bestow. But as officers we were nondescript. There were too many of us; and for the most the object was to acquire a sufficient seaman's knowledge, not an officer's. Yet, curiously enough, so at least it seemed to me, there was a disposition on the part of some to be jealous of any supposed infringement of our prerogative to be treated as "a bit of an officer." Ashore or afloat, we made our own beds or lashed our own hammocks, swept our rooms, tended our clothes, and blacked our boots; our drills were those of the men before the mast, at sails and guns; all parts of a seaman's work, except cleaning the ship, was required and willingly done; but there was a comical rebellion on one occasion when ordered to pull – row – a boat ashore for some purpose, and almost a mutiny when one lieutenant directed us to go barefooted while decks were being scrubbed, a practice which, besides saving your shoe-leather, is both healthy, cleanly, and, in warm weather, exceedingly comforting. Some asserted that the lieutenant in question, who afterwards commanded one of the Confederate commerce-destroyers, and from his initials (Jas. I.) was known to us as Jasseye, had done this because he had very pretty feet which he liked to show bare, and we must do the same; much as Germans are said to train their mustaches with the emperor's. At all events, there was great wrath, which I supposed I should have shared had I not preferred bare feet – not for as sound reasons as the lieutenant's. It stands to reason, however, that that imputation was slanderous, for there were no appreciative observers, unless himself. Why waste such sweetness on the desert air of a lot of heedless midshipmen? With so many details regulated – if not enforced – from the length of our hair to the cut of our trousers, it did seem hypercritical to object to going shoeless for an hour. But who is consistent? The uncertainty of our position kept the chip on the shoulder.

V
MY FIRST CRUISE AFTER GRADUATION – NAUTICAL CHARACTERS

1859-1861

At the moment of graduation, in the summer of 1859, I had a narrow escape from the cutting short of my career, resembling that which a man has from a railway accident by missing the train. To a certain extent the members of classes were favored in forming groups of friends, and choosing the ship to which they would be sent. Myself and two intimates applied for the sloop-of-war *Levant*, destined for the Pacific by way of Cape Horn; our motive being partly the kind of vessel, supposed by us to favor professional opportunity, and partly the friendship existing between one of us and the master of the *Levant*, a graduate of two or three years before, who had just completed his examinations for promotion. Luckily for us, and particularly for me, as the only one of the three who in after life survived middle age, the frigate *Congress* was fitting out, and her requirements for officers could not be disregarded. The *Levant* sailed, reached the Pacific, and disappeared--one of the mysteries of the deep. We very young men had the impression that small vessels were better calculated to advance us professionally, because, having fewer officers, deck duty might be devolved on us, either to ease the regular watch officers or in case of a disability. This prepossession extended particularly to brigs, of which the navy then had several. This was a pretty wild imagining, for I can hardly conceive any one in trusting such a vessel to a raw midshipman. It is scarcely an exaggeration to say they were all canvas and no hull – beautiful as a dream, but dangerous to a degree, except to the skilful. As it was, an unusual proportion of them came to grief. Our views were doubtless largely, if unconsciously, affected by the pleasing idea of prospective early importance as deck officers. The more solid opinion of our seniors was that we would do better to pause awhile on the bottom step, under closer supervision; while as for vessel, the order, dignity, and scale of performance on big ships were more educative, more formative of military character, which, and not seamanship, is the leading element of professional value. "Keep them at sea," said Lord St. Vincent, "and they can't help becoming seamen; but attention is needed to make them learn their business with the guns." I have already mentioned that, at the outbreak of the War of Secession, it was this factor which decided the authorities to give seniority to the very young lieutenants over the volunteers from the merchant service, most of whom had longer experience and (though by no means all of them) consequent ability as seamen.

After graduating, my first cruise was upon what was then known as the Brazil Station; by the British called more comprehensively the Southeast Coast of America. After the war the name and limits were judiciously changed. It became then the South Atlantic Station, to embrace the Cape of Good Hope, and, generally, the coasts of South America and Africa, with the islands lying between, such as St. Helena and the Falklands. From the point of view of healthy activity for the ships and their companies, and specifically for the education of younger officers, this extension was most desirable. In the earlier time long periods were spent in port, because there really was not enough that required doing. Our captain once kept the ship at sea for a fortnight or more, "cruising;" that is, moving about within certain limits back and forth. In war-time this is frequent, if not general; but then it is for a specific purpose, conducive to the ends of war. In peace, cruising ends in itself; it is like a "constitutional;" beneficial, no doubt, but not to most men as healthily beneficial as the walk to the office, with its definite object and the incidental amusement of the streets. A *terminus ad quem* is essential to the perfection of exercise, bodily or mental. As it was, Montevideo, in the river La Plata, and Rio de Janeiro were the two chief ports between which we oscillated, with rare and brief stays elsewhere or at sea.

The *Congress* was a magnificent ship of her period. The adjective is not too strong. Having been built about 1840, she represented the culmination of the sail era, which, judged by her, reached then the splendid maturity that in itself, to the prophetic eye, presages decay and vanishment. In her just but strong proportions, in her lines, fine yet not delicate, she "seemed to dare," and did dare, "the elements to strife;" while for "her peopled deck," when her five hundred and odd men swarmed up for an evolution, or to get their hammocks for the night, it was peopled to the square foot, despite her size. On her forecastle, and to the fore and main masts, each, were stationed sixty men, full half of them prime seamen, not only in skill, but in age and physique – ninety for the starboard watch, and ninety for the port; not to count the mizzen-topmen, after-guard, and marines, more than as many more. I have always remembered the effect produced upon me by this huge mass, when all hands gathered once to wear ship in a heavy gale, the height of one of those furious *pamperos* which issue from the prairies (*pampas*) of Buenos Ayres. The ship having only fore and main topsails, close reefed, the officers, beyond those of the watch, were not summoned; the handling of the yards required only the brute force of muscle, under which, even in such conditions, they were as toys in the hands of that superb ship's company. I had thus the chance to see things from the poop, a kind of bird's-eye view. As the ship fell off before the wind, and while the captain was waiting that smoother chance which from time to time offers to bring her up to it again on the other side with the least shock, she of course gathered accelerated way with the gale right aft – scudding, in fact. Unsteadied by wind on either side, she rolled deeply, and the sight of those four hundred or more faces, all turned up and aft, watching intently the officer of the deck for the next order, the braces stretched taut along in their hands for instant obedience, was singularly striking. Usually a midshipman had to be in the midst of such matters with no leisure for impressions – at least, of an "impressionist" character. Those were the prerogatives of the idlers – the surgeon, chaplain, and marine officers – who obtained thereby not only the benefit of the show, but material for discussion as to how well the thing had been done, or whether it ought to have been done at all. The midshipman's part at "all hands" was to be as much in the way as was necessary to see all needed gear manned, no skulkers, and as much out of the way as his personal stability required, from the rush of the huge gangs of seamen "running away" with a rope.

I never had the opportunity of viewing the ship from outside under way at sea; but she was delightful to look at in port. Her spars, both masts and yards, lofty and yet square, were as true to proportion, for perfection of appearance, as was her hull; and the twenty-five guns she showed on each broadside, in two tiers, though they had abundance of working-room, were close enough together to suggest two strong rows of solid teeth, ready for instant use. Nothing could be more splendidly martial. But what old-timers they were, with the swell of their black muzzles, like the lips of a full-blooded negro. Thirty-two-pounders, all of them; except on either side five eight-inch shell guns, a small tribute to progress. The rest threw solid shot for the most part. Imposing as they certainly looked, and heavier though they were than most of those with which the world's famous sea-fights have been fought, they were already antediluvian. A few years later I saw a long range of them enjoying their last repose on the skids in a navy-yard; and a bystander, with equal truth and irreverence, called them pop-guns. One almost felt that the word should be uttered in a whisper, out of respect for their feelings. But the whole equipment of the ship, though up to date in itself, was so far of the past that I recall it with mingled pathos and interest. What naval officer who may read these words was ever shipmate with rope "trusses" for the lower yards, or with a hemp messenger? A "messenger" was a huge rope, of I suppose eighteen to twenty-four inches circumference, used for lifting the anchor. At the after end of the ship it was passed three times round the capstan, where the men walking round merrily to the sound of the fife, under the eyes of the officer of the deck, were doing the work of weighing; at the forward end it moved round rollers to save friction. Thus one part was taut under the strain of the capstan; and to this the cable of the anchor, as it was hove in, was made fast by a succession of selvagees, for which I will borrow the elaborate description of White Jacket, who tells us the name was applied by the seamen of his ship to one of the lieutenants: "It is a slender, tapering, unstranded piece of rope, prepared with much solicitude; peculiarly flexible; which wreathes and serpentines round the cable and messenger like an elegantly modelled garter-snake round the stalks of a vine." The messenger thus was appropriately named; it went back and forth on its errand of anchor raising, the slack side being helped on its way by a row of twelve or fifteen men seated, pulling it along forward. This gang, by immemorial usage, was composed of the colored servants, and I can see now that row of black faces, with grinning ivories, as they yo-ho'd in undertones together, "lighting forward the messenger."

Like the ship and her equipment, the officers and crew by training and methods were still of the olden time in tone and ideals; a condition, of course, fostered at the moment by the style of vessel. Yet they had that curious adaptability characteristic of the profession, which afterwards enabled them to fall readily into the use of the new constructions of every kind evolved by the War of Secession. Concerning some of these, a naval professional humorist observed that they could be worshipped without idolatry; for they were like nothing in heaven, or on earth, or in the waters under the earth. Adored or not, they were handled to purpose. By a paradoxical combination, the seaman of those days was at once most conservative in temperament and versatile in capacity. Among the officers, however, there was an open vision towards the future. I well remember "Joe" Smith enlarging to me on the merits of Cowper Coles's projected turret ship, much talked about in the British press in 1860; a full year or more before Ericsson, under the exigency of existing war, obtained from us a hearing for the *Monitor*. Coles's turrets, being then a novel project, were likened, explanatorily, to a railway turntable, a very illustrative definition; and Smith was already convinced of the value of the design, which was proved in Hampton Roads the day after he himself fell gloriously on the deck of the *Congress*. There is a double tragedy in his missing by this brief space the clear demonstration of a system to which he so early gave his adherence; and it is another tragedy, which most Americans except naval officers will have forgotten, that

Coles himself found his grave in the ship – the *Captain* – ultimately built through his urgency upon this turret principle. This happened in 1870. The tradition of masts and sails, as economical, still surviving, she was equipped with them, which we from the beginning had discarded in monitors. The *Captain* was a large vessel with low freeboard, her deck only six feet above water. Lying to under sail in a moderate gale, in the Bay of Biscay, she heeled over in a squall, bringing the lee side of the deck under water; and the force of the wind increasing, without meeting the resistance offered ordinarily by the pressure of the water against the lee side of a ship, she went clean over and sank. The incident made the deeper impression upon me because two months before I had visited her, when she was lying at Spithead in company with another iron-clad, the *Monarch*, which soon after was assigned by the British government to bring George Peabody's remains to their final resting-place in America. I then met and was courteously received by the captain of the *Captain*, Burgoyne, of the same family as the general known to our War of Independence. Coles had gone merely as a passenger, to observe the practical working of his designs. I do not know how far the masting was consonant to his wishes. It may have been forced upon him as a concession, necessary to obtain his main end; but nothing could be more incongruous than to embarrass the all-round fire of turrets by masts and rigging.

In 1859 the United States government was coquetting with the title "Admiral," which was supposed to have some insidious connection with

145

monarchical institutions. Even so sensible and thoughtful a man as our sailmaker, who was a devout disciple and constant reader of Horace Greeley, with the advanced political tendencies of the *Tribune*, said to me: "Call them admirals! Never! They will be wanting to be dukes next." We had hit, therefore, on a compromise, quite accordant with the transition decade 1850-1860, and styled them flag-officers; concerning which it might be said that all admirals are flag-officers, but all flag-officers were not admirals – not American flag-officers, at all events. As a further element in the compromise, instead of the broad swallow-tailed pendant of a commodore, our previous flag-rank, we carried the square flag at the mizzen indicative in all navies of a rear-admiral, to which we gave a rear-admiral's salute of thirteen guns, and expected the same from foreigners; while all the time the recipient stood on our *Navy Register* as a captain, only temporarily brevetted Flag-officer. Well do I remember the dismay of our flag-officer when, quitting a British ship of war, she fired the customary salute, and stopped at eleven – a commodore's perquisite. The hit was harder, because the old gentleman was particularly fond of the English, having received from them great hospitality incidental to his commanding the ship of war which carried part of the American exhibition to the World's Fair of 1851. An "*Et tu, Brute*" expression came over his face, as he sank back with a sorrowful exclamation in the stern-sheets of the barge, which, as nautical convention requires, was lying motionless, oars horizontal, a ship's-length away; when, lo and behold,

146

as a kind of appendix to the previous proceedings, bang! bang! went two more guns, filling the baker's dozen. It was, of course, somewhat limping, but the apology was sufficient.

Salutes are as liable to accidents as are other affairs of well-regulated households, and a little more so; a gun misses fire, or somebody counts wrong, or what not. On the *Congress* we rarely had trouble, for the greatest number of guns is twenty-one – a national salute – and on our main deck we had thirty, any part of which could be ready. If one missed fire, the gun next abaft stepped in. If near enough, you might hear the primer snap, but the error of interval was barely appreciable – the effect stood. Laymen may not know that the manner of the salute was, and is, for the officer conducting it to give the orders, "Starboard, fire!" "Port, fire!" the discharges thus ranging from forward, aft, alternately on each side. A man who cannot trust his ear times the interval by watch; most, I presume, trust their counting. I once underwent an amusing *faux pas* in this matter of counting. Of course, the count is a serious matter; gun for gun is diplomatically as important as an eye for an eye. My captain had heard that an excellent precaution was to provide one's self with a number of dried beans – with which, needless to say, a ship abounds – corresponding to the number of guns. The receipt ran: Put them all in one pocket, and with each gun shift a bean to the other pocket. He proposed this to me, but I demurred; I feared I might get mixed on the beans and omit to shift one. He did not press me, but when I began to perform on the main deck he stood near the hatch on the deck above, duly – or unduly – provided with beans. It was a national salute; to the port. When I finished, he called to me: "You have only fired twenty guns." "No, sir," I replied; "twenty-one." "No," he repeated, "twenty; for I have a bean left." "All right!" I returned, and I banged an appendix; after which, upon counting, it was found the captain had twenty-two beans and the French twenty-two guns – a "tiger" which I hope they appreciated, but am sure they did not "return."

Our flag-officer was a veteran of 1812. He had evidently been very handsome, to which possibly he owed three successive wives, the last one much younger than himself. Now, in his sixties, he was still light in his movements. He had a queer way of tripping along on the balls of his feet, with a half-shuffling movement, his hands buried in his pockets, with the thumbs out. He was, I fear, the sort of man capable of wearing a frock-coat unbuttoned. It was amusing to see him walk the poop with the captain of the ship, who out topped him by a head, was ponderous in dimensions, with wide tread and feet like an elephant's; yet, it was said by those who had seen, a beautiful waltzer. His son, who was his clerk, used to say: "The old man's feet really aren't so big, if he would not wear such shoes." When his shoes were sent up to dry in the sun, as all sea-shoes must be at times, the midshipmen knew the occasion as a gunboat parade. The flag-officer was styled familiarly in the navy by the epithet Buckey; I never saw it spelled, but the pronunciation was as given. Report ran that he thus called every one, promiscuously; but, although I was his aide for nearly six months, I only heard him use it once or twice. Possibly he was breaking a bad habit.

Judged by my experience, which I believe was no worse than the average, the life of an aide is literally that of a dog; it was chiefly following round, or else sitting in a boat at a landing, just as a dog waits outside for his master, to all hours of the night, till your superior comes down from his dinner or out from the theatre. A coachman has a "cinch," to use our present-day slang; for he has only his own behavior to look to, while the aide has to see that the dozen bargemen also behave, don't skip up the wharf for a drink, and then forget the way back to the boat. If one or two do, no matter how good his dinner may have been, the remarks of the flag-officer are apt to be unpleasant; not to speak of subsequent interviews with the first-lieutenant. I trace to those days a horror which has never left me of keeping servants waiting. Flag-officers apparently never heard that punctuality is the politeness of kings. There are, however, occasional compensations; bones, I might say, pursuing the dog analogy. One incident very interesting to me occurred. The flag-officer had a well-deserved reputation for great bravery, and in his early career had fought two or three duels. One of these had been at Rio Janeiro, on an island in the harbor, and he had there killed his man. On this occasion, the barge being manned and I along, we pulled over to the island. In the thirty intervening years it must have changed greatly, for many buildings were now on it; but his memory evidently was busy and serving him well. He walked round meditatively, uttering a low, humming whistle, his hands in his pockets, his secretary and myself following. At last he reached a point where he stopped and mused for some moments, after which he went quietly and silently to the boat. Not a word passed from him to us during our stay, nor the subsequent pull to shore; but there can be little doubt where his thoughts were. It is right to add that on the occasion in question not only was the provocation all on the other side, but it was endured by him to the utmost that the standards of 1830 would permit.

To my aideship also I owed an unusual opportunity to see an incident of bygone times – the heaving down of a fair-sized ship of war. One of our sloops, of some eight hundred tons' burden, bound to China, had put into Rio for repairs: a leak of no special danger, but so near the keel as to demand examination. It might get worse. As yet Rio had no dry-dock, and so she must be hove down. This operation, probably never known in these days, when dry-docks are to be found in all quarters, consisted in heeling the ship over, by heavy purchases attached to the top of the lower masts, until the keel, or at least so much of the side as was necessary, was out of water. As the leverage on the masts was extreme, almost everything had to be taken out of the ship, guns included, to lighten her to the utmost; and the spars themselves were heavily backed to bear the strain. The upper works, usually out of water, must on the down side be closed and protected against the proposed immersion. In short, preparation was minute as well as extensive. In the old days, when docks were rare, and long voyages would be made in regions without local resources, a ship would be hove down two or three times in a cruise, to clean her uncoppered bottom or to see what damage worms might be effecting. When frequently done, familiarity doubtless made it comparatively easy; but by 1859 it had become very exceptional. I have never seen another instance. She was taken to a sheltered cove, in one of those picturesque bights which abound in the harbor of Rio, the most beautiful bay in the world, and there, in repeated visits by our flag-officer, I saw most stages of the process. Technical details I will not inflict upon the reader, but there was one amusing anecdote told me by our carpenter, who as a senior in his business was much to the fore. Some general overhauling was also required, and among other things the sloop's captain pointed out that the side-board in the cabin was not well secured. "I have sometimes to get up two or three times in the night to see to it," he said. He had been one of the restored victims of the Retiring Board of 1855, and had the reputation of knowing that sideboards exist for other purposes than merely being secured; hence, at this pathetic remark, the carpenter caught a wink, "on the fly," as it passed from the flag-officer to the captain of the *Congress* and back again. The commander invalided soon after, and the sloop went on her way to China under the charge of the first lieutenant.

The flag-officer, though not a man of particular distinction, possessed strongly that kind of individuality which among seamen of the days before steam, when the world was less small and less frequented, was more common than it is now, when we so cluster that, like shot in a barrel, we are rounded and polished by mere attrition. Formerly, characteristics had more chance to emphasize themselves and throw out angles, as I believe they still do in long polar seclusions. Withal, there came from him from time to time a whiff of the naval atmosphere of the past, like that from a drawer where lavender has been. Going ashore once with him for a constitutional, he caught sight of a necktie which my fond mother had given me. It was black, yes; but with variations. "Humph!" he ejaculated; "don't wear a thing like that with me. You look like a privateersman." There spoke the rivalries of 1812. There had not been a privateersman in the United States for near a half-century. A great chum of his was the senior surgeon of the frigate, a man near his own years. Leaving the ship together for a walk, the surgeon, crossing the deck, smudged his white trousers with paint or coal-tar, the free application of which in unexpected places is one of the snares attending a well-appearing man-of-war. "Never mind, doctor," said the flag-officer, consolingly, falling back like Sancho Panza on an ancient proverb; "remember the two dirtiest things in the world are a clean ship and a clean soldier" – paint and pipeclay, to wit.

Another trait was an extensive, though somewhat mild, profanity which took no account of ladies' presence, although he was almost exaggeratedly deferential to them, as well as cordially courteous to all. His speech was like his gait, tripping. I remember the arrival of the first steamer of a new French line to Rio. Steam mail-service was there and then exceptional; most of our home letters still came by sailing-vessel; consequently, this was an event, and brought the inevitable banquet. He was present; I also, as his aide, seated nearly opposite him, with two or three other of our officers. He was called to respond to a toast. "Gentlemen and ladies!" he began. "No! Ladies and gentlemen – ladies always first, d--n me!" What more he said I do not recall, although we all loyally applauded him. Many years afterwards, when he was old and feeble, an acquaintance of mine met him, and he began to tell of the tombstone of some person in whom he was interested. After various particulars, he startled his auditor with the general descriptive coruscation, "It was covered with angels and cherubs, and the h--l knows what else."

It would be easily possible to overdraw the personal peculiarities of the seamen. I remember nothing corresponding at all to the extravagances instanced in my early reading of Colburn's; such as a frigate's watch – say one hundred and fifty men – on liberty in Portsmouth, England, buying up all the gold-laced cocked bats in the place, and appearing with them at the theatre. Many, however, who have seen a homeward-bound ship leaving port, the lower rigging of her three masts crowded with seamen from deck to top, returning roundly the cheers given by all the ships-of-war present, foreign as well as national, as she passes, have witnessed also the time-honored ceremony of her crew throwing their hats overboard with the last cheer. This corresponded to the breaking of glasses after a favorite toast, or to the bursts of enthusiasm in a Spanish bull-ring, where Andalusian caps fly by dozens into the arena. There, however, the bull-fighter returns them, with many bows; but those of the homeward-bounders become the inheritance of the boatmen of the port. The midshipman of the watch being stationed on the forecastle, my intimates among the crew were the staid seamen, approaching middle-age; allotted there, where they would have least going aloft. The two captains of the forecastle – one, I shrewdly think, Dutch, the other English, though both had English names – would engage in conversation with me at times, mingling deference and conscious superior experience in due proportion. One, I remember, just before the War of Secession began, was greatly exercised about the oncoming troubles. The causes of the difficulty and the political complications disturbed him little; but the probable prospect of the heads of the rebellion losing their property engrossed his mind. He constantly returned to this; it would be confiscated, doubtless; yet the assertion was an evident implied query to me, to which I could give no positive answer. As is known, few of the seamen, as of private soldiers in the army, sympathized sufficiently with the Confederacy to join it. Indeed, the vaunt I have heard attributed to Southern officers of the old navy, which, though never uttered in my ears, was very consonant to the Southern spirit as I then knew it, that Southern officers with Yankee seamen could beat the world, testified at least to the probable attitude of the latter in a war of sections. Considering the great naval names of the past, Preble, Hull, Decatur, Bainbridge, Stewart, Porter, Perry, and Macdonough, the two most Southern of whom came from Delaware and Maryland, this ante-bellum assurance was, to say the least, self-confident; but Farragut was a Southerner. The other captain of the forecastle was less communicative, taciturn by nature; but there ran of him a story of amusing simplicity. It occurred to him on one occasion that he would lay under contribution the resources of the ship's small library. Accordingly he went to the chaplain, in whose care it was; but as he was wholly in the dark as to what particular book he might like, the chaplain, after two or three tries, suggested a *Life of Paul Jones*. Yes, he thought he would like that. "You see, I was shipmates with him some cruises ago; he was with me in the main-top of the ----."

Another forecastle intimate of mine was the boatswain, who, like most boatswains of that day, had served his time before the mast. As is the case with many self-made men, he, on his small scale, was very conscious of the fact, and of general consequent desert. A favorite saying with him was, "Thanks to my own industry and my wife's economy, I am now well beforehand with the world." Like a distinguished officer higher in rank of that day, of whom it was said that he remembered nothing later than 1813, my boatswain's memory dwelt much in the thirties, though he acknowledged more recent experiences. His attitude towards steam, essentially conservative, was strictly and amusingly official. He had served on board one steamer, the *San Jacinto*; and what had pleased him was that the yards could be squared and rigging hauled taut – his own special function – before entering port, so that in those respects the job had been done when the anchor dropped. One of his pet stories, frequently brought forward, concerned a schooner in which he had served in the earlier period, and will appeal to those who know how dear a fresh coat of paint is to a seaman's heart. She had just been thus decorated within and without, and was standing into a West-Indian port to show her fine feathers, when a sudden flaw of wind knocked her off, and over, dangerously close to a rocky point. The first order given was, "Stand clear of the paint-work!" – an instance of the ruling passion strong *in extremis*. He had another woesome account of a sloop-of-war in which he had gone through the Straits of Magellan. The difficult navigation and balky winds made the passage protracted for a sailing-vessel; all were put on short rations, and the day before she entered a Chilian port the bread-room was swept to the last crumbs. "I often could not sleep for hunger when I turned in." In the same ship, the watch-officers falling short, through illness or suspension, the captain set a second lieutenant of marines to take a day watch. Being, as he supposed, put to do something, he naturally wanted to do it, if he only knew what it was, and how it was to be done. The master of the ship was named Peter Wager, and to him, when taking sights, the marine appealed. "Peter, what's the use of being officer of the deck if you don't do anything? Tell me something to do." "Well," Peter replied, "you might send all the watch aft and take in the mizzen-royal" – the mizzen-royal being the smallest of all sails, requiring about two ordinary men, and in no wise missed when in. This was practical "tales for the marines."

This boatswain afterwards saw the last of the *Congress*, when the *Merrimac* – or rather the *Virginia*, to give her her Confederate name – wasted time murdering a ship already dead, aground and on fire. He often afterwards spun me the yarn; for I liked the old man, and not infrequently went to see him in later days. He had borne good-humoredly the testiness with which a youngster is at times prone to assert himself against what he fancies interference, and I had appreciated the rebuke. The *Congress* disaster was a very big and striking incident in the career of any person, and it both ministered to his self-esteem and provided the evening of his life with material for talk. Unhappily, I have to confess, as even Boswell at times did, I took no notes, and cannot reproduce that which to me is of absorbing interest, the individual impressions of a vivid catastrophe.

The boatswain was one of the four who in naval phrase were termed "warrant" officers, in distinction from the lieutenants and those above, who held their offices by "commission." The three others were the gunner, carpenter, and sailmaker, names which sufficiently indicate their several functions. In the hierarchical classification of the navy, as then established by long tradition, the midshipmen, although on their way to a commission, were warrant officers also; and in consequence, though they had a separate mess, they had the same smoking-place, the effect of which in

157

establishing a community of social intercourse every smoker will recognize. I suppose, if there had been three sides to a ship, there would have been three smoking-rendezvous; but in the crude barbarism of those days – as it will now probably be considered – both commissioned and warrant officers had no place to smoke except away forward on the gun-deck – the "eyes" of the ship, as the spot was appropriately named; the superiors on the honor side, which on the gun-deck was the port, the midshipmen and warrant officers on the starboard. The position was not without advantages, when riding head to wind, in hot tropical weather; but under way, close-hauled, with a stiff breeze, a good deal of salt water found its way in, especially if the jackasses were in the hawse-holes. But under such conditions we sat there serenely, the water coursing in a flowing stream under our chairs if the ship had a steady heel, or rushing madly from side to side if she lurched to windward. The stupidity of it was that we didn't even know we were uncomfortable, and by all sound philosophy were so far better off than our better accommodated successors. What was more annoying was the getting forward at night, when the hammocks were in place; but even for that occasional compensations offered. I remember once, when making this awkward journey, hearing a colloquy between two young seamen just about to swing themselves into bed at nine o'clock. "I say, Bill," said one, with voluptuous satisfaction, "too watches in,[9] and beans to-morrow." Can any philosophy soar higher than that, in contentment with small things? Plain living and high thinking! Diogenes wasn't in it.

As the warrant officers of the ship were of the generation before us, we heard from their lips many racy and entertaining experiences of the former navy, most of which naturally have escaped me, while others I have dropped all along the line of my preceding reminiscences where they seemed to come in aptly. Each of the four had very different characteristics, and I fancy they did not agree very well together. All have long since gone to their rest; peace be with them! Four is an awkwardly small number for a mess-table of equals; friction is emphasized by narrowness of sphere. "I didn't like the man," said the boatswain afterwards to me of the sailmaker, narrating the destruction of the *Congress*; "but he is brave, brave as can be. Getting the wounded over the side to put them ashore, he was as cool as though nothing was happening. The great guns weren't so bad," he continued – "but the rifle-bullets that came singing along in clouds like mosquitoes! Yah!" he used to snap, each time he told me the tale, slapping his ears right and left, as one does at the hum of those intrusive insects. He did not like the carpenter, either, for reasons of another kind. They were both humorists, but of a different order. Indeed, I don't think that the boatswain, though slightly sardonic in expression, suspected himself of humor; but he really came at times pretty close to wit, if that be a perception of incongruities, as I have heard said. He was telling one day of some mishap that befell a vessel, wherein the officer in charge showed the happy blending of composure and ignorance we sometimes find; a condition concerning which a sufferer once said of himself, "I never open my mouth but I put my foot in it;" a confusion of metaphor, and suggestion of physical contortion, not often so neatly combined in a dozen words. The boatswain commented: "He didn't mind. He didn't know what to do, but there he stood, looking all the time as happy as a duck barefooted." A duck shod, and the consequent expression of its countenance, presents to my mind infinite entertainment. Our first lieutenant, under whom immediately he worked, was a great trial to him. He was an elderly man, as first lieutenants of big ships were then, great with the paint-brush and tar-pot, traces of which were continually surprising one's clothes; mighty also in that lavish swashing of sea-water which is called washing decks, and in the tropics is not so bad; but otherwise, while he was one of the kindliest of men, the go was pretty well out of him. "Yes," the boatswain used to say grimly, – he seldom smiled, – "the first lieutenant is like an old piece of soap – half wore out. Go day, come day, God send Sunday; that's he."

The carpenter, on the other hand, was always on a broad grin – or rather roar. He breathed farce, both in story and feature. Unlike the boatswain, who was middle-sized and very trig, as well as scrupulously neat, the carpenter was over six feet, broad in proportion, with big, round, red, close-shaven face, framed with abundance of white hair. He looked not unlike one's fancies of the typical English yeoman, while withal having a strong Yankee flavor. Wearing always a frock-

coat, buttoned up as high as any one then buttoned, he carried with it a bluff heartiness of
manner, which gave an impression of solidity not,
I fear, wholly sustained on demand. There was no
such doubt about the fun, however, or his own
huge enjoyment of his own stories, accompanied
by a running fire of guffaws, which pointed the
appreciation we easily gave. But it was all of the
same character, broad farce; accounts of mishaps
such as befall in children's pantomimes, – which
their seniors enjoy, too, – practical jokes equally
ludicrous, and resulting situations to match.
Comical as such tales were at the time, and many
a pleasant pipeful of Lynchburg tobacco in Pow-
hatan clay though they whiled away, they lacked
the catching and fixing power of the boatswain's
shrewd sayings. I can remember distinctly only
one, of two small midshipmen, shipmates of his in
a sloop-of-war of long-gone days, who had a
deadly quarrel, calling for blood. A duel ashore
might in those times have been arranged, unknown to superiors – they often were; but the necessity for speedy satisfaction was too urgent, and
they could not wait for the end of the voyage.
Consequently, they determined to fight from the
two ends of the spritsail-yard, a horizontal spar
which crossed the bowsprit end, and gave, or
could admit, the required number of paces. Seconds, I presume, were omitted; they might have
attracted unnecessary attention, and on the yard
would have been in the way of shot, unless they
sat behind their several principals, like damsels on
a pillion. So these two mites, procuring each a
loaded pistol, crawled out quietly to their respec-

tive places, straddled the yard, and were proceeding to business, when the boatswain caught sight of them from his frequent stand-point between the knightheads. He ran out, got between them in the line of fire, and from this position of tactical advantage, having collared first one and then the other, brought them both in on the forecastle, where he knocked their heads together. The last action, I fancy, must be considered an embellishment, necessary to the dramatic completeness of the incident, though it may at least be admitted it would not have been incongruous. In telling this occurrence, which, punctuated by his own laughter, bore frequent repetition, the carpenter used to give the names of the heroes. One I have forgotten. The other I knew in after life and middle-age, still small of stature, with a red face, in outline much like a paroquet's. He was not a bad fellow; but his first lieutenant, a very competent critic, used to say that what he did not know of seamanship would fill a large book.

At first thought it seems somewhat singular that the six lieutenants of the ship presented no such aggregate of idiosyncrasies as did the four warrant officers. It was not by any means because we did not know them well, and mingle among them with comparative frequency. Midshipmen, we travelled from one side to the other; here at home, there guests, but to both admitted freely. But, come to think of it more widely, the distinction I here note must have had a foundation in conditions. My acquaintance with Marryat, who lived the naval life as no other sea author has, is now somewhat remote, but was once intimate as well as extensive; and recollection deceives me if the same remark does not apply to his characters. He has a full gallery of captains and lieutenants, each differing from the other; but his greatest successes in portrayal, those that take hold of the memory, are his warrant officers – boatswains, gunners, and carpenters. The British navy did not give sailmakers this promotion. By-products though they are, rather than leading characters, Boatswain Chucks, whom Marryat takes off the stage midway, as though too much to sustain to the end, Carpenter Muddle, and Gunner Tallboys, with his aspirations towards navigating, sketched but briefly and in bold outline as they are, survive most of their superiors in clear individuality and amusing eccentricity. Peter Simple, and even Jack Easy himself, whose traits are more personal than nautical, are less vivid to memory. Cooper also, who caricatures rather than reproduces life, seeks here his fittest subjects – Boltrope and Trysail – warrant masters, superior in grade indeed to the others, but closely identified with them on board ship, and essentially of the same class. Such coincidence betokens a more pronounced individuality in the subject-matter. There have been particular eccentric commissioned officers, of whom quaint stories have descended; but in early days, originality was the class-mark of those of whom I am speaking, as many an anecdote witnesses. I fancy few will have seen this, which I picked up in my miscellaneous nautical readings. A boatswain, who had been with Cook in his voyages, chanced upon one of those fervent Methodist meetings common in the eighteenth century. The preacher, in illustration of the abundance of the Divine mercy, affirmed that there was hope for the worst, even for the boatswain of a man-of-war; whereupon the boatswain sprang to the platform and administered a drubbing. True or not, offence and punishment testify to public estimate as to character and action; to a natural exaggeration of feature which lends itself readily to reproduction. This was due, probably, to a more contracted sphere in early life, and afterwards less of that social opportunity, in the course of which angular projections are rounded off and personal peculiarities softened by various contact. The same cause would naturally occasion more friction and disagreement among themselves.

Thus the several lieutenants of our frigate call for no special characterization. If egotism, the most amusing of traits where it is not offensive, existed among them to any unusual degree, it was modified and concealed by the acquired exterior of social usage. Their interests also were wider. With them, talk was less of self and personal experience, and more upon subjects of general interest, professional or external; the outlook was wider. But while all this tended to make them more instructive, and in so far more useful companions, it also took from the salt of individuality somewhat of its pungency. It did not fall to them, either, to become afterwards especially conspicuous in the nearing War of Secession. They were good seamen and gallant men; knew their duty and did it; but either opportunity failed them, or they failed opportunity; from my knowledge of them, probably the former. As Nelson once wrote:

"A sea officer cannot form plans like those of a land officer; his object is to embrace the happy moment which now and then offers; it may be this day, not for a month, and perhaps never." So also Farragut is reported to have said of a conspicuous shortcoming: "Every man has one chance; he has had his and lost it." Certainly, by failure that man lost promotion with its chances. It is somewhat congruous to this train of thought that Smith, whom I have so often mentioned, said one day to me: "If I had a son (he was unmarried), I would put him in the navy without hesitation. I believe there is a day coming shortly when the opportunities for a naval officer will exceed any that our country has yet known." He did not say what contingencies he had in mind; scarcely those of the War of Secession, large looming though it already was, for, like most of us, he doubtless refused to entertain that sorrowful possibility. As with many a prophecy, his was of wider scope than he thought; and, though in part fulfilled, more yet remains on the laps of the gods. He himself, perhaps the ablest of this group, was cut off too early to contribute more than an heroic memory; but that must live in naval annals, enshrined in his father's phrase, along with Craven's "After you, pilot," when the *Tecumseh* sank.

VI
MY FIRST CRUISE AFTER GRADUATION
– NAUTICAL SCENES AND SCENERY
– THE APPROACH OF DISUNION

1859-1861

The absence of the *Congress* lasted a little over two years, the fateful two years in which the elements of strife in the United States were sifting apart and gathering in new combinations for the tremendous outbreak of 1861. The first battle of Bull Run had been fought before she again saw a home port. The cruise offered little worthy of special note. This story is one of commonplaces; but they are the commonplaces of conditions which have passed away forever, and some details are worthy to be not entirely forgotten, now that the life has disappeared. We were in contact with it in all its forms and phases; being, as midshipmen, utilized for every kind of miscellaneous and nondescript duty. Our captain interfered very little with us directly, and I might almost say washed his hands of us. The regulations required that at the expiry of a cruise the commander of a vessel should give his midshipmen a letter, to be presented to the board of examiners before whom they were shortly to appear. Ours, while certifying to our general correct behavior – personal rather than official – limited himself, on the score of professional accomplishments, which should have been under constant observance, to saying that, as we were soon to appear before a board, the intent of which would be to test them, he forbore an opin-

166

ion. This was even more non-committal than another captain, whose certificates came under my eye when myself a member of a board. In these, after some very cautious commendation on the score of conduct, he added, "I should have liked the display of a little more zeal." Zeal, the readers of *Midshipman Easy* will remember, is the naval universal solvent. Although liable at times to be misplaced, as Easy found, it is not so suspicious a quality as Talleyrand considered it to be in diplomacy.

Our captain's zeal for our improvement confined itself to putting us in three watches; that is, every night we had to be on deck and duty through one of the three periods, of four hours each, into which the sea night is divided. Of this he made a principle, and in it doubtless found the satisfaction of a good conscience; he had done all that could be expected, at least by himself. I personally agree with Basil Hall; upon the whole, watch keeping pays, yields more of interest than of disagreeables. It must be conceded that it was unpleasant to be waked at midnight in your warm hammock, told your hour was come, that it was raining and blowing hard, that another reef was about to be taken in the topsails and the topgallant yards sent on deck. Patriotism and glory seemed very poor stimulants at that moment. Still half asleep, you tumbled, somewhat literally, out of the hammock on to a deck probably wet, dressed by a dim, single-wick swinging lantern, which revealed chiefly what you did not want, or by a candle which had to be watched with one eye lest it roll over and, as once in my experience happened, set fire to wood-work. Needless to say, electric lights then were not. Dressed in storm-clothes about as conducive to agility as a suit of mediæval armor, and a sou'wester which caught at every corner you turned, you forced your way up through two successive tarpaulin-covered hatches, by holes just big enough to pass, pushing aside the tarpaulin with one hand while the other steadied yourself. And if there were no moon, how black the outside was, to an eye as yet adjusted only to the darkness visible of the lanterns below! Except a single ray on the little book by which the midshipman mustered the watch, no gleam of artificial light was permitted on the spar – upper – deck; the fitful flashes dazzled more than they helped. You groped your way forward with some certainty, due to familiarity with the ground, and with more certainty of being jostled and trampled by your many watch-mates, quite as blind and much more sleepy than their officers could afford to be. The rain stung your face; the wind howled in your ears and drowned your voice; the men were either intent on going below, or drowsy and ill-reconciled to having to come on deck; in either case inattentive and hard to move for some moments.

In truth, the fifteen minutes attending the change of a watch were a period not only of inconvenience, but of real danger too rarely appreciated. I remember one of the smartest seamen and officers of the old navy speaking feelingly to me of the anxiety those instants often caused him. The lieutenant of an expiring watch too frequently would postpone some necessary step, either from personal indolence or from a good-natured indisposition to disturb the men, who when not needed to work slept about the decks – except, of course, the lookouts and wheel. The other watch will soon be coming up, he would argue; let them do it, before they settle down to sleep. There were times, such as a slowly increasing gale, which might justify delay; especially if the watch had had an unusual amount of work. But tropical squalls, which gather quickly and sweep down with hurricane force, are another matter; and it was of these the officer quoted spoke, suggesting that possibly such an experience had caused the loss of one of our large, tall-sparred sloops-of-war, the *Albany*, which in 1854 disappeared in the West Indies. The men who have been four hours on deck are thinking only of their hammocks; their reliefs are not half awake, and do not feel they are on duty until the watch is mustered. All are mingled together; the very numbers of a ship of war under such circumstances impede themselves and their officers. I remember an acquaintance of mine telling me that once on taking the trumpet, the outward and visible sign of "the deck being relieved," his predecessor, after "turning over the night orders," said, casually, "It looks like a pretty big squall coming up there to windward," and incontinently dived below. "I jumped on the horseblock," said the narrator, "and there it was, sure enough, coming down hand over fist. I had no time to shorten sail, but only to put the helm up and get her before it;" an instance in point of what an old gray-haired instructor of ours used to say, with correct accentuation, "Always the hellum first."

But, when you were awake, what a mighty stimulus there was in the salt roaring wind and the pelting rain! how infectious the shout of the officer of the deck! the answering cry of the topmen aloft – the "Haul out to windward! Together! All!" that reached your ear from the yards as the men struggled with the wet, swollen, thrashing canvas, mastering it with mighty pull, and "lighting to windward" the reef-band which was to be the new head of the sail, ready to the hand of the man at the post of honor, the weather caring! How eager and absorbing the gaze through the darkness, from deck, to see how they were getting on; whether the yard was so braced that the sail lay with the wind out of it, really slack for handling, though still bellying and lifting as the ship rolled, or headed up or off; whether this rope or that which controlled the wilful canvas needed another pull. But if the yard itself had not been laid right, it was too late to mend it. To start a brace with the men on the spar might cause a jerk that would spill from it some one whose both hands were in the work, contrary to the sound tradition, "One hand for yourself and one for the owners." I believe the old English phrase ran, "One for yourself and one for the king." Then, when all was over and snug once more, the men down from aloft, the rigging coiled up again on its pins, there succeeded the delightful relaxation from work well done and finished, the easy acceptance of the quieting yet stimulating effect of the strong air, enjoyed in indolence; for nothing was more unoccupied than the seaman when the last reef was in the topsails and the ship lying-to.

Talking of such sensations, and the idle *abandon* of a whole gale of wind after the ship is secured, I wonder how many of my readers will have seen the following ancient song. I guard myself from implying the full acquiescence of seamen in what is, of course, a caricature; few seamen, few who have tried, really enjoy bad weather. Yet there are exceptions. That there is no accounting for tastes is extraordinarily true. I once met a man, journeying, who told me he liked living in a sleeping-car; than which to me a dozen gales, with their abounding fresh air, would be preferable. Yet this ditty does grotesquely reproduce the lazy satisfaction and security of the old-timers under the conditions:

"One night came on a hurricane, The sea was mountains rolling, When Barney Buntline turned his quid And said to Billy Bowline, 'A strong nor'wester's blowing, Bill: Hark! don't you hear it roar now? Lord help them! how I pities all Unlucky folks on shore now.

"'Foolhardy chaps, that live in towns, What dangers they are all in! And now lie shaking in their beds, For fear the roof should fall in! Poor creatures, how they envies us, And wishes, I've a notion, For our good luck, in such a storm, To be upon the ocean.

"'And often, Bill, I have been told How folks are killed, and undone, By overturns of carriages, By fogs and fires in London. We know what risks all landsmen run, From noblemen to tailors: Then,

Bill, let us thank Providence That you and I are sailors.'"

Tastes differ as to which of the three night watches is preferable. Perhaps some one who has tried will reply they are all alike detestable, and, if he be Irish, will add that the only decent watch on deck is the watch below – an "all night in." But I also have tried; and while prepared to admit that perhaps the pleasantest moment of any particular watch is that in which your successor touches his cap and says, "I'll relieve you," I still maintain there are abundant and large compensations. Particularly for a midshipman, for he had no responsibilities. The lieutenant of the watch had always before him the possibilities of a mischance; and one very good officer said to me he did not believe any lieutenant in the navy felt perfectly comfortable in charge of the deck in a heavy gale. Freedom from anxiety, however, is a matter of temperament; not by any means necessarily of courage, although it adds to courage the invaluable quality of not wasting nerve force on difficulties of the imagination. A weather-brace may go unexpectedly; a topsail-sheet part; an awkward wave come on board. Very true; but what is the use of worrying, unless you are constitutionally disposed to worry. If you are constitutionally so disposed, I admit there is not much use in talking. Illustrative of this, the following story has come down of two British admirals, both men of proved merit and gallantry. "When Howe was in command of the Channel Fleet, after a dark and boisterous night, in which the ships had been in some danger of running foul of each other, Lord Gardner, then the third in command, the next day went on board the *Queen Charlotte* and inquired of Lord Howe how he had slept, for that he himself had not been able to get any rest from anxiety of mind. Lord Howe said he had slept perfectly well, for, as he had taken every possible precaution he could before dark, he laid himself down with a conscious feeling that everything had been done which it was in his power to do for the safety of the ships and of the lives intrusted to his care, and this conviction set his mind at ease." The apprehensiveness with which Gardner was afflicted "is further exemplified by an anecdote told by Admiral Sir James Whitshed, who commanded the *Alligator*, next him in the line. Such was his anxiety, even in ordinary weather, that, though each ship carried three poop lanterns, he always kept one burning in his cabin, and when he thought the *Alligator* was approaching too near, he used to run out into the stern gallery with the lantern in his hand, waving it so as to be noticed." My friend above quoted had only recently quitted a brig-of-war, on board which he had passed several night watches with a man standing by the lee topsail-sheet, axe in hand, to cut if she went over too far, lest she might not come back; and the circumstance had left an impression. I do not think he was much troubled in this way on board our frigate; yet the *Savannah*, but little smaller than the *Congress*, had been laid nearly on her beam-ends by a sudden squall, and had to cut, when entering Rio two years before.

Being even at nineteen of a meditative turn, fond of building castles in the air, or recalling old acquaintance and *auld lang syne*, – the retrospect of youth, though short, seems longer than that of age, – I preferred in ordinary weather the mid-watch, from midnight to four. There was then less doing; more time and scope to enjoy. The canvas had long before been arranged for the night. If the wind shifted, or necessity for tacking arose, of course it was done; but otherwise a considerate officer would let the men sleep, only rousing them for imperative reasons. The hum of the ship, the loitering "idlers," – men who do not keep watch, – last well on to ten, or after, in the preceding watch; and the officers of the deck in sailing-ships had not the reserve – or preserve – which the isolation of the modern bridge affords its occupants. Although the weather side of the quarter-deck was kept clear for him and the captain, there was continued going and coming, and talking near by. He was on the edge of things, if not in the midst; while the midshipman of the forecastle had scarce a foot he could call his very own. But when the mid-watch had been mustered, the lookouts stationed, and the rest of them had settled themselves down for sleep between the guns, out of the way of passing feet, the forecastle of the *Congress* offered a very decent promenade, magnificent compared to that proverbial of the poops of small vessels – "two steps and overboard." Then began the steady pace to and fro, which to me was natural and inherited, easily maintained and consistent with thought – indeed, productive of it. Not every officer has this habit, but most acquire it. I have been told that, however weakly otherwise, the calf muscles of watch-officers were generally well developed. There were exceptions. A lieutenant who was something of a wag on one occasion handed the midshipman of his watch a small instrument, in which the latter did not recognize a pedometer. "Will you kindly keep this in your trousers-pocket for me till the watch is over?" At eight bells he asked for it, and, after examining, said, quizzically, "Mr. ----, I see you have walked just half a mile in the last four hours." Of course, walking is not imperative, one may watch standing; but movement tends to wakefulness – you can drowse upon your feet – while to sit down, besides being forbidden by unwritten law, is a treacherous snare to young eyelids.

How much a watch afforded to an eye that loved nature! I have been bored so often by descriptions of scenery, that I am warned to put here a sharp check on my memory, lest it run away with me, and my readers seek escape by jumping off. I will forbear, therefore, any attempt at portraiture, and merely mention the superb aurora borealis which illuminated several nights of the autumn of 1859, perceptibly affecting the brightness of the atmosphere, while we lay becalmed a little north of the tropics. But other things I shall have some excuse for telling; because what my eyes used to see then few mortal eyes will see again. Travel will not reach it; for though here and there a rare sailing-ship is kept in a navy, for occasional instruction, otherwise they have passed away forever; and the exceptions are but curiosities – reality has disappeared. They no longer have life, and are now but the specimens of the museum. The beauties of a brilliant night at sea, whether starlit or moonlit, the solemn, awe-inspiring gloom and silence of a clouded, threatening sky, as the steamer with dull thud moves at midnight over the waste of waters, these I need not describe; many there are that see them in these rambling days. These eternities of the heavens and the deep abide as before, are common to the steamer as to the sailing-ship; but what weary strain of words can restore to imagination the beautiful living creature which leaped under our feet and spread her wings above us? For a sailing-ship was more inspiring from within than from without, especially a ship of war, which, as usually ordered, permitted no slovenliness; abounded in the perpetual seemliness that enhances beauty yet takes naught from grace. Viewed from without, undeniably a ship under sail possesses attraction; but it is from within that you feel the "very pulse of the machine." No canvas looks so lofty, speaks so eloquently, as that seen from its own deck, and this chiefly has invested the sailing-vessel with its poetry. This the steamer, with its vulgar appeal to physical comfort, cannot give. Does any one know any verse of real poetry, any strong, thrilling idea, suitably voiced, concerning a steamer? I do – one – by Clough, depicting the wrench from home, the stern inspiration following the wail of him who goeth away to return no more:

"Come back! come back! Back flies the foam; the hoisted flag streams back; The long smoke wavers on the homeward track. Back fly with winds things which the winds obey, *The strong ship follows its appointed way*."

Oddly enough, two of the most striking sea scenes that I remember, very different in character, associate themselves with my favorite midwatch. The first was the night on which we struck the northeast trade-winds, outward bound. We had been becalmed for nearly, if not quite, two weeks in the "horse latitudes;" which take their name, tradition asserts, from the days when the West India sugar islands depended for live-stock, and much besides, on the British continental colonies. If too long becalmed, and water gave out, the unhappy creatures had to be thrown overboard to save human lives. On the other side of the northeast trades, between them and the southeast, towards the equator, lies another zone of calms, the doldrums, from which also the *Congress* this time suffered. We were sixty seven or eight days from the Capes of the Delaware to Bahia, a distance, direct, of little more than four thousand miles. Of course, there was some beating against head wind, but we could not have averaged a hundred miles to the twenty-four hours. During much of this passage the allowance of fresh water was reduced to two quarts per man, except sick, for all purposes of consumption – drinking and cooking. Under such conditions, washing had to be done with salt water.

We had worried our weary way through the horse latitudes, embracing every flaw of wind, often accompanied by rain, to get a mile ahead here, half a dozen miles there; and, as these spurts come from every quarter, this involves a lot of bracing – changing the position of the yards; continuous work, very different from the placid restfulness of a "whole gale" of wind, with everything snug aloft and no chance of let-up during the watch. Between these occasional puffs would come long pauses of dead calm, in which the midshipman of the watch would enter in the log: "1 A.M., 0 knots; 2 A.M., 6 fathoms (¾ knot); 3 A.M., 0 knots; 4 A.M., 1 knot, 2 fathoms;" the last representing usually a guess of the officer of the deck as to what would make the aggregate for the four hours nearly right. It did not matter, for we were hundreds of miles from land and the sky always clear for observations. Few of the watch got much sleep, because of the perpetual bracing; and all the while the ship rolling and sending, in the long, glassy ocean swell, unsteadied by the empty sails, which swung out with one lurch as though full, and then slapped back all together against the masts, with a swing and a jerk and a thud that made every spar tremble, and the vessel herself quiver in unison. Nor were we alone. Frequently two or three American clippers would be hull-up at the same moment within our horizon, bound the same way; and it was singular how, despite the apparently unbroken calm, we got away from one another and disappeared. Ships lying with their heads "all around the compass" flapped themselves along in the direction of their bows, the line of least resistance.

I do not know at what hour under such circumstances we had struck the trades, but when I came on deck at midnight we had got them steady and strong. As there was still a good-deal of casting to make, the ship had been brought close to the wind on the port tack; the bowlines steadied out, but not dragged, every sail a good rap full, "fast asleep," without the tremor of an eyelid, if I may so style a weather leach, or of any inch of the canvas, from the royals down to the courses. Every condition was as if arranged for a special occasion, or to recompense us for the tedium of the horse latitudes. The moon was big, and there was a clear sky, save for the narrow band of tiny clouds, massed like a flock of sheep, which ever fringes the horizon of the trades; always on the horizon, as you progress, yet never visible above when the horizon of this hour has become the zenith of the next. After the watch was mustered and the lookouts stationed, there came perfect silence, save for the slight, but not ominous, singing of the wind through the rigging, and the dash of the water against the bows, audible forward though not aft. The seamen, not romantically inclined, for the most part heeded neither moon nor sky nor canvas. The vivid, delicate tracery of the shrouds and ruining gear, the broader image of the sails, shadowed on the moonlit deck, appealed not to them. Recognizing only that we had a steady wind, no more bracing to-night, and that the most that could happen would be to furl the royals should it freshen, they hastened to stow themselves away for a full due between the cannon, out of the way of passing feet, sure that this watch on deck would be little less good than one below. Perhaps there were also visions of "beans to-morrow." I trust so.

The lieutenant of the watch, Smith, and I had it all to ourselves; unbroken, save for the half-hourly call of the lookouts: "Starboard cathead!" "Port cathead!" "Starboard gangway!" "Port gangway!" "Life buoy!" He came forward from time to time to take it all in, and to see how the light spars were standing, for the ship was heeling eight or ten degrees, and racing along, however quietly; but the strain was steady, no whipping about from uneasy movement of the vessel, and we carried on to the end. Each hour I hove the log and reported: one o'clock, eleven knots; two o'clock, eleven; three o'clock, eleven – famous going for an old sailing-ship close-hauled. Splendid! we rubbed our hands; what a record! But, alas! at four o'clock, ten! Commonly, ten used to be a kind of standard of excellence; Nelson once wrote, as expressive of an utmost of hopefulness, "If we all went ten knots, I should not think it fast enough;" but, puffed up as we had been, it was now a sad come-down. Smith looked at me. "Are you *sure*, Mr. Mahan?" With the old hand-log, its line running out while the sand sped its way through the fourteen-seconds glass, the log-beaver might sometimes, by judicious "feeding" – hurrying the line under the plea of not dragging the log-chip – squeeze a little more record out of the log-line than the facts warranted; and Smith seemed to feel I might have done a little better for the watch and for the ship. But in truth, when a cord is rushing through your hand at the rate of ten miles an hour – fifteen feet a second – you cannot get hold enough to hasten the pace. He passed through a struggle of conscience. "Well, I suppose I must; log her ten-four." A poor tail to our beautiful kite. Ten-four meant ten and a half; for in those primitive days knots were divided into eight fathoms. Now they are reckoned by tenths; a small triumph of the decimal system, which may also carry cheer to the constant hearts of the spelling reformers.

A year later, at like dead of night, I witnessed quite another scene. We were then off the mouth of the river La Plata, perhaps two hundred miles from shore. We had been a fortnight at sea, cruising; and I have always thought that the captain, who was interested in meteorology and knew the region, kept us out till we should catch a *pampero*. We caught it, and quite up to sample. I had been on deck at 9 P.M., and the scene then, save for the force of the wind, was nearly the same as that I have just described. The same sail, the same cloudless sky and large moon; but we were going only five knots, with a quiet, rippling sea, on which the moonbeams danced. Such a scene as Byron doubtless had in memory:

"The midnight moon is weaving Her bright chain o'er the deep; Whose breast is gently heaving Like an infant's asleep."

Having to turn out at twelve, I soon started below; but before swinging into my hammock I heard the order to furl the royals and send the yards on deck. This startled me, for I had not been watching the barometer, as the captain had; and I remember, by the same token, that I was then enlarging on the beauties of the outlook above, accompanied by some disparaging remarks about what steamers could show, whereupon one of our senior officers, over-hearing, called me in, and

181

told me quite affably, and in delicate terms, not to make a fool of myself.

But "Linden saw another sight," when I returned to the deck at midnight; sharp, I am sure, for I held to the somewhat priggish saying, first devised, I imagine, by some wag tired of waiting for his successor, "A prompt relief is the pride of a young officer." The quartermaster, who called me and left the lantern dimly burning, had conveyed the comforting assurance that it looked very bad on deck, and the second reef was just taking in the topsails. When I got to my station, the former watch was still aloft, tying their last reef-points, from which they soon straggled down, morosely conscious that they had lost ten minutes of their one watch below, and would have to be on deck again at four. The moon was still up, but, as it were, only to emphasize the darkness of the huge cloud masses which scudded across the sky, with a rapid but steady gait, showing that the wind meant business. The new watch was given no more time than to wake up and shake themselves. They were soon on the yards, taking the third and fourth-last – reefs in the fore and main topsails, furling the mizzen, and seeing that the lower sails and topgallant-sails were securely rolled up against the burst that was to be expected. Before 1.30 A.M. all things were as ready as care could make them, and not too soon. The moon was sinking, or had sunk; the sky darkened steadily, though not beyond that natural to a starless night. In the southwest faint glimmerings of lightning gave warning of what might be looked for; but we had used light well while we had it, and could now bear what was to come. At 2 P.M. it came with a roar and a rush, "butt-end foremost," as the saying is, preceded by a few huge drops of scurrying rain.

"When the rain before the wind, Topsail sheets and halyards mind;"

but that was for other conditions than ours.

A pampero at its ordinary level is no joke; but this was the charge of a wild elephant, which would exhaust itself soon, but for the nonce was terrific. Pitch darkness settled down upon the ship. Except in the frequent flashes of lightning, literally blue, I could not see the forecastle boatswain's mate of the watch, who stood close by my elbow, ready pipe in hand. The rain came down in buckets, and in the midst of all the wind suddenly shifted, taking the sails flat aback. The shrillness of the boatswain's pipes is then their great merit. They pierce through the roar of the tempest, by sheer difference of pitch, an effect one sometimes hears in an opera; and the officer of the deck, our second lieutenant, who bore the name of Andrew Jackson, and was said to have received his appointment from him – which shows how far back he went – had a voice of somewhat the same quality. I had often heard it assert itself, winding in and out through the uproar of an ordinary gale, but on this occasion it went clean away – whistled down the wind. "I always think bad of it," said Boatswain Chucks, "when the elements won't allow my whistle to be heard; and I consider it hardly fair play." Such advantage the elements took of us on this occasion, but the captain came to the rescue. He had the throat of a bull of Bashan, which went the elements one better on their own hand. Under his stentorian shouts the weather head-braces were led along (probably already had been, as part of the preparation, but that was quarter-deck work, outside my knowledge) and manned. All other gear being coiled out of the way, on the pins, there was nothing to confuse or entangle; the fore topsail was swung round on the opposite tack from the main, a-box, to pay the ship's head off and leave her side to the wind, steadied by the close-reefed fore and main topsails, which would then be filled. She was now, of course, going astern fast; but this mattered nothing, for the sea had not yet got up. The evolution, common enough itself, an almost invariable accompaniment of getting under way, was now exciting even to grandeur, for we could see only when the benevolent lightning kindled in the sky a momentary glare of noonday. "Now that's a clever old man," said the boatswain's mate next day to me, approvingly, of the captain; "boxing her off that way, with all that wind and blackness, was handsomely done." After this we settled down to a two days' pampero, with a huge but regular sea.

Whether the *Congress's* helm on this interesting occasion was shifted for sternboard I never inquired. Marryat tells us it was a moot point in his young days. Our captain was an excellent seaman, but had 'doxies of his own. Of these, one which ran contrary to current standards was in favor of clewing up a course or topsail to leeward, in blowing weather. Among the lieutenants was a strong champion of the opposite and accepted dogma, and a messmate of mine, in his division and shining by reflected light, was always prompt to enforce closure of debate by declaiming:

"He who seeks the tempest to disarm Will never first embrail the lee yard-arm."

Whether Falconer, besides being a poet, was also an expert in seamanship, or whether he simply registered the views of his day, may be questioned. The two alternatives, I fancy, were the chance of splitting the sail, and that of springing the yard; and any one who has ever watched a big bag of wind whipping a weather yard-arm up and down in its bellying struggles, after clewing up to windward, will have experienced as eager a desire to call it down as he has ever felt to suppress its congener in an after-dinner oration. Both are much out of place and time.

Days of the past! Certainly a watch spent reefing topsails in the rain was less tedious than that everlasting bridge of to-day: Tramp! Tramp! or stand still, facing the wind blowing the teeth down your throat. Nothing to do requiring effort; the engine does all that; but still a perpetual strain of attention due to the rapid motion of vessels under steam. The very slowness of sailing-ships lightened anxiety. In such a gale you might as well be anxious in a wheel-chair. And then, when you went below, you went, not bored, but healthfully tired with active exertion of mind and body. Yes; the sound was sweet then, at eight bells, the pipe, pipe, pipe, pipe of the boatswain's mates, followed by their gruff voices drawling out, in loud singsong: "A-a-a-all the starboard watch! Come! turn out there! Tumble out! Tumble out! Show a leg!

Show a leg! On deck there! all the starboard watch!" When I went below that morning with the port watch, at four o'clock, I turned over to my relief a forecastle on which he would have nothing to do but drink his coffee at daylight.

That daylight coffee of the morning watch, chief of its charms, need not be described to the many who have experienced the difference between the old man and the new man of before and after coffee. The galley (kitchen) fire of ships of war used to be started at seven bells of the mid-watch (3.30 A.M.); and the officers, and most of the men, who next came on duty, managed to have coffee, the latter husbanding their rations to this end. Since those days a benevolent regulation has allowed an extra ration of coffee to the crew for this purpose, so that no man goes without, or works the morning watch on an empty stomach. For the morning watch was very busy. Then, on several days of the week, the seamen washed their clothes. Then the upper deck was daily scrubbed; sometimes the mere washing off the soap-suds left from the clothes, sometimes with brooms and sand, sometimes the solemn ceremony of holy-stoning with its monotonous musical sound of grinding. Along with these, dovetailed in as opportunity offered, in a sailing-ship under way there went on the work of readjusting the yards and sails; a pull here and a pull there, like a woman getting herself into shape after sitting too long in one position. Yards trimmed to a nicety; the two sheets of each sail close home alike; all the canvas taut up, from the weather-tacks of the courses to the weather-earings of the royals; no slack weather-braces, or weather-leaches, letting a bight of loose canvas sag like an incipient double chin. When these and a dozen other little details had remedied the disorders of the night, due to the invariable slacking of cordage under strain, the ship was fit for any eye to light on, like a conscious beauty going forth conquering and to conquer. I doubt the crew grumbled and d----d a little under their breath, for the process was tedious; yet it was not only a fad, but necessary, and the deck-officer who habitually neglected it might possibly rise to an emergency, but was scarcely otherwise worth his salt. In my humble judgment, he had better have worn a frock-coat unbuttoned.

Occupation in plenty was not the only solace of a morning watch; at least in the trades. While the men were washing their clothes, the midshipman of the watch, amid the exhilaration of his coffee, and with the cool sea-water careering over his bare feet, had ample leisure to watch the break of day: the gradual lighting up of the zenith, the rosy tints gathering and growing upon the tiny, pearly trade-clouds of which I have spoken, the blue of the water gradually revealing itself, laughing with white-caps, like the Psalmist's valleys of corn; until at last the sun appeared, never direct from the sea, but from these white cloud banks which extend less than five degrees above it. Such a scene presents itself day after day, day after day, monotonous but never wearisome, to a vessel running down the trades; that is, steering from east to west, with fixed, fair breeze, as I have more than once had the happiness to do. Then, as the saying was, a fortnight passed without touching brace or tack, because no change of wind; a slight exaggeration, for frequent squalls required the canvas to be handled, but substantially true in impression. Balmy weather and a steady gait, rarely more than seven or eight knots – less than two hundred miles a day; but who would be in haste to quit such conditions, where the sun rose astern daily with the joy of a giant running his course, bringing assurance of prosperity, and sank to rest ahead smiling, again behind the dimpling clouds which he tinged like mother-of-pearl.

Such was not our lot in the *Congress*, for we were bound south, across the trades. This, with some bad luck, brought us close-hauled, that we might pass the equator nothing to the westward of thirty degrees of west longitude; otherwise we might fall to leeward of Cape St. Roque. This ominous phrase meant that we might be so far to the westward that the southeast trades, when reached, would not let the ship pass clear of this easternmost point of Brazil on one stretch; that we would strike the coast north of it and have to beat round, which actually happened. Consequently we never had a fair wind, to set a studding-sail, till we were within three or four days of Bahia. This encouraging incident, the first of the kind since the ship went into commission, also befell in one of my mid-watches, and an awful mess our unuse made of it. All the gear seemed to be bent with a half-dozen round turns; the stun'sail-yards went aloft wrong end uppermost, dangling in the most extraordinary and wholly unmanageable attitudes; everything had to be done over and over again, till at last the case looked desperate.

Finally the lieutenant of the watch came forward in wrath. He was a Kentuckian, very competent, ordinarily very good-tempered; but there was red in his hair. When he got sufficiently near he tucked the speaking-trumpet under his arm, where it looked uncommonly like a fat cotton umbrella, himself suggesting a farmer inspecting an intended purchase, and in this posture delivered to us a stump speech on our shortcomings. This, I fear, I will have to leave to the reader's imagination. It would require innumerable dashes, and even so the emphasis would be lost. My relief had cause to be pleased that those stun'sails were set by four o'clock, when he came on deck. Ours the labor, his the reward.

* * * * *

A few days more saw us in Bahia; and with our arrival on the station began a round of duties and enjoyments which made life at twenty pleasant enough, both in the passage and in retrospect, but which scarcely afford material for narration. Our two chief ports, Rio de Janeiro and Montevideo, were then remote and provincial. They have become more accessible and modern; but at the time of my last visit – already over thirty years ago – they had lost in local color and particular attraction as much as they had gained in convenience and development. Street-cars, double-ended American ferry-boats, electric lights, and all the other things for which these stand, are doubtless good; but they make places seem less strange and so less interesting. But I suppose there must still be in the business streets that pervading odor of rum and sugar which tells that you are in the tropics; still there must be the delicious hot calm of the early morning, before the sea-breeze sets in, the fruit-laden boats plying over the still waters to the ships of war; still that brilliant access of life and animation which comes sparkling in with the sea-breeze, and which can be seen in the offing, approaching, long before it enters the bay. The balance of better and worse will be variously estimated by various minds. The magnificent scenery of Rio remains, and must remain, short of earthquake; the Sugar Loaf, the distant Organ mountains, the near, high, surrounding hills, the numerous bights and diversified bluffs, which impart continuous novelty to the prospect. It is surprising that in these days of travel more do not go just to see that sight, even if they never put foot on shore; though I would not commend the omission. I see, too, in the current newspapers, that Secretary Root has attributed to the women of Uruguay to-day the charm which we youngsters then found in those who are now their grand-mothers. As Mr. Secretary cannot be very far from my own age, we have here the mature confirmation of an impression which otherwise might be attributed to the facility of youth.

An interesting, though not very important, reminiscence of things now passed away was the coming and going of numerous vessels, usually small, carrying the commercial flags of the Hanse cities, Bremen, Hamburg, and Lubeck, now superseded on the ocean by that of the German Empire. Scarcely a morning watch which did not see in its earlier hours one or more of these stealing out of port with the tail of the land breeze. These remnants of the "Easterlings," a term which now survives only in "sterling," were mostly small brigs of some two hundred tons, noticeable mainly for their want of sheer; that is, their rails, and presumably their decks, were level, without rise at the extremities such as most vessels show.

Up to the middle of the last century, Rio, thanks probably to its remoteness, had escaped the yellow-fever. But the soil and climate were propitious; and about 1850 it made good a footing which it never relinquished. At the time of our cruise it was endemic, and we consequently spent there but two or three months of the cooler season, June to September. Even so, visiting the city was permitted to only a few selected men of the foremast hands. The habits of the seamen were still those of a generation before, and drink, with its consequent reckless exposure, was a right-hand man to Yellow Jack. All shore indulgence was confined to Montevideo, where we spent near half of the year; and being limited to one or two occasions only, of two or three days duration each, it was signalized by those excesses which, in conjunction with the absence of half the crew at once, put an end to all ordinary routine and drill on board. My friend, the captain of the forecastle, who apprehended that the Southern leaders would lose their property, a self-respecting, admirably behaved man in ordinary times, was usually hoisted on board by a tackle when he returned: for Montevideo affords only an open roadstead for big ships, and frequently a rough sea. The story ran that he secured a room on going ashore, provided for the safety of his money, bought a box of gin, and went to bed. This I never verified; but I remember a nautical philosopher among the crew enlarging, in my hearing, on the folly of drink. To its morality he was indifferent; but from sad experience he avouched that it incapacitated you for other enjoyments, regular and irregular, and that he for one should quit. To-day things are changed – revolutionized. There may be ports too sickly to risk lives in; but the men to be selected now are the few who cannot be trusted, the percentage which every society contains. This result will be variously interpreted. Some will attribute it to the abolition of the grog ration, the removal of temptation, a change of environment. Others will say that the extension of frequent leave, and consequent opportunity, has abolished the frenzied inclination to make the most – not the best – of a rare chance; has renewed men from within. Personally, I believe the last. Together with the gradual rise of tone throughout society, rational liberty among seamen has resulted in rational indulgence. "Better England free than England sober."

In the end it was from Montevideo that we sailed for home in June, 1861. During the preceding six months, mail after mail brought us increasing ill tidings of the events succeeding the election of Lincoln. Somewhere within that period a large American steamboat, of the type then used on Long Island Sound, arrived in the La Plata for passenger and freight service between Montevideo and Buenos Ayres. Her size and comfort, her extensive decoration and expanses of gold and white, unknown hitherto, created some sensation, and gave abundant supply to local paragraphists. Her captain was a Southerner, and his wife also; of male and female types. He commented to me briefly, but sadly, "Yes, we have now two governments"; but she was all aglow. Never would she lay down arms; M. Ollivier's light heart was "not in it" with hers; her countenance shone with joy, except when clouded with contempt for the craven action of the *Star of the West*, a merchant-steamer with supplies for Fort Sumter which had turned back before the fire of the Charleston batteries. Never could she have done such a thing. What influence women wield, and how irresponsible! And they want votes!

In feeling, most of us stood where this captain did, sorrowful, perplexed; but in feeling only, not in purpose. We knew not which became us most, grief, or stern satisfaction that at last a doubtful matter was to be settled by arms; but, with one or two exceptions, there was no hesitancy, I believe, on the part of the officers as to the side each should take. There were four pronounced Southerners: two of them messmates of mine, from New Orleans. The other two were the captain and lieutenant of marines. None of these was extreme, except the captain, whom, though well on in middle life, I have seen stamp up and down raging with excitement. On one occasion, so violent was his language that I said to him he would do well to put ice to his head; an impertinence, considering our relative ages, but almost warranted. I think that he possibly took over the lieutenant, who was from a border State, and, like the midshipmen, rather sobered than enthusiastic at the prospects; though these last had no doubts as to their own course. There was also a sea lieutenant from the South, who said to me that if his State was fool enough to secede, she might go, for him; he would not fight against her, but he would not follow her. I believe he did escape having to fight in her waters, but he was in action on the Union side elsewhere, and, I expect, revised this decision. This halting allegiance, thinking to serve two masters, was not frequent; but there were instances. Of one such I knew. He told me himself that he on a certain occasion had said in company that he would not leave the navy, but would try for employment outside the country; whereon an officer standing by said to him that that appeared a pretty shabby thing, to take pay and dodge duty. The remark sank deep; he changed his mind, and served with great gallantry. It seems to me now almost an impiety to record, but, knowing my father's warm love for the South, I hazarded to the marine captain a doubt as to his position. He replied that there could be no doubt whatever. "All your father's antecedents are military; there is no military spirit in the North; he must come to us." Many Southerners, not by any means most, had formed such impressions.

The remainder of the officers were not so much Northern as Union, a distinction which meant much in the feeling that underlies action. Our second lieutenant, with soberer appreciation of conditions than the marine, said to me, "I cannot understand how those others expect to win in the face of the overpowering resources of the

Northern States." The leaders of the Confederacy, too, understood this; and while I am sure that expected dissension in the North, and interference from Europe, counted for much in their complicated calculations, I imagine that the marine's overweighted theory, of incompatibility between the mercantile and military temperaments, also entered largely. My Kentuckian expressed the characteristic, if somewhat crude, opinion, that the two had better fight it out now, till one was well licked; after which his head should be punched and he be told to be decent hereafter. We had, however, one Northern fire-eater among the midshipmen. He was a plucky fellow, but with an odd cast to his eyes and a slight malformation, which made his ecstasies of wrath a little comical. His denunciations of all half measures, or bounded sentiments, quite equalled those of the marine officer on the other side. If the two had been put into the same ring, little could have been left but a few rags of clothes, so completely did they lose their heads; but, as often happens with such champions, their harangues descended mostly on quiet men, conveniently known as doughfaces.

Doughfaces I suppose we must have been, if the term applied fitly to those who, between the alternatives of dissolving the Union and fighting one another, were longing to see some third way open out of the dilemma. In this sense Lincoln, with his life-long record of opposition to the extension of slavery, was a doughface. The marine could afford to harden his face, because he believed there would be no war – the North would not fight; while the midshipman, rather limited intellectually, was happy in a mental constitution which could see but one side of a case; an element of force, but not of conciliation. The more reflective of my two Southern messmates, a man mature beyond his years, said to me sadly, "I suppose there will be bloodshed beyond what the world has known for a long time;" but he naturally shared the prevalent opinion – so often disproved – that a people resolute as he believed his own could not be conquered, especially by a commercial community – the proverbial "nation of shopkeepers." Napoleon once had believed the same, to his ruin. Commercial considerations undoubtedly weigh heavily; but happily sentiment is still stronger than the dollar. An amusing instance of the pocket influence, however, came to my knowledge at the moment. Our captain's son received notice of his appointment as lieutenant of marines, and sailed for home in an American merchant-brig shortly before the news came of the firing on Fort Sumter. When I next met him in the United States, he told me that the brig's captain had been quite warmly Southern in feeling during the passage; but when they reached home, and found that Confederate privateers had destroyed some merchant-vessels, he went entirely over. He had no use for people who would "rob a poor man of his ship and cargo."

Our orders home, and tidings of the attack on Fort Sumter, came by the same mail, some time in June. There were then no cables. The revulsion of feeling was immediate and universal, in that distant community and foreign land, as it had been two months before in the Northern States. The doughfaces were set at once, like a flint. The grave and reverend seigniors, resident merchants, who had checked any belligerent utterance among us with reproachful regret that an American should be willing to fight Americans, were converted or silenced. Every voice but one was hushed, and that voice said, "Fight." I remember a tempestuous gathering, an evening or two before we sailed, and one middle-aged invalid's excited but despondent wish that he was five hundred men. Such ebullitions are common enough in history, for causes bad or good. They are to be taken at their true worth; not as a dependable pledge of endurance to the end, but as an awakening, which differs from that of common times as the blast of the trumpet that summoned men at midnight for Waterloo differs from the lazy rubbing of the eyes before thrusting one's neck into the collar of a working day. The North was roused and united; a result which showed that, wittingly or unwittingly, the Union leaders had so played the cards in their hands as to score the first trick.

Our passage home was tedious but uneventful. I remember only the incident that the flag-officer on one occasion played at old-time warfare of his youth, by showing to a passing vessel a Spanish flag instead of the American. The common ship life went on as though nothing had happened. On an August evening we anchored in Boston lower harbor, and Mr. Robert Forbes, then a very prominent character in Boston, and in most nautical matters throughout the country, came down in a pilot-boat, bringing newspapers to our captain, with whom he was intimate. Then we first learned of Bull Run; and properly mortified we of the North were, not having yet acquired that indifference to a licking which is one of the first steps towards success. Some time after the war was over an army officer of the North repeated to me the comment on this affair made to him by a Southern acquaintance, both being of the aforetime regular army. "I never," he said, "saw men as frightened as ours were – except yours." The after record of both parties takes all the sting out of these words, without lessening the humor.

Immediately upon arrival, the oath of allegiance was tendered, and, of course, refused by our four Southerners. They had doubtless sent in their resignations; but by that time resignations were no longer accepted, and in the following *Navy Register* they appeared as "dismissed." They were arrested on board the ship and taken as prisoners to Fort Lafayette. I never again saw any of them; but from time to time heard decisively of the deaths of all, save the lieutenant of marines. One of the midshipmen drew from my father an action which I have delighted to recall as characteristic. He wrote from the fort, stating his comradeship with me in the past, and asking if he could be furnished with certain military reading, for his improvement and to pass time. Though suspicions of loyalty were rife, and in those days easily started by the most trivial communication, the books were sent. The war had but just ended, when one morning my father received a letter expressing thanks, and enclosing money to the supposed value of the books. The money was returned; but I, happening to be at home, replied on my own account in such manner as a very young man would. My father saw the addressed envelope, and remonstrated. "Do you think it quite well and prudent to associate yourself, at your age and rank, with one so recently in rebellion? Will it not injure your standing?" I was not convinced; but I yielded to a solicitude which under much more hazardous conditions he had not admitted for himself, though known to be a Virginian. Shortly after his death, while our sorrow was still fresh, I met a contemporary and military intimate of his. "I want," he said, "to tell you an anecdote of your father. We were associated on a board, one of the members of which had proposed, as his own suggestion, a measure which I thought fundamentally and dangerously erroneous. I prepared a paper contesting the project and took it to your father. He read it carefully, and replied, 'I agree with you entirely; but ---- will never forgive you, and he is persistent and unrelenting towards those who thwart him. You will make a life-long and powerful enemy. If I were you, I should not lay this upon myself.' I gave way to his judgment, and kept back the paper; but you may imagine my surprise when at the next meeting he took upon himself the burden which he had advised me to shun. He made an argument substantially on my lines, and procured the rejection of the proposition. The result was a hostility which ceased only with his life, but between which and me he had interposed."

VII
INCIDENTS OF WAR AND BLOCKADE SERVICE

1861-1862

The *Congress*, upon her return, was retained in commission, though entirely useless, either for fighting or blockade, under modern conditions. I suppose there were not yet enough of newer vessels to spare her value as a figure-head. She was sent afterwards to Hampton Roads, where in the following March she, with another sailing-frigate, the *Cumberland*, fell helpless victims to the first Confederate iron-clad. The staff of combatant sea officers was much changed; the captain, the senior three lieutenants, and the midshipmen being detached. Smith, the fourth lieutenant, remained as first; and, in the absence of her captain on other duty, commanded and fell at her death agony. I was sent first to the *James Adger*, a passenger-steamer then being converted in New York for blockade duty, for which she was very fit; but in ten days more I was moved on to the *Pocahontas*, a ship built for war, a very respectable little steam-corvette, the only one of her class – if such a bull as a class of one may be excused. She carried one ten-inch gun and four 32-pounders, all smooth-bores. There was, besides, one small nondescript rifled piece, upon which we looked with more curiosity than confidence. Indeed, unless memory deceive, the projectiles from it were quite as apt to go end over end as true. It was rarely used.

When I joined, the *Pocahontas* was lying off the Washington Navy-Yard, in the eastern branch of the Potomac, on duty connected with the patrol of the river; the Virginia bank of which was occupied by the Confederates, who were then erecting batteries to dispute the passage of vessels. After one excursion down-stream in this employment, the ship was detached to the combined expedition against Port Royal, South Carolina, the naval part of which was under the command of "Flag-Officer" Dupont. The point of assembly was Hampton Roads, whither we shortly proceeded, after filling with stores and receiving a new captain, Percival Drayton, a man greatly esteemed in the service of the day, and a South-Carolinian. Coincidently with us, but independently as to association, the steam-sloop *Seminole*, slightly larger, also started. We outstripped her; and as we passed a position where the Confederates were believed to be fortifying, our captain threw in a half-dozen shells. No reply was made, and we went on. Within a half-hour we heard firing behind us, apparently two-sided. The ship was turned round and headed up-river. In a few minutes we met the *Seminole*, her men still at the guns, a few ropes dangling loose, showing that she had, as they say, not been exchanging salutes. We had stirred up the hornets, and she had got the benefit; quite uselessly, her captain evidently felt, by his glum face and short answers to our solicitous hail. He was naturally put out, for no good could have come, beyond showing the position of the enemy's guns; while an awkward hit might have sent her back to the yard and lost her her share in the coming fray, one of the earliest in the war, and at that instant the only thing in sight on the naval horizon. As no harm resulted, the incident would not be worth mentioning except for a second occasion, which I will mention later, in which we gave the *Seminole's* captain cause for grim dissatisfaction.

The gathering of the clans, the ships of war and the transports laden with troops, in the lower Chesapeake had of course a strange element of excitement; for war, even in its incipiency, was new to almost all present, and the enthusiasm aroused by a great cause and approaching conflict was not balanced by that solemnizing outlook which experience gives. We lived in an atmosphere of blended exaltation and curiosity, of present novelty and glowing expectation. But business soon came upon us, in its ordinary lines; for we were not two days clear of the Capes, in early November, when there came on a gale of exceptional violence, the worst of it at midnight. It lasted for forty-eight hours, and must have occasioned great anxiety to the heads of the expedition; for among the curious conglomerate of heterogeneous material constituting both the ships of war and transports there were several river steamers, some of them small. Being utterly unpractised in such movements, an almost entire dispersal followed; in fact, I dare say many of the transport captains asked nothing better than to be out of other people's way. The *Pocahontas* found herself alone next morning; but, though small and slow, she was a veritable sea-bird for wind and wave. Not so all. One of our extemporized ships of war, rejoicing in the belligerent name of *Isaac Smith*, and carrying eight fairly heavy guns, which would have told in still water, had to throw them all overboard; and her share in the subsequent action was limited to a single long piece, rifled I believe, and to towing a sailing-corvette in the column.

There were some wrecks and some gallant rescues, the most conspicuous of which was that of the battalion of marines, embarked on board the *Governor*; a steamer, as I recollect, not strictly of the river order, but like those which ply outside on the Boston and Maine coast. She went down, but not before her living freight had been removed by the sailing-frigate *Sabine*. The first lieutenant of the latter, now the senior rear-admiral on the retired list of the navy, soon afterwards relieved Drayton in command of the *Pocahontas*; so that I then heard at first hand many particulars which I wish I could now repeat in his well-deserved honor. His distinguished share in the rescue was of common notoriety; the details only we learned from his modest but interesting account. The deliverance was facilitated by the two vessels being on soundings. The *Governor* anchored, and then the *Sabine* ahead of her, dropping down close to. The ground-tackle of our naval ships, as we abundantly tested during the war, would hold through anything, if the bottom let the anchor grip.

With very few exceptions all were saved, officers and privates; but their clothes, except those they stood in, were left behind. The colonel was a notorious martinet, as well as something of a character; and a story ran that one of the subalterns had found himself at the start unable to appear in some detail of uniform, his trunks having gone astray. "A good soldier never separates from his baggage," said the colonel, gruffly, on hearing the excuse. After various adventures, common to missing personal effects, the lieutenant's trunks turned up at Port Royal. He looked sympathetically at the colonel's shorn plumes and meagre array, and said, reproachfully, "Colonel, where are your trunks? A good soldier should never separate from his baggage." But, doubtless, to follow it to the bottom of the sea would be an excess of zeal.

Not long afterwards I was shipmate with an assistant surgeon who had been detailed for duty on board the *Governor*, and had passed through the scenes of anxiety and confusion preceding the rescue. He told me one or two amusing incidents. An order being given to lighten the ship, four marines ran into the cabin where he was lying, seized a marble-top table, dropped the marble top on deck, and threw the wooden legs overboard. There was also on board a very young naval officer, barely out of the Academy. He was of Dutch blood and name – from central Pennsylvania, I think. Although without much experience, he was of the constitutionally self-possessed order, which enabled him to be very useful. After a good deal of exertion, he also came into the cabin. The surgeon asked him how things looked. "I think she will last about half an hour," he replied, and then composedly lay down and went to sleep.

There was in the hero of this anecdote a vein of eccentricity even then, and he eventually died insane and young. I knew him only slightly, but familiarly as to face. He had mild blue eyes and curly brown hair, with a constant half-smile in eyes as well as mouth. In temperament he was Dutch to the backbone – at least as we imagine Dutch. A comical anecdote was told me of him a few years later, illustrating his self-possession – cool to impudence. He was serving on one of our big steam-sloops, a flag-ship at the time, and had charge of working the cables on the gun-deck when anchoring. Going into a port where the water was very deep – Rio de Janeiro, I believe – the chain cables "got away," as the expression is; control was lost, and shackle after shackle tore out of the hawse-holes, leaping and thumping, rattling and roaring, stirring a lot of dust besides. Indeed, the violent friction of iron against iron in such cases not infrequently generates a stream of sparks. The weight of twenty fathoms of this linked iron mass hanging outside, aided by the momentum already established by the anchor's fall through a hundred feet, of course drags after it all that lies unstopped within. I need not tell those who have witnessed such a commotion that the orderly silence of a ship of war breaks down somewhat. Every one who has any right to speak shouts, and repeats, in rapid succession, "Haul-to that chain! Why the something or other don't you haul-to?" while the unhappy compressor-men, saving their own wind to help their arms, struggle wildly with the situation, under a storm of obloquy. The admiral – by this time we had admirals – was a singular man, something of a lawyer, acute, thinking he knew just how far he might go in any case, and given at times to taking liberties with subordinates, which were not to them always as humorous as they seemed to him. In this instance he miscalculated somewhat. He was on deck at the moment, and when the chain had been at last stopped and secured, he said to the captain, "Alfred, send for the young man in charge of those chains, and give him a good setting-down. Ask him what he means by letting such things happen. Ride him down like a main-tack, Alfred – like the main-tack!" The main-tack is the chief rope controlling the biggest sail in the ship, and at times, close on the wind, it has to be got down into place by the brute force of half a hundred men, inch by inch, pull by pull. That is called riding down, and is clearly a process the reverse of conciliatory. The Dutchman was sent for, and soon his questioning blue eyes appeared over the hatch coaming. Alfred – as my own name is Alfred, I may explain that I was not that captain – Alfred was a mild person, and clearly did not like his job; he could not have come up to the admiral's standard. The latter saw it, and intervened: "Perhaps you had better leave it to me. I'll settle him." Fixing his eyes on the offender, he said, sternly, "What do you mean by this, sir? Why the h--l did you not stop that chain?" This exordium was doubtless the prelude to a fit oratorical display; but the culprit, looking quietly at him, replied, simply, "How the h--l could I?" This was a shift of wind for which the admiral was unprepared. He was taken flat back, like a screaming child receiving a glass of cold water in his face. After a moment's hesitation he turned to the captain, and said meekly, yet with evident humorous consciousness of a checkmate, "That's true, Alfred; how the h--l could he?"

Still, while the defence implied in the lieutenant's question is logically unimpeachable, it does not follow that the method of the admiral – as distinct from his manner, which need not be excused – was irrational. The impulse of reprimand, applied at the top, where ultimate responsibility rests, is transmitted through the intervening links down to the actual culprits, and takes effect for future occasions. As Marryat in one of his amusing passages says: "The master's violence made the boatswain violent, which made the boatswain's mate violent, and the captain of the forecastle also; all which is practically exemplified by the laws of motion communicated from one body to another; and as the master swore, so did the boatswain swear, and the boatswain's mate, and the captain of the forecastle, and all the men." An entertaining practical use of this transmission of energy was made by an acquaintance of mine in China. Going to bed one night, he found himself annoyed by a mosquito within the net. He got up, provided himself with the necessities for his own comfort during the period of discomfort which he projected for others, and called the servant whose business it was to have crushed the intruder. Him he sent in search of the man next above him, him in turn for another, and so on until he reached the head of the domestic hierarchy. When the whole body was assembled, he told them that they were summoned to receive the information that "one piecee mosquito" was inside his net, owing to the neglect of – pointing to the culprit. This done, they were dismissed, in calm assurance that in future no mosquito would disturb his night's rest, and that the desirable castigation of the offender might be intrusted to his outraged companions.

After the gale subsided, the *Pocahontas* proceeded for the rendezvous, just before reaching which we fell in with a coal-schooner. Though a good fighting-ship, she carried only sixty-three tons of coal, anthracite; for that alone we then used to burn. The amount seems too absurd for belief, and it constituted a very serious embarrassment on such duty as that of the South Carolina and Georgia coasts. To economize, so as to remain as long as possible away from the base at Port Royal, and yet to have the ship ready for speedy movement, was a difficult problem; indeed, insoluble. We used to meet it by keeping fires so low, when lying inside the blockaded rivers, that we could not move promptly. This was a choice between evils, which the event justified, but which might have been awkward had the Confederates ever made a determined attempt at boarding with largely superior force in several steamers, as happened at Galveston, and once even by pulling boats in a Georgia river. Under steam, the battery could be handled; anchored, an enemy could avoid it. With this poor "coal endurance," as the modern expression has it, the captain decided to fill up as he could. We therefore took the schooner in tow, and were transferring from her, when the sound of cannonading was heard.

Evidently the attack had begun, and it was incumbent to get in, not only on general principles, but for the captain's own reputation; for although in service he was too well known to be doubted, the outside world might see only that he was a South Carolinian. It was recognition of this, I doubt not, that led Admiral Dupont, when we passed the flag-ship after the action, to hail aloud, "Captain Drayton, I knew you would be here;" a public expression of official confidence. We were late, however, as it was; probably because our short coal supply had compelled economical steaming, though as to this my memory is uncertain. The *Pocahontas* passed the batteries after the main attack, in column on an elliptical course, had ceased, but before the works had been abandoned; and being alone we received proportionate attention for the few moments of passage. The enemy's fire was "good line, but high;" our main-mast was irreparably wounded, but the hull and crew escaped.

After the action there followed the usual scene of jollification. The transports had remained outside, and now steamed up; bands playing, troops hurrahing, and with the general expenditure of wind from vocal organs which seems the necessary concomitant of such occasions. And here the *Pocahontas* again brought the *Seminole* to grief. She had anchored, but we kept under way, steaming about through the throng. Drayton had binoculars in hand; and, while himself conning the ship, was livelily interested in what was passing around. I believe also that, though an unusually accomplished officer professionally, he had done a good deal of staff duty; had less than the usual deck habit of his period. Besides, men used mostly to sails seemed to think steamers could get out of any scrape at any moment. However that be, after a glance to see that we were rightly headed for a clear opening, he began gazing about through his glasses, to the right hand and to the left. He had lost thought of the tide, and in such circumstances as ours a very few seconds does the business. When he next looked, we were sweeping down on the *Seminole* without a chance of retreat; there was nothing but to go ahead fast, and save the hulls at least from collision. Her flying jib-boom came in just behind our main-mast (we had only two masts); and as the current of course was setting us down steadily, the topping-lifts of our huge main boom caught her jib-boom. Down came one of the big blocks from our mast-head, narrowly missing the captain's head, while we took out of her all the head booms as far as the bowsprit cap, leaving them dragging in helpless confusion by her side. Then we anchored.

It is a nuisance to have to clear a wreck and repair damages; and the injured party does not immediately recover his equanimity after such a mishap, especially coming fresh upon a former instance of trouble occasioned barely a fortnight before. But after a victory all things are forgiven, and the more so to a man of Drayton's well-deserved popularity. A little later in the day he went on board the flag-ship to visit the admiral. When I met him at the gangway upon his return, I had many questions to ask, and among others, "Have you learned who commanded the enemy?" "Yes," he replied, with a half-smile; "it was my brother."

Very soon afterwards he left us, before we again quitted port. He was dissatisfied with the *Pocahontas*, partly on account of her coal supply; and the captain of the *Pawnee* then going home, he obtained command of her. The *Pawnee* was *sui generis*; in this like the *Pocahontas*, only a good deal more so, representing somebody's fad. I cannot vouch for the details of her construction; but, as I heard, she was not only extremely broad in the beam, giving great battery space, – which was plain to see, – but the bilge on each side was reported to come lower than the keel, making, as it were, two hulls, side by side, so that a sarcastic critic remarked, "One good point about her is, that if she takes the ground, her keel at least is protected." Like all our vessels at that time, she was of wood. Owing to her build, she had for her tonnage very light draught and heavy battery, and so was a capital fighting-ship in still, shoal waters; but in a seaway she rolled so rapidly as to be a wretched gun platform. Her first lieutenant assured me that in heavy weather a glass of water could not get off the table. "Before it has begun to slide on one roll, she is back on the other, and catches it before it can start." This description was perhaps somewhat picturesque – impressionist, as we now say; but it successfully conveyed the idea, the object of all speech and impressions. However satisfactory for glasses – not too full – it may be imagined that under such conditions it would be difficult to draw sight on a target between rolls. Whatever her defects, the *Pawnee* was admirably adapted for the inland work of which there was much in those parts, behind the sea islands; and she continued so employed throughout the war. I met her there as late as the last six months of it. But she was not reproduced, and remains to memory only; an incident of the speculative views and doubting progresses of the decade before the War of Secession.

Drayton's successor was one of the senior lieutenants of the fleet, George B. Balch, late the first of the *Sabine* frigate. His services in saving the people of the *Governor* have already been mentioned. He still survives in venerable old age; but Drayton, who later on was with Farragut at Mobile, being captain of the flag-ship *Hartford* and chief of staff at the time of the passage of the forts, was cut off prematurely by a short illness within six months after hostilities ended. Balch remained with us till the *Pocahontas* returned North, ten months later. He was an officer of varied service, and like all such, some more, some less, abounded in anecdote of his own experiences. A great deal that might be instructive, and more still that is entertaining, is lost by our slippery memories and the rarity of the journal-keeping habit. I remember distinctly only two of his stories. One related to a matter which now belongs to naval archæology, – "backing and filling in a tideway," by a ship under sail. In this, in a winding channel, the ship sets towards her destination with the current, up or down, carrying only enough canvas, usually the three topsails, to be under control; to move her a little ahead, or a little astern, keeping in the strength of the stream, or shifting position as conditions of the navigation require. Backing is a term which explains itself; filling applies to the sails when so trimmed as to move the vessel ahead. Sometimes a reach of the river permits the sails to be braced full, and she bowls along merrily under way; anon a turn comes where she can only lie across, balanced as to headway by the main top-sail aback. Then the smallest topsail, the mizzen, has a game in its hands. The ship, as she drifts up or down, may need to be moved a little astern, more or less, to avoid a shoal or what not; and to do this the sail mentioned is braced either to shake, neutralizing it, or to bring it also aback, as the occasion demands. This rather long preamble is perilously like explaining a joke, but it is neces-sary. Balch had seen a good deal of this work in China, and he told us that the Chinese pilot's ex-pression, if he wanted the sail shaken, was "Makee sick the mizzen topsail;" but if aback, he added, "Kill him dead." I wonder does that give us an insight into the nautical idiom of the Chinese, who within the limitations of their needs are prime seamen.

By the time I got to China, two years after the War of Secession, steam had relieved naval vessels from backing and filling. I once, however, saw the principle applied to a steamer in the Paraguay River. We were returning from a visit to Asun-cion, and had a local pilot, who was needed less for the Paraguay, which though winding is fairly clear, than for the Paraná, the lower stream, which finally merges in the Rio de la Plata and is con-stantly changing its bed. We had anchored for the night just above a bend, head of course up-stream, for the tide does not reach so far. The next morning the pilot was bothered to turn her round, for she was a long paddle steamer, not very handy. He seemed to be in a nautical quandary, similar to that which the elder Mr. Weller described as "being on the wrong side of the road, backing into the palings, and all manner of unpleasantness." The captain watched him fuming for a few minutes, and then said, "Is there any particular trouble on either hand, or is it only the narrowness?" The pilot said no; the bottom was clear. "Well," said the captain, "why not cast her to port, and let her drift till she heads fair for the turn below?" This was done easily, and indeed was one of those things which would be almost foolishly simple did we not all have experience of overlooking expedients that lie immediately under our noses.

Balch's other story which I recall was at the moment simply humorous, but has since seemed to me charged with homely wisdom of wide application. He had made a rather longish voyage in a merchant-steamer, and during it used to amuse himself doing navigation work in company with her master, or mate. On one occasion a discussion arose between them as to some result, and Balch in the course of the argument said, "Figures won't lie." "Yes, that's all right," rejoined the other, "figures won't lie, if you work them right; but you must work them right, Mr. Balch." I was too young then to have noted a somewhat similar remark about statistics; and I think now, after a pretty long observation of mankind, its records and its statements, that I should be inclined to extend that old seaman's comments to facts also.

Facts won't lie, if you work them right; but if you work them wrong, a little disproportion in the emphasis, a slight exaggeration of color, a little more or less limelight on this or that part of the grouping, and the result is not truth, even though each individual fact be as unimpeachable as the multiplication table.

After the capture of Port Royal, and the establishment there of the naval base, and until the arrival of monitors a year later, operations of the South Atlantic Blockading Squadron, as it was styled, were confined to blockading. This took two principal forms. The fortifications of Charleston and Savannah being still in the hands of the enemy, and intact, these two chief seaports of that coast were unassailable by our fleet. Even after Fort Sumter had been battered to a shapeless heap of masonry, and Fort Pulaski had surrendered, neither city fell until Sherman's march took it in the rear. But the numerous inlets were substantially undefended against naval attack; and for them the blockade, that tremendously potent instrument of the national pressure, the work of which has been too little commemorated, was instituted almost universally within. Even Fort Pulaski, before its fall, though it sealed the highway to Savannah, could not prevent the Union vessels from occupying the inside anchorage off Tybee Island, completely closing the usual access from the sea to the town. During the ensuing ten months there were very few of these entrances, from Georgetown, the northernmost in South Carolina, down to Fernandina, in Florida, into which the *Pocahontas* did not penetrate, alone or in

215

company. I do not know whether people in other parts of the country realize that these various inlets are connected by an inside navigation, behind the sea islands, as they are called, the whole making a system of sheltered intercommunication. The usefulness of this was reinforced by the numerous navigable rivers which afford water roads to the interior, and gave a vessel, once entered, refuge beyond the reach of the blockaders' arm, with ready means for distribution. Such a gift of nature to a community, however, has the defects of its qualities. Ease of access, and freedom of movement in all directions, now existed for foe as it had for friend, and the very facility which such surroundings bestow had prevented the timely creation of an alternative. Deprival consequently was doubly severe.

It thus came to pass that, by a gradual process of elimination, blockade in the usual sense of the word, blockade outside, became confined to Charleston and its approaches. It is true that much depended on the class of vessel. It was obviously inexpedient to expose sailing-ships where they might be attacked by steamers, in ground also too contracted for manoeuvring; and two years later I found myself again blockading Georgetown, in a paddle steamer from the merchant service, the size and unwieldiness of which prevented her entering. Moreover, torpedoes had then begun to play a part in the war, though still in a very primitive stage of development. But in 1862 there was little outside work except at Charleston. The very reasons which determine the original selection of a port – facility for entrance, abundant anchorage, and ease of access to the interior for distribution and receipt of the articles of commerce – determine also the accumulation of defences, to the exclusion of other less favored localities. All these conditions, natural and artificial, combined with the Union occupancy of the other inlets to concentrate blockade-running upon Charleston. This in turn drew thither the blockaders, which had to be the more numerous because the harbor could be entered by two or more channels, widely separated. There was thus constituted a blockade society, which contrasted agreeably with the somewhat hermit-like existence of the smaller stations. The weather was usually pleasant enough – many Northerners now know the winter climate of South Carolina – so during the daytime the ships would lift their anchors and get more or less together; the officers, and to a less extent the crews, exchanging visits. Old acquaintanceships were renewed, former cruises discussed, "yarns" interchanged; and then there was always the war with its happenings. Fort Henry, Fort Donelson, Shiloh, the *Monitor* and *Merrimac* fight, the capture of New Orleans by Farragut, all occurred during the stay of the *Pocahontas* upon the blockade in 1862. Our news was apt to be ten days old, but to us it was as good as new; indeed, somewhat better, for we heard of the first reverses at Shiloh, and by the hands of the *Merrimac*, by the same mail which brought word of the final decided victory. Thus we were spared the anxiety of suspense. Even the disasters about Richmond were not by us fairly appreciated until the ship returned North, when the mortification of defeat was somewhat solaced, and the tendency to despondency lessened, by the happiness of being again at home; in my case after a continuous absence of more than three years, in the *Congress* and *Pocahontas*.

Talking of despondency, I had an odd experience of the ease with which people forget their frames of mind. While Burnside was engaged in the movements preceding Fredericksburg, I was in conversation with a veteran naval officer at his own house. Speaking of the probable outcome of the operations in progress, which then engrossed all thoughts, he said to me, "I think, Mr. Mahan, that if we fail this time, we may as well strike"; the naval phrase "strike the colors" being the equivalent of surrender – give up. I dissented heartily; not from any really reasoned appreciation of conditions, but on general principles, as understood by a man still very young. More than two years later, when the war had just drawn to its triumphant close, I again met the same gentleman. Amid our felicitations, he said to me, "There is one thing, Mr. Mahan, which I have never allowed myself to doubt – the ultimate success of our just cause."

After all, it was very natural. When you are cold, you're cold, and when you're hot, you're hot; and if you are indiscreet enough to say so to some one who feels differently, he remembers it against you. What business have you to feel other than he? If, with the thermometer at zero, I chance to say that I wish it were warmer, I am sure of some one, a lady usually, bursting in upon me when it is ninety-five, with the jeer, "Well! I hope, now, *you* are satisfied." I recall distinctly the long faces we pulled when we reached Philadelphia on our return, and realized, by the withdrawal of McClellan's army to Washington, the full extent of our disasters on the Peninsula; my old commodore might then have found some to say, Amen. But this did not keep our hats any lower when we chucked them aloft over Vicksburg and Gettysburg, and forgot that we had ever felt otherwise.

Vicksburg and Gettysburg, by the way, and their coincidence with the Fourth of July, have furnished me with a reminiscence quite otherwise agreeable. The ship in which I then was spent that Fourth at Spithead, England. We dressed ship with multicolored signals, red, white, and blue, at every yard-arm, big American ensigns at the three mast-heads and the peak, presenting a singularly gay and joyful aspect, which could profitably be viewed from as many points as Mr. Pecksniff looked at Salisbury Cathedral. At noon we fired a national salute, all the more severely punctilious and observant, because by the last mail things at home seemed to be looking particularly blue. The British ships of war, though I fear few of their officers then were other than pleased with our presumed discomfiture, dressed likewise, as by naval courtesy bound, and also fired a salute. The *Times* of the day arrived from London in due season, and had improved the occasion to moralize upon the sad condition to which the Republic of Bunker Hill and Yorktown was reduced: Grant held up at Vicksburg,[10] Lee marching victoriously into Pennsylvania, no apparent probability of escaping disaster in either quarter. The conclusion was couched in that vein of Pecksniffian benevolence of which we hear so much in life. "Let us *hope* that so much adversity may be tempered to a nation, afflicted with evil as unprecedented as its former prosperity; and this will indeed be the case if America ... is led on this day of festivity, now converted into a day of humiliation, to review past errors, and to consider that, if her present policy has led her so near ruin, in its reversal must lie the only path that can conduct her to safety." I wonder, if there had been a cable, would that editorial have been headed off. It was not.

"And there it stands unto this day, To witness if I lie."

It was bitter then to my taste; but sweet were the chuckles which I later had, when the actual transactions of that anniversary came to hand.

Whatever their sympathies, the British naval officers during that stay in British waters had no difficulty in paying us all the usual personal attentions; but a particular incident showed for our susceptibilities a nicety of consideration, which could not have been exacted and was very grateful at the time. We were at Plymouth, under the breakwater, but some distance from the inner anchorage, when a merchant-vessel lying inside hoisted a Confederate flag at her mizzen masthead. We saw it, but of course could do nothing. It was a clear case of intended insult, for the ship had no claim to the flag, and could only mean to flaunt us. It flew for perhaps an hour, and then disappeared. The same day, and not long afterwards, a British lieutenant from a vessel in the harbor came on board, and told me that he had had it hauled down, acting in place of his captain, who was absent. The communication to me, also momentarily in command, was purely personal; indeed, there was nothing official in the whole transaction, nor do I know by what means or by what authority he could insist upon the removal of the flag. However managed, the thing was done, and with the purpose of stopping a rudeness which, it is true, reflected more upon the port than upon us, for I think the offending vessel was British. Very many years afterwards I had occasion to quote this, when, during the Boer War, on the visit of a British squadron to one of our seaside resorts, a resident there thought to show American breeding by hoisting the Four-Color. In the late winter of 1863-64 I again met this officer and his ship in New Orleans. In conversation then he told me he did not believe the Union cause could succeed; that he, with others, looked to see three or four nations formed. In the same month of 1863 this anticipation would not have surprised me; but in 1864 it did, although Grant had not yet begun his movement upon Richmond.

Blockading was desperately tedious work, make the best one could of it. The largest reservoir of anecdotes was sure to run dry; the deepest vein of original humor to be worked out. I remember hearing of two notorious tellers of stories being pitted against each other, for an evening's amusement, when one was driven as a last resource to recounting that "Mary had a little lamb." We were in about that case. Charleston, however, was a blooming garden of social refreshment compared with the wilderness of the Texas coast, to which I found myself exiled a year or so later; a veritable

Siberia, cold only excepted. Charleston was not very far from the Chesapeake or Delaware, in distance or in time. Supply vessels, which came periodically, and at not very long intervals, arrived with papers not very late, and with fresh provisions not very long slaughtered; but by the time they reached Galveston or Sabine Pass, which was our station, their news was stale, and we got the bottom tier of fresh beef. The ship to which I there belonged was a small steam-corvette, which with two gunboats constituted all the social possibilities. Happily for myself, I did not join till midway in the corvette's stay off the port, which lasted in all nearly six months, before she was recalled in mercy to New Orleans. I have never seen a body of intelligent men reduced so nearly to imbecility as my shipmates then were.

One of my captains used to adduce, as his conception of the extreme of isolation, to be the keeper of a lightship off Cape Horn; a professional conceit rivalling the elder Mr. Weller's equally profound recognition of the connection between keeping a pike and misanthropy. We off Sabine Pass were banished about equally with the keeper of a turnpike or of a remote lightship. We ought, of course, to have improved the leisure which weighed so heavily on our hands; but the improvement of idle moments is an accomplishment of itself, as many a retired business man has found out too late. There is an impression, derived from the experience of passengers on board ocean steamers, that naval officers have an abundance of spare time. The ship, it seems assumed, runs itself; the officers have only to look on and enjoy. As a matter of fact, sea officers under normal conditions are as busy as the busiest house-keeper, with the care to boot of two, three, four, or five hundred children, to be kept continually doing as they should; the old woman who lived in the shoe had a good thing in comparison. Thus occupied, the leisure habit of self-improvement, other than in the practice of the calling, is not formed. At sea, on a voyage, the vicissitudes of successive days provide the desultory succession of incidents, which vary and fill out the tenor of occupations, keeping life full and interesting. In port, besides the regular and fairly engrossing routine, there are the resources of the shore to fill up the chinks. But the dead monotony of the blockade was neither sea nor port. It supplied nothing. The crew, once drilled, needed but a few moments each day to keep at the level of proficiency; and there was practically nothing to do, because nothing happened that required either a doing or an undoing.

Under such conditions even a gale of wind was a not unwelcome change. Although little activity was required to meet it, it at least presented new surroundings – something different from the daily outlook. After a very brief period, it became the rule to ride out the storms at anchor; and I remember one of our volunteer officers, who had commanded a merchant-ship for some years, saying that he would have been spared a good deal of trouble, on occasions, had he had our experience of holding on with an anchor instead of keeping under way. It was, however, an old if forgotten expedient, where anchorage ground was good – bottom sticky and water not too deep. In the ancient days of the French wars, the British fleets off Brest and Toulon had to keep under way, but that blockading Cadiz, in 1797-98, used to hold its position at anchor, and under harder conditions than ours; for there the worst gales blew on shore, whereas ours swept chiefly along the coast. A standing dispute in the British navy, in those days of hemp cables, used to be whether it was safer to ride with three anchors down, or with one only, having to it three cables, bent together, so as to form one of thrice the usual length. The balance of opinion leaned to the latter; the dead weight of so much hemp held the ship without transmitting the strain to the anchor itself. She "rode to the bight," as the expression was; that is, to the cable, curved by its own weight and length, lying even in part on the bottom, which prevented its tightening and pulling at the anchor. What was true of hemp was yet more true of iron chains. The *Pocahontas* used to veer to a hundred fathoms, and there lie like a duck in fifty or sixty feet of water. I remember on one occasion, however, that when we next weighed the anchor, it came up with parts polished bright, as in my childhood we used sometimes to burnish a copper cent. This seemed to show that it had been scoured hard along a sandy bottom. We had had no suspicion of the ship's dragging during the gale, and I have since supposed that it may have started from its bed as we began to heave, and so been scrubbed along towards us.

The problem of maintaining the health of ships' companies condemned to long months of salt provisions, and to equally depressing short allowance of social salt for the intellect, which reasonable beings crave, has to be ever present to those charged with administration. Nelson's "cattle and onions" sums up in homely phrase the first requirement; while, for the others, his policy during a weary two years, in which he himself never left the flag-ship, was to keep the vessels in constant movement, changing scene, and thereby maintaining expectation of something exciting turning up. "Our men's minds," he said, "are always kept up with the daily hopes of meeting the enemy." As the Confederacy had practically no navy, this particular distraction was debarred our blockaders; but in the matter of food, we in the early sixties had not got beyond his prescription for the opening years of the century. The primitive methods then still in vogue, for preserving meats and vegetables fresh, accomplished chiefly the making them perfectly tasteless, and to the eye uninviting; the palate, accustomed to the constant stimulant of salt, turned from "bully" (bouilli) beef and "desecrated" (dessicated) potatoes, jaded before exercise. Like liquor, salt, long used in large measures, at last becomes a craving. I have heard old seamen more than once say, "I must have my salt;" and I have even known one to express his utter weariness of the fresh butter France sends up with its morning coffee and rolls. So we on the blockade depended more upon the good offices of salt than upon those of tin cans, for giving us acceptable food; the consequence being, with us as with our British forebears, a keen physical demand for "cattle and onions." In one principal respect our supplies differed from theirs – in the profusion of ice afforded by our country. Our beef, therefore, came to us already butchered, while theirs was received on the hoof. Many of my readers doubtless will recall the adventures of Mr. Midshipman Easy, when in charge of the transport from Tetuan with bullocks for the fleet off Toulon. Onions – blessings on their heads, if they have any – came to both us and our predecessors as easily as they were welcome. I have sometimes heard the plea, that Nature is the best guide in matters of appetite, advanced for indulgences which, so construed, seemed to reflect upon her parental character; but there can be no such doubt concerning onions to a system well saturated with salt. When you see them you know what you want; and a half-dozen raw, with a simple salad dressing, were little more than a whetter on the blockade. Would it be possible now to manage a single one?

VIII
INCIDENTS OF WAR AND BLOCKADE
SERVICE – CONTINUED

1863-1865

The *Pocahontas* came North for repairs in the late summer of 1862, and after a brief leave I was ordered to the Naval Academy. Under the stress of the war, this had been broken out from its regular seat at Annapolis and transferred for the moment to Newport. All the arrangements were temporary and extemporized. The principal establishment, housing the three older classes, was in a building in the town formerly known as the Atlantic Hotel; while the new entries, who were very numerous, were quartered on two sailing-frigates, moored head and stern in the inner harbor, off Goat Island. This duplex arrangement necessitated a double set of officers, not easy to be had with war going on; the more so that the original corps had been depleted by the resignations of Southern men. The embarrassment arising from the immediate scantness of officers led naturally, if perhaps somewhat irreflectively, to a great number of admissions to the Naval Academy, disregardful of past experience with the '41 Date, and of the future, when room at the top would be lacking to take in all these youngsters as captains and admirals. Thus was constituted the "hump," as it came to be called, which, like a tumor on the body, engaged at a later day the attention of many professional practitioners. As it would not absorb, and as the rough-and-ready methods by which civil

227

life and the survival of the fittest deal with such conditions could not be applied, it had to be dissipated; a process ultimately carried out with indifferent success. While it lasted it caused many a heartache from postponement. As one of the sufferers said, when hearing the matter discussed, "I don't know about this or that. All I know is that I have been a lieutenant for twenty years." Owing to the slimness of the service in the lower grades they became lieutenants young; but there they stuck. Every boom is followed by such reaction, and for a military service war is a boom. Expansion sets in; and when contraction follows somebody is squeezed. At the end of the Napoleonic Wars there were over eight hundred post-captains in the British navy. What could peace do for them?

Eight pleasant months I spent on shore at the Academy, and then was again whisked off to sea, there to remain for substantially all the rest of the war. Although already prominent as a fashionable watering-place, Newport then was very far from its present development; but in winter it had a settled and pleasant, if small, society. At this time I met the widow of Captain Lawrence of the *Chesapeake*, who survived until two years later. She was already failing, and not prematurely; for it was then, 1862-63, the fiftieth year since her husband fell. She lived with a sister, also the widow of an officer, and was frequently visited by her granddaughter, the child of Lawrence's daughter, a singularly beautiful girl. I remember her pointing to me a picture of the defeat of the *Peacock*, by the *Hornet*, under her grandfather's command; on which, she laughingly said, she had been brought up. This meeting had for me not only the usual interest which a link with the distant past supplies, but a certain special association; for my grandmother, then recently dead, had known several of Lawrence's contemporaries in the navy, and my recollection is that she told me she had seen him leaving his wife at their doorstep, when departing to take command of the *Chesapeake*.

When the summer of 1863 drew nigh, the question of the usual practice cruise came up. I have before stated the two opinions: one favoring a regular ocean voyage, with its customary routine and accidents of weather; the other more disposed to contracted cruising in our own waters, anchoring at night, and by day following a formulated programme of varied practical exercises. For this year both plans were adopted. There were two practice-ships, one of which was to remain between Narragansett and Gardiner's Bay, in Long Island. I was ordered as first lieutenant of the other, which was to go to Europe. The advisability of this step for a sailing-ship was on this occasion doubly questioned, for the *Alabama* had already begun her career. In fact, one of the officers then stationed at the school had been recently captured by her, when making a passage to Panama in a mail-steamer. I remember his telling me, with glee, that when the *Alabama* fired a shot in the direction of the packet, called, I think, the *Ariel*, a number of the passengers took refuge behind the bulkheads of the upper-deck saloons, which, being of light pine, afforded as much protection as the air, with the additional risk of splinters. He hoped to escape observation, but the Confederate boarding-officer had been a classmate of his, and spotted him at once. Being paroled, he was for the time shut off from war service, and was sent to the Academy. He was a singular man, by name Tecumseh Steece, and looked with a certain disdain upon the navy as a profession. In his opinion, it was for him only a stepping-stone to some great future, rather undefined. At bottom a very honest fellow, with a sense of duty which while a midshipman had led him to persist defiantly in a very unpopular – though very proper – course of action, he yet seemed to see no impropriety in utterly neglecting professional acquirement, rather boasting of his ignorance. The result was that, having been detailed for the European cruise, he was subsequently detached; I think from doubt of his fitness for the deck of a sailing-vessel. While at the Academy at this time, he took a first step in his proposed career by writing a pamphlet, the title and scope of which I now forget; but unluckily, by a slip of the pen, he wrote on the first page, "We judge the *known* by the *unknown*." This, being speedily detected, raised a laugh, and I fear prevented most from further exploration of a somewhat misty thesis. He was rather chummy with me, and tried mildly to persuade me that I also should stand poised on the navy for a flight into the empyrean; but, if fain to soar, which I do not think I was, like Raleigh, I feared a fall. For himself, poor fellow, weighted by his aspirations, he said to me, "I don't fear death, I fear life;" and death caught him early, in 1864, in the shape of yellow-fever. One of his idiosyncrasies was a faith in coffee as a panacea; and I heard that while sickening he deluged himself with that beverage, to what profit let physicians say.

The decision that one of the practice-ships should go to Europe had, I think, been determined by the officer who was to have commanded the *Macedonian*, the vessel chosen for that purpose. She was not the one of that name captured in 1812 by the *United States*, – the only one of our frigate captures brought into port, – but a successor to the title. Before she went into commission, the first commander was detached to service at the front; but no change was made in her destination, even if any misgivings were felt. One of my fellow-officers at the Academy, who was not going, remarked to me pleasantly that, if we fell in with the *Alabama*, she would work round us like a cooper round a cask; an encouraging simile to one who has looked upon that cheerful and much one-sided performance. We were all too young – I, the senior lieutenant, was but twenty-two – and too light-hearted to be troubled with forebodings; and, indeed, there was in reason no adequate inducement for the Confederate cruiser to alter her existing plans in order to take the *Macedonian*. Had we come fairly in her way, to gobble a large percentage of the Naval Academy might have been a fairly humorous practical joke; but it could have been no more. I remember Mr. Schuyler Colfax, afterwards Vice-President, then I think a member of the House, being on board, and mentioning the subject to me. "After all," he said, "I suppose it would scarcely do for one of our vessels to be deterred from a cruise by regard for a

Confederate cruiser." Considering the disparity of advantage, due to steam, I should say this would scarcely be a working theory, in naval life or in private. Our military insignificance was our sufficient protection. During my cruise in the *Congress*, a ship much heavier every way than the *Macedonian*, the commander of one of our corvettes, substantially of the *Alabama* class, said to our captain, "I suppose, if I fell in with you as an enemy, I ought to attack you." "Well," replied the other, "if you didn't, you should pray not to have me on your court-martial."

The officer originally designated to command the *Macedonian* had been very greatly concerned about the midshipmen's provisions: the quality of which they should be, and the room to be kept for their stowage. I wonder would his soul have been greatly vexed had he accompanied me the first evening out, as I inspected the steerage while they were at supper? "What!" shouted one of them to a servant, as I passed. "What! No milk?" The mingled consternation, bereavement, and indignation which struggled for full expression in the words beggar description. I can see his face and hear his tones to this day. Laughable to comedy; yet to a philosophizing turn of mind what an epitome of life! Do we not at every corner of experience meet the princess who felt the three hard peas under the fifty feather-beds? Sydney Smith's friend, who had everything else life could give, but realized only the disappointing view out of one of his windows? We might dispense with Hague Conferences. War is going to cease because people adequately civilized will not endure hardness.

Whether in the end we shall have cause to rejoice in the double event remains to be seen. The Asiatic can endure.

Among the *Macedonian's* lieutenants was the late Admiral Sampson. We had also for deck officers two who had but just graduated; one of them a young Frenchman belonging to the royal house of Orléans, who had been permitted to take the course at our naval school, I presume with a view on his part to possible contingencies recalling the monarchy to France. Under Louis Philippe, a member of the family had been prominent in the French navy, as the Prince de Joinville; and had commanded the squadron which brought back the body of Napoleon from St. Helena. The representative with us was a very good-tempered, amiable, unpresuming man, too young as yet to be formed in character. As messmates we were, of course, all on terms of cordial equality, and one of our number used frequently to greet him with effusion as "You old King." He spoke English easily, though scarcely fluently, and with occasional eccentricity of idiom. At the Academy, before graduation, he took his turn with others of his class as officer of the day, one of whose duties was to keep a journal of happenings. I chanced once to inspect this book, and found over his signature an entry which began, "The weather was a dirty one."

While at the school, the young duke had been provided with a guide, philosopher, and friend, in the person of an accomplished ex-officer of the French navy, who had been obliged to quit that service, under the Empire, because of his attachment to the exiled monarchy. I knew this gentleman very well at Newport, exchanging with him occasional visits, though he was much my senior in years. His name was Fauvel, which the midshipmen, or other, had promptly Anglicized into Four Bells – a nautical hour-stroke. I suppose this propensity to travesty foreign or difficult names is not merely maritime; but naturally enough my reading has brought me more in contact with it in connection with naval matters. Thus the *Ville de Milan*, captured into the British service, became to their seamen the "Wheel 'em along;" and the *Bellerophon*, originally their own, is historically reported to have passed current as the "Bully Ruffian." Captain Fauvel accompanied us in the *Macedonian*; but after arriving in England, as we were to go to Cherbourg, his charge and he left us, neither being *persona grata* at that date in a French harbor. When we reached Cherbourg, Fauvel's wife was there, either resident or for the moment, and at our captain's invitation visited the ship to see where her husband had been living, and would again be when we reached a more friendly port. As contrary luck would have it, while she was on board, the French admiral and the general commanding the troops came alongside to return the official call paid them. The awkwardness, of course, was merely that her presence obtruded the fact, otherwise easily and discreetly ignored, that when out of French waters we were hospitably entertaining persons politically distasteful to the French government, the courtesies of which we were now accepting; and there was a momentary impulse to keep her out of sight. A better judgment prevailed, however, and a very courteous exchange of French politeness ensued between the officials and the lady, to whom doubtless political significance attached. A more notable circumstance, in the light of the then future, was that during our few days in Cherbourg arrived the news of the capture of the city of Mexico by the French troops; and before our departure took place the official celebration, with flags and salutes, of that crowning event in an enterprise which in the end proved disastrous to its originator, and fatal to his protégé, Maximilian.

The *Macedonian*, for a sailing-vessel, had a quite rapid run across from Newport to Plymouth, eighteen days from anchor to anchor, though I believe one of our frigates, after the war, made it in twelve. This was the only occasion, during my fairly numerous crossings, that. I have ever seen icebergs under a brilliant sky. Usually the scoundrels come skulking along masked by a fog, as though ashamed of themselves, as they ought to be. They are among the most obnoxious of people who do not know their place. This time we passed several, quite large, having a light breeze and perfectly clear horizon. After that it again set in thick, with the usual anxiety which ice, unseen but surely near, cannot but cause. Finally we took a very heavy gale of wind, which settled to southwest, hauling gradually to northwest and sending us rejoicing on our way a thousand miles in four days, much of this time under close-reefed topsails.

I am not heedless of the great danger of merely prosing along in the telling of the days of youth, so I will shut off my experience of the *Macedonian* with an incident which amused me greatly at the time, and still seems to have a moral that one needs not to point. While lying at Spithead, a number of the midshipmen were sent ashore to visit the dock yard, – professional improvement. When they returned, the lieutenants in charge were full of the block-making processes. The ingenuity of the machinery, the variety and beauty of the blocks, the many excellences, had the changes rung upon them, meal after meal, till I could hear the whir of the wheels in my head and see the chips fly. Meantime, our captain went to London, having completed his official visiting, and an English captain came on board to return a call. Declining my invitation to enter the cabin, he walked up and down the quarter-deck with me, discussing many things; under his arm his sword. Suddenly he stopped short, and pointing with it to a big iron-strapped leading-block, he said, "Now that is what I call a sensible block; I wonder why it is we cannot get blocks like that in our ships." I was not prepared with a reason for their defects, then or since; but my unreadiness has not marred my enjoyment of these divergent points of view. Perhaps the captain was a professional malcontent; for, looking at a Parrott rifled hundred-pounder gun which we carried on the quarter-deck, he said, interrogatively, "Not breech-loading?" "No," I answered, "breech-loading is not in favor with us at present." "And very right you are," he rejoined. I think they then (1863) still had the Armstrong breech-loading system. This incident may deserve a place in the palæontology of gun-making. There are now, I presume, no muzzle-loaders left; unless in museums, as specimens.

Very shortly after the *Macedonian's* return home I was sent to New Orleans, for a ship on the Texas blockade; transportation being given me on one of the "beef-boats," as the supply-vessels were familiarly known. Among fellow-passengers was one of my class; for a while, indeed, my roommate at the Academy. When we reached New Orleans the chief of staff said to me, "There is a vacancy on board the *Monongahela*," a ship larger and in every way better than the *Seminole* to which I was ordered; moreover, she was lying off Mobile, a sociable blockade, instead of at a jumping-off place, the end of nowhere, Sabine Pass, where the *Seminole* was. He advised me to apply for her, which I did; but Commodore Bell, acting in Farragut's absence in the North, declined. I must go to the ship to which the Department had assigned me, and for which it doubtless had its reasons. So my classmate was ordered to her instead, and on board her was killed in the passage of the Mobile forts the following August. I can scarcely claim a miraculous escape, as it does not appear that I should have got in the way of the ball which finished him; but for him, poor fellow, who had not been long married, the commodore's refusal to me was a sentence of death.

I shall not attempt to furbish up any intellectual entertainment for readers from the excessively dry bones of my subsequent blockading, especially off the mouth of the Sabine. Only a French cook could produce a passable dish out of such woful material; and even he would require concomitant ingredients, in remembered incidents, wherein, if there were any, my memory fails me. Day after day, day after day, we lay inactive – roll, roll; not wholly ineffective, I suppose, for our presence stopped blockade-running; but even in this respect the Texas coast had largely lost importance since the capture of Vicksburg and Port Hudson, the previous summer, had cut off the trans-Mississippi region from the body of the Confederacy. We used to see the big, light-draught steamers coming up the river, or crossing the lagoon-like bay, sometimes crowded with people; and the possibility was discussed of their carrying troops, and of their coming out to attack us, as not long before had been successfully done against our vessels *inside* Galveston Bay. In a norther, possibly, such a thing might have been tried, for the sea was then smooth; but in the ordinary ground-swell I imagine the soldiers would have been incapacitated by sea-sickness. The chances were all against success, and no attempt was ever made; but it was something to talk about.

The ensuing twelve or fifteen months to the close of the war were equally uneventful. Long before they ended I had got back to the South Atlantic coast. To this I was indebted for the opportunity of being present when the United States flag was ceremoniously hoisted again over what then remained of Fort Sumter, by General Robert Anderson, who, as Major Anderson, had been forced to lower it just four years before. Henry Ward Beecher delivered the address, of which I remember little, except that, citing the repeated question of foreigners, why we should wish to re-establish our authority over a land where the one desire of the people was to reject it, he replied, "We so wish, because it is ours." The sentiment was obvious enough, one would think, to any man who had a country to love and objected to seeing it dismembered, but to many of our European critics it then seemed monstrous in an American; at least they said so. The orator on such an occasion has only to swim with the current. The enthusiasm is already there; he needs not to elicit it. Here and again a blast of eloquence from him may start the fire roaring, but the flame is already kindled. The joy of harvest, the rejoicing of men who divide the spoil, the boasting of them who can now put off their harness, need not the stimulation of words.

The exact coincidence of raising the flag over Sumter on the anniversary of its lowering was artificial, but the date of the surrender of Charleston, February 18th, was just opportune to complete the necessary arrangements and preparations without holding back the ceremony, on the night of which – Good Friday – within twelve hours, President Lincoln was murdered. Joy and grief were thus brought into immediate and startling contrast. A perfectly natural and quite impressive coincidence came under my notice in close connection with these occurrences. I was at this time on the staff of Admiral Dahlgren, commander-in-chief of the South Atlantic Blockading Squadron during the last two years of the war, and accompanied him when he entered Charleston Harbor, which he had so long assailed in vain.

The following Sunday I attended service at one of the Episcopal churches. The appointed first lesson for the day, Quinquagesima, was from the first chapter of Lamentations, beginning, "How doth the city sit solitary, that was full of people!... She that was great among the nations, and princess among the provinces, how is she become tributary!" Considering the conspicuous, and even leading, part played by Charleston in the Southern movement, "the cradle of secession," her initiation of hostilities, her long successful resistance, and her recent subjugation, the words and their sequence were strikingly and painfully applicable to her present condition; for the Confederate troops in evacuating had started a large destruction of property, and the Union forces on entering found public buildings, stores, warehouses, private dwellings, and cotton, on fire – a scene of distress to which some of them also further contributed.[11] I myself remember streets littered with merchants' correspondence, a mute witness to other devastation. My recollection is that the officiating clergyman saw and dodged the too evident application, reading some other chapter. Many still living may recall how apposite, though to a different mood, was the first lesson of the Sunday – the third after Easter – which in 1861 followed the surrender of Sumter and the excited week that witnessed "the uprising of the North," – Joel iii., v. 9: "Proclaim ye this among the Gentiles: Prepare war, wake up the mighty men, let all men of war draw near; let them come up. Beat your ploughshares into swords, and your pruning-hooks into spears; let the weak say, I am strong." I was not in the country myself at that time, and my attention was first drawn to this in 1865 by a clergyman, who told me of his startled astonishment upon opening the Book. In the then public temper it must have thrilled every nerve among the hearers, already strained to the utter-most by events without parallel in the history of the nation.

Being on Dahlgren's staff gave me also the opportunity of seeing, gathered together in social assembly, all the general officers who had shared in the March to the Sea. This was at a reception given by Sherman in Savannah, within a week after entering that city, which may be considered the particular terminus of one stage in his pro-gress through the heart of the Confederacy. The admiral had gone thither in a small steamer, which served as flag-ship, to greet the triumphant chief. Few, if any, of the more conspicuous of Sherman's subordinates were absent from the rooms, thronged with men whose names were then in all mouths, and who in honor of the occa-sion had changed their marching clothes for full uniform, rarely seen in campaign. From the heads of the two armies, the union of which under him constituted his force, down through the brigade commanders, all were there with their staffs; and many besides. The tone of this gathering was more subdued than at Fort Sumter, if equally ex-ultant. Success, achievement, the clear demonstra-tion of victory, such as the occupation of Savan-nah gave, uplifts men's hearts and swells their breasts; but these men had worked off some of their heat in doing things. Besides, there yet remained for them other and weighty things to do. It could be felt sympathetically that with them the pervading sensation was relaxation – repose. They had reached their present height by prolonged labor and endurance, and were enjoying rather the momentary release from strain than the intoxication of triumph.

In expectation of the victorious arrival of the army in Savannah, I had been charged with two messages, in pathetic contrast with each other. The first was from my father to Sherman himself, who twenty years before had been under his teaching as a cadet at the Military Academy. I cannot now recall whether I bore with me a letter of congratulation which my father wrote him, and to which he pleasantly replied that he had from it as much satisfaction as when in far-away days he had been dismissed from the blackboard with the commendation, "Very well done, Mr. Sherman." My reception by him, however, was in the exact spirit of this remark, and characteristic of the man. When I mentioned my name he broke into a smile – all over, as they say – shook my hand forcibly, and exclaimed, "What, the son of old Dennis?" reverting instinctively to the familiar epithet of school-days.

My other errand was to a former school-mate of my mother's, resident in Savannah, with whom she had long maintained affectionate relations, which the war necessarily suspended. The next day I sought her out. When I found the house, she was at the door, in conversation with some of the subordinate officials of the invading army, probably with reference to the necessity of yielding rooms for quarters. The men were perfectly respectful, but the situation was perturbing to a middle-aged lady brought for the first time into contact with the rough customs of war, and she was very pale, worried in look, and harassed in speech; evidently quite doubtful as to what latent possibilities of harm such a visit might portend – whether ultimately she might not find herself houseless. I made myself known, but she was not responsive; courteous, for with her breeding she could not be otherwise, but too preoccupied with the harsh present to respond to the gentler feelings of the past. It was touchingly apparent that she was trying hard to keep a stiff upper lip, and her attempted frame of mind finally betrayed itself in the words, uttered tremulously, with excitement or mortification, "I don't admit yet that you have beaten us." I could scarcely contest the point, but it was very sad. At the moment I could almost have wished that we had not.

At the mouths of the Georgia rivers Sherman's soldiers struck tide-water, many of them for the first time in their lives; and a story was current that two, foraging, lay down to sleep by the edge of a stream, and were astounded by waking to find themselves in the water. To consider the tide, however, is an acquired habit. Sherman's approach to the Atlantic had given rise to a certain amount of naval and military activity on the part of the forces already stationed there. In connection with this I had been sent on some staff errand that caused me to spend a couple of days on board the *Pawnee*, which had just been carrying about army officers for reconnoissances. "By George!" said her captain, laughing and bringing down his fist on the table, "you can't make those fellows understand that a ship has to look out for the tide. I would say to them, 'See here, the tide is running out, and if we don't move very soon we shall be left aground, fast till next high-water.' 'Oh yes, yes,' they would reply, 'all right'; and then they would forget all about it, and go on as if they had unlimited time." But of course the captain did not forget.

The fall of Richmond and Charleston, and the surrender of Lee's army, assuring the early termination of hostilities on any grand scale, the admiral had kindly transferred me from his staff back to the ship on board which I had joined the squadron a year before, and which was soon to return North. War service, nominal at least, was not, however, quite over; for after some brief repairs we were sent down to Haïti to take up the duty of convoying the Pacific Mail steamers from the Windward Passage (between Cuba and Haïti) some distance towards Panama. It is perhaps worth recording that such an employment incident to the war was maintained for quite a while, consequent upon the capture of the *Ariel*, before mentioned. Upon my personal fortunes it had the effect of producing a severe tropical fever, engendered probably during the years of Southern service, and brought to a head by the conditions of Haïti. Whatever its cause, this led to my being invalided for six months, at the expiration of which, to my grievous disappointment, I was again assigned to duty in the Gulf of Mexico. The War of Secession then – December, 1865 – was entirely over; but the Mexican expedition of Napoleon III., the culminating incident of which, the capture of Mexico, we had seen celebrated at Cherbourg in 1863, was still lingering. Begun in our despite, when our hands were tied by intestine troubles, it now engaged our unfriendly interest; and part of the attention paid to it was the maintenance of a particular squadron in those waters – observant, if quiescent. Here again sickness pursued, not me, but my ship; from the mouth of the Rio Grande we returned to Pensacola, with near a hundred men, half the ship's company, down with fever. It was not malignant – we had but three deaths – but one of those was our only doctor, and we were sent to the far North, and so out of commission, in September, 1866. The particular squadron was continued till the following spring, when, under diplomatic pressure, the French expedition was withdrawn; but by then I was again in Rio de Janeiro on my way to China.

The headquarters of this temporary squadron was at Pensacola; but until her unlucky visit to the Rio Grande my ship, the *Muscoota*, one of the iron double-ender paddle steamers which the war had evolved among other experiments, lay for some months at Key West, then, as always from its position, a naval station of importance. I suppose most people know that this word "Key," meaningless in its application to the low islands which it designates, is the anglicized form of the Spanish "Cayo." Among the valued acquaintances of my life I here met a clergyman, whose death at the age of eighty I see as these words pass from my pen.

As chaplain to the garrison, he had won the esteem and praise of many, including General Sherman, for his devotion during an epidemic of yellow-fever, and he was now rector of the only Episcopal parish. He told me an anecdote of one of his flock. Key West, from its situation, had many of the characteristics of an outpost, a frontier town, a mingling of peoples, with consequent rough habits, hard drinking, and general dissipation. The man in question, a good fellow in his way, professed to be a very strong churchman, and constantly so avowed himself; but the bottle was too much for him. The rector remonstrated. "----, how can you go round boasting yourself a churchman when your life is so scandalous? You are doing the Church harm, not good, by such talk." "Yes, Mr. Herrick," he replied, "I know it's too bad; it is a shame; but, you see, all the same, I *am* a good churchman. I fight for the Church. If I hear a man say anything against her, I knock him down." It was at Mr. Herrick's table I heard criticised the local inadequacy of the prayer-book petition for rain. "What we want," said the speaker, "is not 'moderate rain and showers, that we may receive the fruits of the earth,' but a hard down-pour to fill our tanks." Key West and its neighbors then depended chiefly, if not solely, upon this resource for drinking-water.

IX
A ROUNDABOUT ROAD TO CHINA

1867

With the termination of the War of Secession, which had concentrated the entire effort of the navy upon our own coasts and inland waters, the policy of the government reverted, irreflectively perhaps, to the identical system of distribution in squadrons that had existed before. The prolonged tension of mind and effort during four years of overwrought activity was followed by a period of reaction, to which, as far as the administration of the navy was concerned, the term collapse would scarcely be misapplied. Of course, for a few years the evil effects of this would not be observable in the military resources of the government. Only the ravages of time could deprive us of the hundreds of thousands of veterans just released from the active practice of war; and the navy found itself in possession of a respectable fleet, which, though somewhat over-specialized in order to meet the peculiar conditions of the hostilities, was still fairly modern. There was a body of officers fully competent in numbers and ability, and comparatively young. In the first ship on board which I made a long cruise, beginning in 1867, of ten in the ward-room, three only, the surgeon, paymaster, and chief engineer, were over thirty; and they barely. I myself, next to the captain, was twenty-six; and there was not a married man among us. The seamen, though professionally more liable to dispersion than the land forces, were not yet

247

scattered. Thus provided against immediate alarms, and with the laurels of the War of Secession still fresh, the country in military matters lay down and went to sleep, like the hare in the fable, regardless of the incessant progress on every side, which, indeed, was scarcely that of the tortoise. Our ships underwent no change in character or armament.

Twenty years later, in the Pacific, I commanded one of these old war-horses, not yet turned out to grass or slaughter, ship-rigged to royals, and slow-steamed. One day the French admiral came on board to return my official visit. As he left, he paused for a moment abreast one of our big, and very old, pivot guns. "Capitaine," he said, "les vieux canons!" Two or three days later came his chief of staff on some errand or other. That discharged, when I was accompanying him to his boat at the gangway, he stopped in the same spot as the admiral. His gaze was meditative, reminiscent, perhaps even sentimental. "Où sont les neiges d'antan?" Whatever their present merits as fighting-machines, he saw before him an historical memento, sweeping gently, doubtless, the chords of youthful memories. "Oui, oui!" he said at last; "l'ancien systême. Nous l'avons eu." It was a summary of American naval policy during the twenty years following 1865; we "hail" things which other nations "had had," until Secretary Chandler started the movement of renovation by the first of all necessary steps, the official exposure of the sham to which we had allowed ourselves to be committed. There is an expression, "quaker guns," applied to blackened cylinders of wood, intended to simulate cannon, and mounted upon ramparts or a ship's broadside to impose upon an enemy as to the force before him. We made four such for the *Macedonian*, to deceive any merchant-men we spoke as to our battery, in case she should report us to an *Alabama*; and, being carried near the bows, much trouble they gave us, being usually knocked overboard when we tacked ship, or set a lower studding-sail. Well, by 1885 the United States had a "quaker" navy; the result being that, not the enemy, but our own people were deceived. Like poor Steece's passengers on board the *Ariel*, we were blissfully sheltering behind pine boards.

In 1867, however, these old ships and ancient systems were but just passing their meridian, and for a brief time might continue to live on their reputation. They were beautiful vessels in outline, and repaid in appearance all the care which the seamen naturally lavishes on his home. One could well feel proud of them; the more so that they had close behind them a good fighting record. It was to one such, the *Iroquois*, which had followed Farragut from New Orleans to Vicksburg, that I reported on the second day of that then new year. She was destined to China and Japan, the dream of years to me; but, better still, there was chalked out for her an extensive trip, "from Dan to Beer-sheba," as a British officer enviously commented in my hearing. We were to go by the West Indies to Rio de Janeiro, thence by the Cape of Good Hope to Madagascar, to Aden at the mouth of the Red Sea, to Muscat at the entrance of the Persian Gulf, and so by India and Siam to our first port in

Chinese waters, Hong Kong. The time, too, was apposite, for Japan had not yet entered upon the path of modernization which she has since pursued with such revolutionary progress. Some eight or ten years ago there lunched with me a young Japanese naval officer, who I understand has occupied a position of distinguished responsibility during the recent war with Russia. I chanced to ask him if he had ever seen a two-sworded man. He replied, Never. He belonged to the samurai class, who once wore them; but in actual life they have disappeared. When the *Iroquois* reached Japan, and throughout her stay, two-sworded men were as thick almost as blackberries. To European prepossessions it was illuminating to see half a dozen riding down a street, hatless, crown of the head shaved, with a short pigtail at the back tied tight near the skull and then brought stiffly forward close to the scalp; their figures gowned, the handles of the two swords projecting closely together from the left side of their garments, and the feet resting in stirrups of slipper form, which my memory says were of straw-work; but of that I am less sure. This equipment was completed by a painted fan stuck in the belt, and at times an opened paper umbrella. I have been passenger in the same boat with some of these warriors, accoutred as above, and using their fans as required, while engaged in animated conversation with the courtesy and smiling affability characteristic of all classes in Japan. Such, in outward seeming, then was the as yet raw material, out of which have been evolved the heroic soldiery who have recently astonished the world by the practical development they have given to modern military ideas; then as unlike the troops which now are, except in courage, as the ancient Japanese war-junk is to the present battle-ship. I was in Japan at the arrival of their first iron-clad, purchased in the United States, and doubtless long since consigned to the scrap-heap; but of her hereafter.

A glance over the list of vessels in the *Navy Register* of 1907 shows me that the once abundant Indian names have disappeared, except where associated with some State or city; or, worse, have been degraded to tugboats, a treatment which the Indian, with all his faults, scarcely deserves. They no longer connote ships of war. *Iroquois*, *Seminole*, *Mohican*, *Wyoming*, *Oneida*, *Pawnee*, and some dozens more, are gone with the ships, and like the tribes, which bore them. Yet what more appropriate to a vessel meant for a scout than the tribal epithet of a North American Indian! *Dacotah*, alone survives; while for it the march of progress in spelling has changed the *c* to *k*, and phonetically dropped the silent, and therefore supposedly useless, *h*. As if silence had no merits! is the interjection, *ah*, henceforth to be spelled *a*? Since they with their names have passed into the world of ghosts – can there be for them a sea in the happy hunting-grounds? – it may be historically expedient to tell what manner of craft they were. If only some contemporary had done the same by the trireme, what time and disputation might have been saved!

The *Iroquois* and her sisters, built in the fifties, were vessels of the kind to which I have applied the term corvette, then very common in all navies;

cruisers only; scouts, or commerce-destroyers. Not of the line of battle, although good fighting-ships. Ours were of a thousand tons, as size was then stated, or about seven hundred tons "displacement," as the more modern expression runs; displacement being the weight of the water displaced by the hull which rests in and upon it. Thus measured, they were from one-third to one-fourth the dimensions of the vessels called third-class cruisers, which now correspond to them; but their serviceableness in their time was sufficiently attested by the Confederate *Alabama*, substantially of this general type, as was her conqueror, the *Kearsarge*. For external appearance, they were something over two hundred feet long, with from one-fifth to one-sixth that width, and sat low in the water. Low and long are nautical features, suggestive of grace and speed, which have always obtained recognition for beauty; and the rail of these vessels ran unbroken, but with a fine sweep, from bow to stern. Along the water-line, and extending a few inches above it, shone the burnished copper, nearly parallel to the rail, between which and it glistened the saucy black hull.

Steam had not yet succeeded in asserting its undivided sway; but the *Iroquois* and her mates marked a stage in the progress, for they carried sails really as auxiliary, and were intended primarily to be fast steamers, as speed was reckoned in their time. The larger vessels of the service were acceptedly slow under steam. They had it chiefly to fight with, and to help them across the places where wind failed or weakened. These corvettes carried sails with a view to saving coal, by utilizing the well-defined wind zones of the ocean when fair for their course. Though the practical result for both was much the same, the underlying idea was different. In the one, sail held the first place; in the other, steam; and it is the idea which really denotes and maintains intellectual movement and material progress. This was represented accordingly in the rig adopted. Like a ship, they had three masts, yes; but only the two forward were square-rigged, and on each of them but three sails. The lofty royals were discarded. The general result was to emphasize the design of speed under steam, and the use of sails with a fresh, fair wind only; a distinct, if partial, abandonment of the "auxiliary" steam reliance which so far had governed naval development. It may be added that the shorter and lighter masts, by a common optical effect, increased the impression of the vessel's length and swiftness, as was the case with the old-time sailing-frigate when her lofty topgallant-masts were down on deck.

Under sail alone the *Iroquois* could never accomplish anything, except with a fair wind. We played with her at times, on the wind and tacking, but she simply slid off to leeward – never fetched near where she looked. Consonant with the expedient of using sails where the wind served, the screw could be disconnected from its shaft and hoisted; held in position, clear of the water, by iron pawls. In this way the hinderance of its submerged drag upon the speed of the ship was obviated. We did this on occasions, when we could reckon on a long period of favorable breezes; but it was a troublesome and somewhat anxious operation. The chance of a slip was not great, but the possibility was unpleasant to contemplate. When I add that for armament we carried one 100-pounder rifled gun on a pivot, and four 9-inch smooth-bore shell guns – these being the naval piece which for the most part fought the War of Secession, then just closed – I shall have given the principal distinguishing features of a class of vessel which did good service in its day, and is now a much of the past as is the Spanish Armada. Yet it is only forty years since.

After being frozen up and snowed under, during a very bitter and boisterous January, we at last got to sea, and soon ran into warmer weather. Our first stop was at the French West India island Guadeloupe, and there I had set for me amusingly that key-note of travelling experience which most have encountered. I was dining at a café, and after dinner got into conversation with an officer of the garrison. I asked him some question about the wet weather then reigning. "C'est exceptionnel," he replied; and exceptional we found it "from Dan to Beersheba." At our next port, Ciará, there was drought when every resident said it should have rained constantly – a variation a stranger could endure; while at Rio it was otherwise peculiar – "the warmest April in years." The currents all ran contrary to the books, and the winds which should have been north hung obstinately at south. Whether for natural productions, or weather, or society, we were commonly three months too late or two months too soon; or, as one of "ours" put it, we should have come in the other monsoon. Nevertheless, it was impossible for youth and high spirits to follow our schedule and not find it spiced to the full with the enjoyment of novelty; if not in season, at least well seasoned.

However, every one travels nowadays, and it is time worse than wasted to retell what many have seen. But do many of our people yet visit our intended second port, that most beautiful bay of Rio de Janeiro? I fancy not. It is far out of the ordinary line, and the business immigration to South America is much more from Europe than from our own continent; but, having since visited many harbors, in many lands, I incline to agree with my old captain of the *Congress*, there is none that equals Rio, viewed from the anchorage. Like Japan, I was happy enough to see Rio before it had been much improved, while the sequestered, primitive, tropical aspect still clung to it. I suppose the red-tiled roofs still rise as before from among the abundant foliage and the orange-trees, in the suburb of Bota Fogo; that the same deliciously suggestive smell of the sugar and rum hogsheads hangs about the streets; that the long, narrow Rua do Ouvidor is still brilliant with its multicolored feather flowers; and that at night the innumerable lights dazzle irregularly upward, like the fireflies which also there abound, over the hill-sides and promontories that so charmingly break the shore line. But already in 1867 the strides since 1860 were strikingly visible. In the earlier year I used frequently to visit a friend living at Nichtherohy, on the opposite shore of the bay. The ferriage then was by trig, long, sharp-bowed, black paddle steamers, with raking funnels. They were tremendously fussy, important, puffing little chaps, with that consequential air which so frequently accompanies moderate performance. The making a landing was a complicated and tedious job, characterized by the same amount of needless action and of shortcoming in accomplishment. We would back and stop about twenty feet away from the end of a long, projecting pier. Then ropes would be got ashore from each extremity of the vessel; which done, she would back again, and the bow line would be shortened in. Then she would go ahead, and the like would be done by the stern line. This would fetch her, say, ten feet away, when the same processes must be repeated. I never timed, for why should one be in a hurry in the tropics, where no one else is? but it seemed to me that sometimes ten minutes were thus consumed. In 1867 these had disappeared, and had been replaced by Yankee double-ended boats, which ran into slips such as we have. Much more expeditious and sensible, but familiar and ugly to a degree, and not in the least entertaining; nor, I may add, congruous. They put you at once on the same absurd "jump" that we North Americans practise; whereas in the others we placidly puffed our cigars in an atmosphere of serenity. Time and tide may be so ridiculous as not to wait; we knew that waiting was enjoyment. The boat had time to burn, and so had we. At the later date, street-cars also had been introduced, and we were told were doing much to democratize the people. The man whose ability to pay for a cab had once severed him from the herd now went along with it, and saved his coppers. The black coats and tall black silk hats, with white trousers and waistcoats, which always struck me as such an odd blend, were still in evidence.

The *Iroquois* did not succeed in making Rio without a stop. The northeast trades hung well to the eastward after we left Guadeloupe, and blew hard with a big sea; for it was the northern winter. Running across them, as we were, the ship was held close to the wind under fore and aft canvas. For a small vessel nothing is more uncomfortable. Rolling and butting at waves which struck the bow at an angle of forty-five degrees made walking, not impossible, indeed, to practised sea legs, but still a constant succession of gymnastic balancings that took from it all pleasure. For exercise it was not needed. You had but to sit at your desk and write, with one leg stretched out to keep your position. The varied movements of the muscles of that leg, together with those of the rest of the body, in the continued effort "to correct the horizontal deviation," as Boatswain Chucks phrased it, sent you to bed wearily conscious that you had had constitutional enough. The large consumption of coal in proportion to the ground covered made a renewal necessary, and we went into Ciará, an open roadstead sheltered only by submerged coral reefs, on the northeast coast of Brazil. Here the incessant long trade swell sets in upon a beach only partly protected; and boating is chiefly by catamarans, or *jangadas*, as the Portuguese word is, – three or four long trunks of trees, joined together side by side, without keel, but with mast. These are often to be seen far outside, and ride safely over the heavy breakers.

From Rio to Capetown, being in the month of May, corresponding to our northern November, we had a South Atlantic passage which in bois- terousness might hold its own with that between the United States and Europe, now familiar to so many. When clear of the tropics, one strikes in both hemispheres the westerly gales which are, so to say, the counter-currents of the atmosphere responding to the trade-winds of the equatorial belt – almost as prevalent in direction, though much more variable in force. The early Spanish navigators characterized them as "vientos bravos," an epithet too literally and flatteringly rendered into English by our seamen as "the brave west winds;" the Spanish "bravo" meaning rude. For a vessel using sail, however, "brave" may pass; for, if they hustled her somewhat unceremoniously, they at least did speed her on her way. On two successive Thursdays their prevalence was inter- rupted by a tempest, which in each case surpassed for suddenness, violence, and shortness anything that I remember; for I have never met a tropical hurricane, nor the full power of a China typhoon. On the first occasion the sun came up yellow and wet, with a sulky expression like that of a child bathed against its will; but, as the wind was mod- erate, sail was made soon after daylight. Immedi- ately it began to freshen, and so rapidly that we could scarce get the canvas in fast enough. By ten it was blowing furiously. To be heard by a person standing at your elbow, you had to shout at the top of your voice. The wind shifted rapidly, a cy- clone in miniature as to dimensions, though not as to strength; but the *Iroquois* had been hove-to on the right tack according to the law of storms. That is, the wind hauled aft; and as she followed, close to it, she headed to the sea instead of falling into the trough. When square sails are set, this gradual movement in the same direction is still more important; for, should the wind fly suddenly ahead, the sails may be taken aback, a very awkward situation in heavy weather. By five o'clock this gradual shifting had passed from east, by north, to west, where the gale died out; having lasted only about eight hours, yet with such vehemence that it had kicked up a huge sea. By 10 P.M. the stars were shining serenely, a gentle breeze barely steadying the ship, under increased canvas, in the huge billows which for a few hours continued to testify that things had been nasty. A spoiled child that has carried a point by squalling could scarcely present a more beaming expression than did the heavens; but our wet decks and clothes assured us that our discomfort had been real and was not yet over.

Throughout the ordeal the little *Iroquois* – for small she was by modern standards – though at a stand-still, lay otherwise as unconcerned as a duck in a mill-pond; her screw turning slowly, a triangular rag of storm-sail showing to steady her, rolling deeply but easily, and bowing the waves with gentle movement up or down, an occasional tremor alone betraying the shock when an unusually heavy comber hit her in the eyes. Then one saw admiringly that the simile "like a sea-fowl" was no metaphor, but exact. None were better qualified to pronounce than we, for the South Atlantic abounds in aquatic birds. We were followed continuously by clouds of them, low flying, skirting the water, of varied yet sober plumage. The names of these I cannot pretend to give, except the monarch of them all, in size and majesty of flight, the albatross, of unsullied white, as its name implies – the king of the southern ocean. Several of these enormous but graceful creatures were ever sweeping about us in almost endless flight, hardly moving their wings, but inclining them wide-spread, now this way, now that, like the sails of a windmill, to catch the breeze, almost never condescending to the struggle of a stroke. By this alone they kept up with us, running eight or nine knots. As a quiet demonstration of reserve power it was most impressive; while the watching of the intricate manoeuvres of these and their humbler companions afforded a sort of circus show, a relief always at hand to the monotony of the voyage.

As this has remained my only crossing of the South Atlantic, my experience cannot claim to be wide; but, as far as it goes, these animating accompaniments of a voyage under sail are there far more abundant and varied than in the northern ocean. How far the steamer in southern latitudes may still share this privilege, I do not know; but certainly I now rarely see the petrel, unfairly called stormy, numbers of which hung ever near in the wake of a sailing-ship on her way to Europe, keeping company easily with a speed of seven or eight knots, and with spare power enough to gyrate continually in their wayward flight. What instinct taught them that there was food there for them? and, if my observation agree with that of others, why have they disappeared from steamers? Is it the greater pace that wearies, or the commotion of the screw that daunts them?

Our second Thursday gale, May 16th, exceeded the first in fury and duration. Beginning at daybreak, it lasted till after sundown, twelve hours in all; and during it the *Iroquois* took on board the only solid sea that crossed her rail during my more than two years' service in her. We sprung also our main mast-head, which made us feel flatteringly like the ancient mariners, who, as we had read, were always "springing" (breaking) some spar or other. Ancient mariners and albatrosses are naturally mutually suggestive. Except for the greater violence, the conditions were much the same as a week before; with the exception, however, that the sun shone brightly most of the time from a cloudless sky, between which and us there interposed a milky haze, the vapor of the spoon-drift. During the height of the storm the pressure of the wind in great degree kept down the sea, which did not rise threateningly till towards the end. For the rest, our voyage of thirty-three hundred miles, while it afforded us many samples of weather, presented as a chief characteristic perpetual westerly gales, with gloomy skies and long, high following swell. Although the wind was such that close to it we should have been reduced to storm-sails, the *Iroquois* scudded easily before it, carrying considerable canvas. "Before it" must not be understood to mean ahead of the waves. These, as they raced along continually, swept by the ship, which usually lifted cleverly abaft as they came up; though at rare intervals a tiny bit of a crest would creep along over the poop and fall on the quarter-deck below – nothing to hurt. The onward movement of the billows, missing thus the stern, culminated generally about half-way forward, abreast the main-mast; and if the ship, in her continual steady but easy roll, happened just then to incline to one side, she would scoop in a few dozen buckets of water, enough to keep the decks always sloppy, as it swashed from side to side.

From Rio to the Cape took us thirty-two days. This bears out the remark I find in an old letter that the *Iroquois* was very slow; but it attests also a series of vicissitudes which have passed from my mind, leaving predominant those only that I have noted. Among other experiences, practically all our mess crockery was smashed; the continual rolling seemed to make the servants wilfully reckless. Also, having an inefficient caterer, our sea stores were exhausted on the way, with the ludicrous exception of about a peck of nutmegs. Another singular incident remains in my memory. At dawn of the day before our arrival, a mirage presented so exactly, and in the proper quarter, the appearance of Table Mountain, the landmark of Cape Town, that our captain, who had been there more than once, was sure of it. As by the reckoning it must be still over a hundred miles distant, the navigating officer was summoned, to his great disconcertment, to be eye-witness of his personal error; and the chronometers fell under unmerited suspicion. The navigator was an inveterate violinist. He had a curious habit of undressing early, and then, having by this symbolic act laid aside the cares of the day, as elbow space was lacking in his own cabin, he would play in the open ward-room for an hour or more before turning in; always standing, and attired in a white night-shirt of flowing dimensions. He was a tall, dark, handsome man, the contrast of his full black beard emphasizing the oddness of his costume; and so rapt was he in his performance that remarks addressed directly to him were unheard. I often had to remind him at ten o'clock that music must not longer trouble the sleep of the mid-watch officers. On this occasion, with appearances so against him, perplexed but not convinced, after looking for a few moments he went below and sought communion with his beloved instrument; nor did the fading of the phantasm interrupt his fiddling. When announced, he listened absently, and continued his aria unmoved by such trivialities. Cape Flyaway, as counterfeits like this are called, had lasted so long and looked so plausible that the order was given to raise steam; and when it vanished later, after the manner of its kind, the step was not countermanded, for the weather was calm and there were abundant reasons in our conditions for hurrying into port.

At the season of our stay, May and June, the anchorage at Cape Town itself, being open to the northward, is exposed to heavy gales from that quarter, often fatal to shipping. I believe this defect has now been remedied by a breakwater, which in 1867 either had not been begun or was not far enough advanced to give security. Vessels therefore commonly betook themselves to Simon's Bay, on the other side of the Cape, where these winds blew off shore. Thither the *Iroquois* went;

and as communication with Cape Town, some twenty miles away, was by stage, the opportunity for ordinary visiting was indifferent. We went up by detachments, each staying several days. The great local natural feature of interest, Table Mountain, has since become familiar in general outline by the illustrations of the Boer War; from which I have inferred that similar formations are common in South Africa, just as I remember at the head of Rio Bay, on the road to Petropolis, a re-production in miniature, both in form and color, of the huge red-brown Sugar-Loaf Rock that dominates the entrance from the sea. Seen as a novelty, Table Mountain was most impressive; but it seems to me that Altar Mountain would more correctly convey its appearance. With rocky sides, which rose precipitate as the Palisades of the Hudson, the sky-line was horizontal, and straight as though drawn by a ruler. At times a white cloud descends, covering its top and creeping like loose drapery down the sides, resembling a ta-ble-cloth; which name is given it. I believe that is reckoned a sign of bad weather.

I recall many things connected with our stay there, but chiefly trivialities. Most amusing, be-cause so embarrassing to the unprepared, was an unlooked-for and startling attention received from the British soldiery, whom I now met for the first time: for the war at home had hitherto prevented the men of my date from having much foreign cruising. I was in uniform in the streets, confining myself severely to my own business, when I saw approaching a squad of redcoats under a non-commissioned officer. Being used to soldiers,

I was observing them only casually, but still with the interest of novelty, when wholly unexpectedly I heard, "Eyes right!" and the entire group, as one man, without moving their heads, slewed their eyes quickly round and fastened them steadily on me; the corporal also holding me with his glittering eye, while carrying his hand to his cap. Of course, in all salutes, from a civilian lifting his hat to a lady, to a military passing in review, the person saluting looks at the one saluted; but to find one's self without warning the undivided recipient of the steady stare of some half-dozen men, transfixed by what Mr. Snodgrass called "the mild gaze of intelligence beaming from the eyes of the defenders of their country," was, however flattering, somewhat disturbing to one not naturally obtrusive. With us the salute would have been given, of course; but only by the non-commissioned officer, touching his cap. Afterwards I was on the lookout for this, and dodged it when I could.

Both in Rio and at the Cape the necessity for repairs occasioned delays which militated somewhat against the full development of our cruise. Through this, I believe, we missed a stop at Siam, which, consequently, I have never visited; and I know that towards the end our captain felt pressed to get along. Our next destination was Madagascar; to reach which, under sail, it was necessary to run well to the eastward, in a latitude farther south than that of Cape Town, before heading north. We left somewhat too soon the westerly winds there prevailing, and in consequence did not go to Tamatave, the principal port, on the east side of the great island, but passed instead through the Mozambique Channel. It was in attempting this same passage that the British frigate *Aurora*, in which was serving the poet Falconer, the author of "The Shipwreck," disappeared with all on board; by what nautical fate overtaken has never been known. His first shipwreck, which he celebrated in verse, was on the coast of Greece, off Cape Colonna; the second in these far southern seas.

The French occupation of Madagascar postdates our visit to it. The harbor we entered, St. Augustine's Bay, on the west side, was only nominally under control of the native dynasty at Antananarivo, in the centre of the island; and the local inhabitants were little, if at all, above barbarism. Though dark in color, they had not the flat negro features. Wandering with a companion through a jungle, having lost our way, we came unexpectedly upon a group of brown people, scantily dressed, the most conspicuous member of which was a woman carrying a spear a little taller than herself, the head of which was burnished till it shone like silver; whether a weapon, or simply a badge of rank, I do not know. They rose to meet us in friendly enough fashion, and had English sufficient to set us on our way. The place was frequented by whalers, who occasionally shipped hands from among the natives; one such came on board the *Iroquois*, and within a limited range spoke English fluently. Our chief acquaintance was known to us as Prince George, and I presume had some personal importance in the neighborhood. He was of use in obtaining supplies, hanging about the deck all day, obligingly ready at any moment to take a glass of wine or a cigar, and seemingly even a little sulky that he was not asked to table. The men dressed their hair in peculiar fashion, gathered together in little globes about the size of a golf ball, distributed somewhat symmetrically over the skull, and plastered with a substance which looked like blue mud. As I refrained from close inspection, I cannot pronounce certainly what it was.

From St. Augustine's Bay we went on to the Comoro Islands, between the north end of Madagascar and the African main-land. I do not know what was then the precise political status of this pleasant-looking group, except that one of them had for some years been under French control. Johanna, at which we stopped, possessed at the least a qualified self-government. We had a good sight of its surface, approaching from the south and skirting at moderate distance westward, to reach the principal anchorage, Johanna Town, on the north. The island is lofty – five thousand feet – and of volcanic origin; bearing the family likeness which I have found in all such that I have seen. On a bright day, which we had, they are very picturesque to look on from the sea, with their deep gullies, ragged precipices, and varied hues; especially striking from the effects of light and shadow produced by the exaggerated inequalities of the ground. It is hard to say which are the more attractive, these or the totally different low coral islands of the tropics, with their brilliant white sand, encircled by which, as by a setting of silver, the deep-green brush glows like an emerald. It is hard, however, to make other than a pleasing picture with a combination of blue water and land. Like flowers, they may be more or less tastefully arranged, but scarcely can be less than beautiful.

In the way of landscape effect, Johanna had a special feature of its own. Up to a height of about fifteen hundred feet from the sea-level, the slopes were of a tawny hue, the color of grass when burned up by drought. Except scattered waving cocoanut palms which grew even on these hill-sides, no green thing was apparent, save in the ravines, where trees seemed to thrive, and so broke the monotony of tint with streaks of sombre verdure. Farther up, the peaks were thickly covered with a forest, which looked impenetrable. The abrupt contrast of the yellow lower land with this cap of tanglewood, itself at times covered, at times only dotted, with fleecy clouds, was singularly vivid.

The inhabitants of the island were Arabs, mixed with some negro blood, and wore the Oriental costume now so familiar to us all in this age of illustration. The ship was besieged by them at once, and throughout our stay, at all hours that they were permitted to come on board. They were cleanly in person, as their religion prescribes, and applied no offensive substance to their hair; on the contrary, some pleasant perfume was perceptible about their clothing. The coloring generally was dark, although some, among whom was the ruler, called the sultan, have olive skins; but the features were clear and prominent, the stature and form good, the bearing manly; nor did they seem other than intelligent. The teeth, too, were fine, when not disfigured by the chewing of the betel nut, which, when long continued, stains them a displeasing dark red. Like all barbarians, they talked, talked, talked, till one was nearly deafened. On one occasion, a group of them favored us with a theological exposition, marked by somewhat elementary conceptions. The ship was a perfect Babel at meal-times, when the intermission of work allowed the freest visiting. Every man who came brought at least a half-dozen fowl, with sweet potatoes, fruit, and eggs, to match; and as, in addition to our own crew bargaining, there were on the deck some fifty or sixty natives, all vociferating, bartering, beseeching, or yelling to the fifty others in canoes alongside, the tumult and noise may be conceived. The chickens, too, both cocks and hens, present by the hundred in basket-work cages, made no small contribution to the general uproar. Chickens, indeed, numerous though not large, are among the chief food commodities of that region; the usual price, as I recollect, being a dollar the dozen. When we left Johanna, we must have had on board several hundred as sea-stock. Not infrequently one would get out of its cage, and if pursued would often end by flapping overboard, so by drowning anticipating its appointed doom; but it was a pathetic sight to see the poor creature, upborne by its feathers so long as dry, floating on the waste of waters in the wake of the ship which seemed almost heartlessly to forsake it.

The faith of the island being Mohammedan, we found it safe to give a large liberty to the crew.

Especially, if I rightly recall, I availed myself of the circumstance to let go certain ne'er-do-wells whose conduct under temptation was not to be depended on. We had the unprecedented experience that they all came back on time and sober; thus avouching that the precepts of the Prophet concerning rum were obeyed in Johanna. Exemplary in this, it would be difficult to say, otherwise, on what precise rung of the ladder stretching from barbarism to civilization these people stood. In manner towards us they were pleasant and smiling; not averse to the arts of diplomacy, but perhaps a little transparent in their approaches to a desired object. I went on shore one Friday, their Sunday, which was inadvertent on my part, for their religious duties interfered with customary routine; one and another excused themselves to me on the plea that they must go to pray. I was known, however, to be in authority on board, which produced for me some simple hospitality, principally not very inviting lemonade – attentions that I soon found to be not wholly disinterested. Next day one of my hosts came on board and interviewed me with many bows. "The *Iroquois* very fine ship, much better than English ship. Captain English very good man; and first lieutenant [myself] he *very good* man;" and the complimenter would like certain articles within the gift of the said very good man, together with a note to bearer, permitting him to come aboard at any time.

Being by this some weeks away from Cape Town, we sent our wash ashore; a resort of desperation. It came back clean enough, but for ironing – well; and as to starch, much in the predicament of Boatswain Chuck's frilled shirts after the gale, upon which, while flying in the breeze, he looked with a degree of professional philosophy that could express itself only by thrashing the cooper. Crumpled would be a mild expression for our linen. We remonstrated, but were met with a shrug of the shoulders and a deprecatory but imperturbable smile – "Yes; Johanna wash!" And "Johanna" we found we were expected to receive as a sufficient explanation for any deficiencies in any line. If not satisfactory to us, it was at least modest in them.

Grave courtesies, ceremonious in conception, if rather rudimentary in execution, were exchanged between us and the authorities of Johanna. Our captain returned the visit of the official in charge of the place, and subsequently called upon the sultan, who came to the town while we were there. I went along on the first occasion. Upon reaching the beach we found a guard of some forty negro soldiers, whose equipment, as to shoes, resembled that of the Barbadian company immortalized in Peter Simple; but in this instance there was no attempt at that decorous regard for externals which ordered those with both shoes and stockings to fall in in the front rank, and those with neither to keep in the rear. They were commanded by a young Arab, who seemed very anxious to do all in style, rising on tiptoe at the several orders, which he jerked out with vim, and to my surprise in English. When duly pointed, we marched off to the sound of a drum, accompanied by a peculiar monotonous wail on a kind of trumpet; the order of the procession being, 1, music; 2, the soldiers, led by an old sergeant in a high state of excitement and coat-collar, which held the poor fellow's head like a vise; and, 3, our captain and his attendants. The visit to the sultan, two days later, was marked by additional features, indicative, I presume, of the greater dignity of the event; the captain being now carried in a chair with a red silk umbrella over his head.

Between three and four years before our visit, the Confederate steamer *Alabama* had stopped at Johanna, and, so at least our friends told us, Semmes had promised them a Yankee whaler or two. Whether he found the whalers or not I cannot say; but to the Johannese it was a Barmecide feast, or like the anticipation of Sisera's ladies – "to every man a damsel or two." To use their own quaint English, the next thing they heard of the *Alabama*, "he go down."

We left Johanna with the southwest monsoon, which in the Indian Ocean and China Sea blows from June to September with the regularity of the trade-winds of the Atlantic, both in direction and force. There the favorable resemblance ends; for, in the region through which we were passing, this monsoon is overcast, usually gloomy, and excessively damp. The northeast monsoon, which prevails during the winter months, is clear and dry. The consequent struggle with shoe-leather, and the deterioration of the same, is disheartening. But, though surcharged with moisture, rain does not fall to any great extent in the open sea, nor until the atmospheric current impinges on land, when it seems to be squeezed, like a sponge by the hand, with resultant precipitation. Our conditions were therefore pleasant enough. Being under sail only, the wind went faster than we, giving a cooling breeze as it passed over; and it was as steady and moderate as it was fair for our next destination, Aden, to reach which we were now pointing for Cape Guardafui. The *Iroquois* ran along steadily northward, six to eight knots, followed by a big sea, but so regular that she rolled only with a slow, steady swing, not disagreeable. The veiled sun showed sufficiently for sights, without burning heat, and by the same token we passed that luminary on our course; that is, he was north of us while at Johanna, and one day on this run we got north of him. This must have been after we had crossed the equator; for, being August, the sun was still north of the "Line."

This reminds me that, the day we thus passed the sun, our navigator, usually very exact, applied his declination wrong at noon, which gave us a wrong latitude. For a few minutes the discrepancy between the observation and the log caused a shaking of heads; the log doubtless fell under an unmerited suspicion, or else we had encountered a current not hitherto noted in the books, the usual solvent in such perplexities. I may explain for the unlearned in navigation that declination of a heavenly body corresponds in the celestial sphere to the latitude of an object on the terrestrial. The sun, being a leisurely celestial globe-trotter, continually varies his latitude – declination – within a zone bounded by the two tropics; and the rule runs that when his declination is of the same name (north or south) as his direction from the ship at noon, the declination is added or subtracted, I now forget which, in the computation that ascertains the vessel's precise position. This has to be remembered when he is passed overhead, in the zenith; for then the bearing changes, while his declination remains of the same name. If the resulting error is large, of course the mistake is detected immediately; a slight difference might pass unnoted with dangerous consequences.

At Johanna, or possibly at St. Augustine's, some of our officers and men, moved by that queer propensity of mankind to acquire strange objects, however useless, had bought animals of the kind called mongoos. There were perhaps a half-dozen of these in all. The result was that most of them, one way or another, escaped and took refuge aloft in the rigging, where it was as hopeless to attempt recapture as for a man to pursue a gray squirrel in a tree. The poor beggars had achieved their liberty, however, without the proverbial crust of bread or cup of water; and in consequence, after fasting all day, gave themselves to predatory nocturnal forays, which were rather startling when unexpectedly aroused by them from sleep. The ward-room pantry was near my berth, and I remember being awaked by a great commotion and scuffling, as one or more utensils were upset and knocked about in the unhappy beast's attempt to get at water kept there in a little cask. No reconcilement between them and man was effected, and one by one they dropped overboard, the victims of accident or suicide, noted or unnoted, to their deliverance and our relief. While they lasted it was pathetic to watch their furtive movements and unrelaxed vigilance, jealously guarding the freedom which was held under such hopeless surroundings and must cost them so dear at last.

When the ship had rounded Cape Guardafui and fairly entered the Strait of Bab-el-Mandeb, the alteration of weather conditions was immediate and startling. The heat became all at once intense and dry. From the latter circumstance the relief was great. I remember that many years afterwards, having spent a month or more determining a site for a navy-yard in Puget Sound, where the temperature is delightful but the atmosphere saturated, I experienced a similar sense of bodily comfort, when we reached Arizona, returning by the Southern Pacific Railroad. One morning I got up from the sleeper and walked out into the rare, crisp air of a way station, delighted to find myself literally as dry as a bone, and a very old bone, too; tertiary period, let us say. The sudden change in the strait proved fatal to one of our officers. He had been ailing for a few days, but on the night after we doubled the cape woke up from a calm sleep in wild delirium, and in a brief period died from the bursting of an aneurism; an effect which the surgeon attributed to the abrupt increase of heat. I may add that, though dry, the air was felt by us to be debilitating. During the ten days passed in the gulf, young as I then was, I was indisposed to any unusual bodily or mental effort. What breeze reached us, coming over desert from every direction, was like the blast of a furnace, although the height of the thermometer was not excessive.

It was scarcely fair to Aden to visit it in mid-summer, but our voyage had not been timed with reference to seasons or our comfort. I shall not weary a reader with any attempt at description of the treeless surroundings and barren lava crags that constitute the scenery; which, moreover, many may have seen for themselves. What chiefly interested me were the Jews and the camels. Like Gibraltar, and in less measure Key West, Aden is a place where meet many and divers peoples from Asia, from Africa, and from Europe. Furthermore, it has had a long and checkered history; and this, at an important centre on a commercial route, tends to the gathering of incongruous elements. English, Arabs, Parsees from India, Somâlese from Africa, – across the gulf, – sepoy soldiers, and Jews, all were to be met; and in varieties of cos-tume for which we had not been prepared by our narrow experience of Oriental dress in Johanna. The Jews most attracted my attention – an attrac-tion of repulsion to the type there exhibited, though I am without anti-Semitic feeling. That Jesus Christ was a Jew covers His race for me. These were reported to have enjoyed in earlier times a period of much prosperity, which had been destroyed in one of the dramatic political reverses frequent in Eastern annals. Since then they had remained a degraded and abject class. Certainly, they were externally a very peculiar and unprepossessing people. The physiognomy commonly associated with the name Jew was very evident, though the cast of feature had been bru-talized by ages of oppression and servility. A sin-gular distinctive mark was the wearing on both sides of the forehead long curls falling to the shoulders. Cringing and subservient in manner, and as traders, there was yet apparent behind the Uriah Heap exterior a fierce cruelty of expression which would make a mob hideous, if once let loose. A mob, indeed, is ever terrible; but these men reconstituted for me, with added vividness, the scene and the cry of "Crucify Him!"

Although I was new to the East, camels in their uncouth form and shambling gait had been made familiar by menageries; but in Aden I first saw them in the circumstances which give the sense of appropriateness necessary to the completeness of an impression, and, indeed, to its enjoyment. Environment is assuredly more essential to appreciation than is commonly recognized. Does beer taste as good in America as in England? I think not, unless perhaps in Newport, Rhode Island. Climatic, doubtless. I have been told by Englishmen that the very best pineapples to be had are raised in England under glass. Very good; but where is your tropical heat to supply the appreciative palate? I remember, in a railway train in Guatemala, some women came along with pineapples. I gave five cents, expecting one fruit; she, unwilling to make change, forced upon me three. Small, yes; pygmies doubtless to the hot-house aristocrats; but at a dinner-table with artificial heat could one possibly want them as much, or enjoy them as keenly, as under the burning southern sun, eaten like an apple, the juice streaming to the ground? A camel sauntering down Broadway would be odd only; a camel in an Eastern street has the additional setting needed to fix him accurately in your gallery of mental pictures; though, for the matter of that, I suppose a desert would be a still more fitting surrounding. Aden has no natural water supply for daily use; one of the sights are the great tanks for storing it, constructed by some bygone dynasty. When we were there the place relied for emergencies upon the more modern expedient of condensers, but for ordinary consumption was mainly dependent upon that brought in skins from the adjacent country on the backs of camels, which returned charged with merchandise. I watched one of these ships of the desert being laden for the homeward voyage. He was on his knees, placidly chewing the cud of his last meal, but with a watchful eye behind him upon his master's movements. Eternal vigilance the price of liberty, or at least the safeguard against oppression, was clearly his conviction; nor did he believe in that outworn proverb not to yell before you are hurt. As each additional package, small or big, was laid on the accumulating burden, he stretched out his long neck, craned it round to the rear, opening his mouth as though to bite, to which he seemed full fain, at the same time emitting a succession of cries more wrathful even than dolorous, though this also they were. But the wail of the sufferer went unheeded, and deservedly; for when the load was complete to the last pound he rose, obedient to signal, and stepped off quietly, evidently at ease. He had had his grumble, and was satisfied.

An impression which accumulates upon the attentive traveller following the main roads of maritime commerce is the continual outcropping of the British soldier. It is not that there is so much of him, but that he is so manywhere. In our single voyage, at places so apart as Cape Town, Aden, Bombay, Singapore, Hong Kong. Although not on our route, nevertheless linked to the four last named by the great ocean highway between East and West, consecutive even in those distant days before the Suez Canal, he was already in force in Gibraltar and Malta; since which he is to be found in Cypress also and in Egypt. He is no chance phenomenon, but an obvious effect of a noteworthy cause; an incident of current history, the exponent, unconsciously to himself, of many great events. In our country we have wisely learned to scrutinize with distrust arguments for manifest destiny; but it is, nevertheless, well to note and ponder a manifest present, which speaks to a manifest past.

From Aden the *Iroquois* ran along the southern coast of Arabia to Muscat, within the entrance of the Persian Gulf. Here, after leaving the open sea, we met a recurrence of the heat, and, in general features, of the scenery we had left at Aden; the whole confirming the association of the name Arabia with scorching and desert. The Cove of Muscat, though a mere indentation of the shoreline, furnishes an excellent harbor, being sheltered by a rocky island which constitutes a natural breakwater. There is considerable trade, and the position is naturally strong for defence, with encircling cliffs upon which forts have been built; but from our experience, told below, it is probable that their readiness did not correspond to their formidable aspect. From the anchorage of the *Iro-*

quois the town was hardly to be descried, the gray color of the stone used in construction blending with the background of the mountains, from which probably it had been quarried; but nearer it is imposing in appearance, there being several minarets, and some massive buildings, among which the ruins of a Portuguese cathedral bear their mute testimony to a transitory era in the long history of the East. During our stay there was some disturbance in the place. Our information was that the reigning sovereign had killed his father two years before; and that in consequence, either through revenge or jealousy, his father's brother kept him constantly stirred up by invasion, or threats of invasion, from the inner country. Such an alarm postponed for the moment a ceremonious visit which our captain was to pay, but it took place next day. As it called for full uniform, I begged off. Those who went returned with unfavorable reports, both of the town and of the sultan.

A rather funny incident here attended our exchange of civilities. In ports where there is cause to think that the expenditure of powder may be inconvenient to your hosts, or that for any reason they may not return a salute, it is customary first to inquire whether the usual national honors "to the flag" will be acceptable and duly answered, gun for gun. In Aden, being British, of course no questions were asked; but in Muscat I presume they were, for failure to give full measure creates a diplomatic incident and correspondence. At all events, we saluted – twenty-one guns; to which the castle replied. When the tale was but half complete there came from one of its cannon a huge puff of smoke, but no accompanying report. "Shall I count that?" shouted the quartermaster, whose special duty was to keep tally that we got our full pound of flesh. A general laugh followed; the impression had resembled that produced by an impassioned orator, the waving of whose arms you see, without hearing the words which give point to his gesticulations, and the quartermaster's query drove home the absurdity. It was solemnly decided, however, that that should be reckoned a gun. The intention was good, if result was imperfect. We had been done out of our noise, but we had had our smoke; and, in these days of smokeless powder, it is hopeful to record an instance of noiseless.

In those few indolent days which we drowsed away in the heat of Muscat, one thing I noticed was the vivid green of the water, especially in patches near the shore, and in the crevices of the rocky basin. I wonder did Moore have a hint of this, or draw upon his imagination? Certainly it was there – a green more brilliant than any I have ever seen elsewhere, and of different shade.

"No pearl ever lay under Oman's green water, More pure in its shell than thy spirit in thee."

After the comparatively sequestered series of St. Augustine's Bay, the Comoros, Aden, and Muscat, our next port, Bombay, seemed like returning to city hubbub and accustomed ways. True, Indian life was strange to most of our officers, if not to all; but there was about Bombay that which made you feel you had got back into the world, albeit in many particulars as different from that you had hitherto known as Rip Van Winkle found after his long slumber. Then, a decade only after the great mutiny, travel to India for travel's sake was much more rare than now. The railway system, that great promoter of journeyings, was not complete. Two years later, when returning from China, I found opportunity to go overland from Calcutta to Bombay; but in the interior had to make a long stage by carriage between Jubbulpore and Nagpore. Since that time many have visited and many have written. I shall therefore spare myself and my possible readers the poor portrayal of that which has been already and better described. Johnson's advice to Boswell, "Tell what you have observed yourself," I take to mean something different from those externals the sight of which is common to all; unless, as in the Corsica of Boswell, few go to see them. What you see is that which you personally have the faculty of perceiving; depends upon you as much as upon the object itself. It may not be worth reporting, but it is all you have. I do not think I remember of Bombay anything thus peculiarly my own. I do recall the big snakes we saw lying apparently asleep on the sea, fifty or sixty miles from land. Perhaps readers who have not visited the East may not know that such modified sea-serpents are to be seen there, as is a smaller variety in the Strait of Malacca.

From Bombay we made a long leg to Singapore. We had sailed in early February; it was now late September, and our captain, as I have said before, began to feel anxious to reach the station. Owing to this haste, we omitted Ceylon and Calcutta, which did not correspond to the expectation or the wishes of the admiral; and we missed – as I think – orders sent us to take in Siam before coming to Hong Kong. It is very doubtful whether, had we received them, we should have seen more of interest than awaited us shortly after our arrival in Japan. At all events, as in duty bound, I shall imitate my captain, and skip rapidly over this intervening period. There is in it nothing that would justify my formed intention not to enlarge upon that which others have seen and told.

We made the run to Singapore at the change of the monsoon, towards the end of September; and at that time a quiet passage is likely, unless you are so unlucky as to encounter one of the cyclones which frequently attend the break-up of the season at this transition period. There is a tendency nowadays to discredit the equinox as a storm-breeder. As regards the particular day, doubtless recognition of a general fact may have lapsed into superstition as to a date; but in considering the phenomena of the monsoons, the great fixed currents of air blowing alternately to or from the heated or cooled continent of Asia, it seems only reasonable, when the two are striving for predominance, to expect the uncertain and at times terrific weather which as a matter of experience does occur about the period of the autumnal equinox in the India and China seas. But after we had made our southing from Bombay our course lay nearly due east, with a fresh, fair, west wind, within five degrees of the equator, a zone wherein cyclonic disturbance seldom intrudes. One of the complaints made by residents against the climate of Singapore, so pleasant to a stranger, is the wearisome monotony. Close to the equator, it has too much sameness of characteristic; *toujours perdrix*. Winter doubtless adds to our appreciation of summer. For all that, I personally am ready to dispense with snow.

From Singapore, another commercial centre with variety of inhabitants, we carried the same smooth water up to Manila, where we stopped a few days for coal. This was the first of two visits paid while on the station to this port, which not our wildest imagination expected ever to see under our flag. Long as American eyes had been fixed upon Cuba, in the old days of negro slavery, it had occurred to none, I fancy, to connect possession of that island with these distant Spanish dependencies. Here our quiet environment was lost. The northeast monsoon had set in in full force when we started for Hong Kong, and the run across was made under steam and fore-and-aft canvas, which we were able to carry close on the wind; a wet passage, throwing a good deal of water about, but with a brilliant sky and delightful temperature. It would be hard to exaggerate the beauty of the weather which this wind brings. In the northern American states we have autumnal spells like it; but along the Chinese coast it continues in uninterrupted succession of magnificent days, with hardly a break for three or four months; an invigorating breeze always blowing, the thermometer ranging between 50° and 60°, a cloudless sky, the air perfectly dry, so that furniture and wood fittings shrink, and crack audibly. As rain does not fall during this favored season, the dust becomes objectionable; but that drawback does not extend to shipboard. The man must be unreasonable who doubts life being worth living during the northeast monsoon. Hong Kong is just within the tropics, and experiences probably the coolest weather of any tropical port. Key West, in the same latitude, is well enough in a Gulf of Mexico norther; that is, if you too are well. The last time I ever saw General Winfield Scott, once our national military hero, was there, during a norther. I had called, and found him in misery; his gigantic frame swathed in heavy clothing, his face pallid with cold. He explained that he liked always to be in a gentle perspiration, and had come to Key West in search of such conditions. These the place usually affords, but the houses are not built to shut out the chill Which accompanies a hard norther. The general was then eighty, and died within the year.

X
CHINA AND JAPAN

1867-1869

The *Iroquois* had been as nearly as possible nine months on her way from New York to Hong Kong. A ship of the same class, the *Wachusett*, which left the station as we reached it, had taken a year, following much the same route. Her first lieutenant, who during the recent Spanish War became familiarly known to the public as Jack Philip, told me that she was within easy distance of Hong Kong the day before the anniversary of leaving home. Her captain refused to get up steam; for, he urged, it would be such an interesting coincidence to arrive on the very date, month and day, that she sailed the year before. I fear that man would have had no scruple about contriving an opportunity.

As the anchor dropped, several Chinese boats clustered alongside, eager to obtain their share of the ship's custom. It is the habit in ships of war to allow one or more boatmen of a port the privilege of bringing off certain articles for private purchase; such as the various specialties of the place, and food not embraced in the ship's ration. From the number of consumers on board a vessel, even of moderate size, this business is profitable to the small traders who ply it, and who from time immemorial have been known as bumboatmen. A good name for fair dealing, and for never smuggling intoxicants, is invaluable to them; and when thus satisfactory they are passed on from ship to ship, through long years, by letters of recommendation from first lieutenants. Their dealings are chiefly with the crew, the officers' messes being provided by their stewards, who market on shore; but at times officers, too, will in this way buy something momentarily desired. I remember an amusing experience of a messmate of mine, who, being discontented with the regular breakfast set before him, got some eggs from the bumboat. Already on a growl, he was emphatic in directing that these should be cooked very soft, and great was his wrath when they came back hard as stones. Upon investigation it proved that they were already hard-boiled when bought. The cable was not yet secured when these applicants crowded to the gangway, brandishing their certificates, and seeking each to be first on deck. The captain, who had not left the bridge, leaned over the rail, watching the excited and shouting crowd scrambling one over another, and clambering from boat to boat, which were bobbing and chafing up and down, rubbing sides, and spattering the water that was squeezed and squirted between them. The scene was familiar to him, for he was an old China cruiser, only renewing his acquaintance. At length, turning to me, he commented, "There you have the regular China smell; you will find it wherever you go." And I did; but how describe it – and why should I?

At this time the Japanese had conceded two more treaty ports, in the Inland Sea – Osaka and Kobé; and as the formal opening was fixed for the beginning of the new year – 1868 – most of the squadron had already gone north. We therefore found in Hong Kong only a single vessel, the *Monocacy*, an iron double-ender; a class which had its beginning in the then recent War of Secession, and disappeared with it. Some six weeks before she had passed through a furious typhoon, running into the centre of it; or, more accurately, I fancy, having the centre pass over her. Perhaps it may not be a matter of knowledge to all readers that for these hurricanes, as for many other heavy gales, the term cyclone is exact; that the wind does actually blow round a circle, but one of so great circumference that at each several point it seems to follow a straight line. Vessels on opposite sides of the circle thus have the wind from opposite directions. In the centre there is usually a calm space, of diameter proportioned to that of the general disturbance. As the whole storm body has an onward movement, this centre, calm or gusty as to wind, but confused and tumultuous as to wave, progresses with it; and a vessel which is so unhappy as to be overtaken finds herself, after a period of helpless tossing by conflicting seas, again subjected to the full fury of the wind, but from the quarter opposite to that which has already tried her. Although at our arrival the *Monocacy* had been fully repaired, and was about to follow the other vessels, her officers naturally were still full of an adventure so exceptional to personal experience. She owed her safety mainly to the strength and rigidity of her iron hull. A wooden vessel of like construction would probably have gone to pieces; for the wooden double-enders had been run up in a hurry for a war emergency, and were often weak. As the capable

288

commander of one of them said to me, they were "stuck together with spit." Battened down close, with the seas coming in deluges over both bows and both quarters at the same time, the *Monocacy* went through it like a tight-corked bottle, and came out, not all right, to be sure, but very much alive; so much so, indeed, that she was carried on the Navy Register for thirty years more. She never returned home, however, but remained on the China station, for which she was best suited by her particular qualities.

By the time the *Iroquois*, in turn, was ready to leave Hong Kong – November 26th – the northeast monsoon had made in full force, and dolorous were the prognostications to us by those who had had experience of butting against it in a northward passage. It is less severe than the "brave" west winds of our own North Atlantic; but to a small vessel like the *Iroquois*, with the machinery of the day, the monsoon, blowing at times a three-quarters gale, was not an adversary to be disregarded, for all the sunshiny, bluff heartiness with which it buffeted you, as a big boy at school breezily thrashes a smaller for his own good. To-day we have to stop and think, to realize the immense progress in size and power of steam-vessels since 1867. We forget facts, and judge doings of the past by standards of the present; an historical injustice in other realms than that of morals.

In our passage north, however, we escaped the predicted disagreeables by keeping close to the coast; for currents, whether of atmosphere or of water, for some reason slacken in force as they sweep along the land. I do not know why, unless it be the result of friction retarding their flow; the fact, however, remains. So, dodging the full brunt of the wind, we sneaked along inshore, having rarely more than a single-reef topsail breeze, and with little jar save the steady thud of the machinery. A constant view of the land was another advantage due to this mode of progression, and it was the more complete because we commonly anchored at night. Thus, as we slowly dragged north, a continuous panorama was unrolled before our eyes.

Another very entertaining feature was the flight of fishing-boats, which at each daybreak put out to sea, literally in flocks; so numerous were they. As I was every morning on deck at that hour, attending the weighing of the anchor, the sight became fixed upon my memory. The wind being on their beam, and so fresh, they came lurching along in merry mood, leaping livelily from wave to wave, dashing the water to either hand. Besides the poetry of motion, their peculiar shape, their hulls with the natural color of the wood, – because oiled, not painted, – their bamboo mat sails, which set so much flatter than our own canvas, were all picturesque, as well as striking by novelty. Most characteristic, and strangely diversified in effect, as they bowled saucily by, were the successive impressions produced by the custom of painting an eye on each side of the bow. An alleged proverb is in pigeon English: "No have eye, how can see? no can see, how can sail?" When heading towards you, they really convey to an imagination of ordinary quickness the semblance of some unknown sea monster, full of life and purpose. Now you see a fellow charging along, having the vicious look of a horse with his ears back. Anon comes another, the quiet gaze of which suggests some meditative fish, lazily gliding, enjoying a siesta, with his belly full of good dinner. Yet a third has a hungry air, as though his meal was yet to seek, and in passing turns on you a voracious side glance, measuring your availability as a morsel, should nothing better offer. The boat life of China, indeed, is a study by itself. In very many cases in the ports and rivers, the family is born, bred, fed, and lives in the boat. In moving her, the man and his wife and two of the elder children will handle the oars; while a little one, sometimes hardly more than an infant, will take the helm, to which his tiny strength and cunning skill are sufficient. Going off late one night from Hong Kong to the ship, and having to lean over in the stern to get hold of the tiller-lines, I came near putting my whole weight on the baby, lying unperceived in the bottom. Those sedate Chinese children, with their tiny pigtails and their old faces, but who at times assert their common humanity by a wholesome cry; how funny two of them looked, lying in the street fighting, fury in each face, teeth set and showing, nostrils distended with rage, and a hand of each gripping fast the other's pigtail, which he seemed to be trying to drag out by the roots; at the moment not "Celestials," unless after the pattern of Virgil's Juno.

The habit of whole families living together in a boat, though sufficiently known to me, was on one occasion realized in a manner at once mortifying and ludicrous. The eagerness for trade among the bumboatmen, actual and expectant, sometimes becomes a nuisance; in their efforts to be first they form a mob quite beyond the control of the ship, the gangways and channels of which they none the less surround and grab, deaf to all remonstrance by words, however forcible. This is particularly the case the first day of arrival, before the privilege has been determined. In one such instance my patience gave way; the din alongside was indescribable, the confusion worse confounded, and they could not be moved. There was working at the moment one of those small movable hand-pumps significantly named "Handy Billy," and I told the nozzle-man to turn the stream on the crowd. Of course, nothing could please a seaman more; it was done with a will, and the full force of impact struck between the shoulders of a portly individual standing up, back towards the ship. A prompt upset revealed that it was a middle-aged woman, a fact which the pump-man had not taken in, owing to the misleading similarity of dress between the two sexes. I was disconcerted and ashamed, but the remedy was for the moment complete; the boats scattered as if dynamite had burst among them. The mere showing of the nozzle was thereafter enough.

The *Iroquois* was about a week in the monsoon, a day or so having been expended in running into Fuchau for coal. She certainly seemed to have lost the speed credited to her in former cruises; the cause for which was plausibly thought to be the decreased rigidity of her hull, owing to the wear and tear of service. In the days of sailing-ships there was a common professional belief that lessened stiffness of frame tended to speed; and a chased vessel sometimes resorted to sawing her beams and loosening her fastenings to increase the desired play. But, however this may have been, the thrust of the screw tells best when none of its effect is lost in a structural yielding of the ship's body; when this responds as a solid whole to the forward impulse. In this respect the *Iroquois* was already out of date, though otherwise serviceable.

On the eleventh day, December 7th, we reached Nagasaki, whence we sailed again about the middle of the month for Hiogo, or Kobé, where the squadrons of the various nations were to assemble for the formal opening. With abundant time before us, we passed in leisurely fashion through the Inland Sea, at the eastern end of which lay the newly opened ports. Anchoring each night, we missed no part of the scenery, with its alternating breadths and narrows, its lofty slopes, terraced here and wooded there, the occasional smiling lowlands, the varied and vivid greens, contrasting with the neutral tints of the Japanese dwellings; all which combine to the general effect of that singular and entrancing sheet of water. The Japanese junks added their contribution to the novelty with their single huge bellying sail, adapted apparently only to sailing with a free wind, the fairer the better.

Hiogo and Kobé, as I understood, are separate names of two continuous villages; Kobé, the more eastern, being the destined port of entry. They are separated by a watercourse, broad but not deep, often dry, the which is to memory dear; for following along it one day, and so up the hills, I struck at length, well within the outer range, an exquisite Japanese valley, profound, semicircular, and terraced, closed at either end by a passage so narrow that it might well be called a defile. The suddenness with which it burst upon me, like the South Sea upon Balboa, the feeling of remoteness inspired by its isolation, and its own intrinsic beauty, struck home so forcible a prepossession that it remained a favorite resort, to which I guided several others; for it must be borne in mind that up to our coming the hill tracks of Kobé knew not the feet of foreigners, and there was still such a thing as first discovery. Some time afterwards, when I had long returned home, a naval officer told me that the place was known to him and others as Mahan's Valley; but I have never heard it has been so entered on the maps. Shall I describe it? Certainly not. When description is tried, one soon realizes that the general sameness of details is so great as quite to defy convincing presentation, in words, of the particular combination which constitutes any one bit of scenery. Scenery in this resembles a collection of Chinese puzzles, where a few elementary pieces, through their varied assemblings, yield most diverging forms. Given a river, some mountains, a few clumps of trees, a little sloping field under cultivation, an expanse of marsh – in Japan the universal terrace – and with them many picturesque effects can be produced; but description, mental realization, being a matter of analysis and synthesis, is a process which each man performs for himself. The writer does his part, and thinks he has done well. Could he see the picture which his words call up in the mind of another, the particular Chinese figure put together out of the author's data, he might be less satisfied. And should the reader rashly become the visitor, he will have to meet Wordsworth's disappointment. "And is this – Yarrow? this the scene?" "Although 'tis fair, 'twill be another Yarrow." Should any reader of mine go hereafter to Kobé, and so wish, let him see for himself; he shall go with no preconceptions from me. If the march of improvement has changed that valley, Japan deserves to be beaten in her next war.

As I recall attending a Christmas service on board the British flag-ship *Rodney* at Kobé, we must have anchored there a few days before that fixed for the formal opening; but, unless my memory much deceive me, visiting the shore after the usual fashion was permitted without awaiting the New Year ceremony. At this time Kobé and Hiogo were in high festival; and that, combined with the fact that the inhabitants had as yet seen few foreigners, gave unusual animation to the conditions. We were followed by curious crowds, to whom we were newer even than they to us; for the latest comers among us had seen Nagasaki, but strangers from other lands had been rare to these villagers. In explanation of the rejoicings, it was told us that slips of paper, with the names of Japanese deities written on them, had recently fallen in the streets, supposed by the people to come from the skies; and that different men had found in their houses pieces of gold, also bearing the name of some divinity. These tokens were assumed to indicate great good luck about to light upon those places or houses. By an easy association of ideas, the approaching opening of the port might seem to have some connection with the expected benefits, and inclines one to suspect human instrumentality in creating impressions which might counteract the long-nurtured jealousy of foreign intrusion. Whatever the truth, the external rollicking celebrations were as apparent as was the general smiling courtesy so noticeable in the Japanese, and which in this case was common to both the throng in ordinary dress and the masqueraders. Men and women, young and old, in gay, fantastic costumes, faces so heavily painted as to have the effect of masks, were running about in groups, sometimes as many as forty or fifty together, dancing and mumming. They addressed us frequently with a phrase, the frequent repetition of which impressed it upon our ears, but, in our ignorance of the language, not upon our understandings. At times, if one laughed, liberties were taken. These the customs of the occasion probably justified, as in the carnivals of other peoples, which this somewhat resembled; but there was no general concourse, as in the Corso at Rome, which I afterwards saw – merely numerous detachments moving with no apparent relation to one another. Once only a companion and myself met several married women, known as such by their blackened teeth, who bore long poles with feathers at one end, much like dusters, with which they tapped us on the head. These seemed quite beside themselves with excitement, but all in the best of humor.

Viewed from the distance, the general effect was very pretty, like a stage scene. The long main street, forming part of the continuous imperial highway known as the Tokaido, was jammed with people; the sober, neutral tints of the majority in customary dress lighted up, here and there, by the brilliant, diversified colors the performers, as showy uniforms do an assembly of civilians. The weather, too, was for the most part in keeping. The monsoon does not reach so far north, yet the days were like it; usually sunny, and the air exhilarating, with frequent frost at dawn, but towards noon genial. Such we found the prevalent character of the winter in that part of Japan, though with occasional spells of rain and high winds, amounting to gales of two or three days' duration.

Unhappily, these cheerful beginnings were the precursors of some very sad events; indeed, tragedies. A week after the New Year ceremonies at Kobé, the American squadron moved over some twelve miles to Osaka, the other opened port, at which our minister then was. Unlike Kobé, where the water permits vessels to lie close to the beach, Osaka is up a river, at the mouth of which is a bar; and, owing to the shoalness of the adjacent sea, the anchorage is a mile or two out. From it the town cannot be seen. The morning after our arrival, a Thursday, it came on to blow very hard from the westward, dead on shore, raising a big sea which prevented boats crossing the bar. The gale continued over Friday, the wind moderating by the following daylight. The swell requires more time to subside; but it was now Saturday, the next day would be Sunday, and the admiral, I think, was a religious man, unwilling to infringe upon the observance of the day, for himself or for the men. His service on the station was up, and, indeed, his time for retirement, at sixty-two, had arrived; there remained for him only to go home, and for this he was anxious to get south. Altogether, he decided to wait no longer, and ordered his barge manned. Danger from the attempt was apprehended on board the flag-ship by some, but the admiral was not one of those who encourage suggestions. Her boatswain had once cruised in whalers, which carry to perfection the art of managing boats in a heavy sea, and of steering with an oar, the safest precaution if a bar must be crossed; and he hung round, in evidence, hoping that he might be ordered to steer her, but she shoved off as for an ordinary trip. The mishap which followed, however, was not that most feared. Just before she entered the breakers, the flag-lieutenant, conscious of the risk, was reported to have said to the admiral, "If you intend to go in before the sea, as we are now running, we had better take off our swords;" and he himself did so, anticipating an accident. As she swept along, her bow struck bottom. Her way being thus stopped for an instant, the sea threw her stern round; she came broadside to and upset. Of the fifteen persons hurled thus into the wintry waves, only three escaped with their lives. Both the officers perished.

The gale continued to abate, and the bodies being all soon recovered, the squadron returned to Kobé to bury its dead. The funeral ceremonies were unusually impressive in themselves, as well as because of the sorrowful catastrophe which so mournfully signalized the entry of the foreigner into his new privilege. The day was fair and cloudless, the water perfectly smooth; neither rain nor wave marred the naval display, as they frequently do. Thirty-two boats, American and British, many of them very large, took part in the procession from the ships to the beach. The ensigns of all the war-vessels in port, American and other, were at half-mast, as was the admiral's square blue flag at the mizzen, which is never lowered while he remains on duty on board. As the movement began, a first gun was fired from the *Hartford*, which continued at minute intervals until she had completed thirteen, a rear-admiral's salute. When she had finished, the *Shenandoah* took up the tale, followed in turn by the *Oneida* and *Iroquois*, the mournful cadence thus covering almost the whole period up to the customary volleys over the graves. As saluting was the first lieutenant's business, I had remained on board to attend to it; and consequently, from our closeness to the land, had a more comprehensive view of the pageant than was possible to a participant. Our ships were nearly stripped of their crews; the rank of the admiral and the number of the sufferers, as well as the tragic character of the incident, demanding the utmost marks of reverent observance. As the march was taken up on shore, the British seamen in blue uniforms in the left column, the American in white in the right, to the number of several hundred each, presented a striking appearance; but more imposing and appealing, the central feature and solemn exponent of the occasion, was the long line of twelve coffins, skirting the sandy beach against a background of trees, borne in single file on men's shoulders in ancient fashion, each covered with the national colors. The tokens of mourning, so far as ships' ensigns were concerned, continued till sunset, when the ceremonial procedure was closed by a simple form, impressive in its significance and appropriateness. Following the motions of the American flag-ship, the chief mourner, the flags of all the vessels, as by one impulse, were rounded up to the peaks, as in the activities of every-day life; that of the dead admiral being at the same time mast-headed to its usual place. By this mute gesture, vessels and crews stood at attention, as at a review, for their last tribute to the departed. The *Hartford* then fired a farewell rear-admiral's salute, at the thirteenth and final gun of which his flag came down inch by inch, in measured dignity, to be raised no more; all others descending with it in silent haulage.

Admiral Henry Bell, who thus sadly ended his career when on the verge of an honored retirement, was in a way an old acquaintance of mine. It was he who had refused me a transfer to the *Monongahela* during the war; and he and my father, having been comrades when cadets at the Military Academy in the early twenties of the last century, had retained a certain interest in each other, shown by mutual inquiries through me. Bell had begun life in the army, subsequently quitting it for the navy for reasons which I do not know. He had the rigidity and precision of a soldier's carriage, to a degree unusual to a naval officer of his period. This may have been due partly to early training, but still more, I think, in his case, was an outcome and evidence of personal character; for, though kindly and just, he was essentially a martinet. He had been further presented to me, colloquially, by my old friend the boatswain of the *Congress*, some of whose shrewd comments I have before quoted, and who had sailed with him as a captain. "Oh! what a proud man he was!" he would say. "He would walk up and down the poop, looking down on all around, thus" – and the boatswain would compress his lips, throw back his shoulders, and inflate his chest; the walk he could not imitate because he had a stiff knee. Bell's pride, however it may have seemed, was rather professional than personal. He was thorough and exact, with high standards and too little give. An officer entirely respectable and respected, though not brilliant.

Upon the funeral of our wrecked seamen followed a dispersion of the squadron. The *Hartford* and *Shenandoah*, both bound home, departed, leaving the *Oneida* and *Iroquois* to "hold the fort." Conditions soon became such that it seemed probable we might have to carry out that precept somewhat literally. This was the period of the overthrow of the Tycoon's power by the revolt of the great nobles, among whom the most conspicuous in leadership were Chiosiu and Satsuma; names then as much in our mouths as those of Grant, Sherman, and Lee had been three years before. Hostilities were active in the neighborhood of Osaka and Kobé, the Tycoon being steadily worsted. So far as I give any account, depending upon some old letters of that date, it will be understood to present, not sifted historical truth, but the current stories of the day, which to me have always seemed to possess a real value of their own, irrespective of their exactness. For example, the reports repeated by Nelson at Leghorn of the happenings during Bonaparte's campaign of 1796 in upper Italy, though often inaccurate, represent correctly an important element of a situation. Misapprehension, when it exists, is a factor in any circumstances, sometimes of powerful influence. It is part of the data governing the men of the time.

While a certain number of foreigners, availing themselves of the treaty, were settling for business in Kobé, a large proportion had gone to Osaka, a more important commercial centre, of several hundred thousand inhabitants. Its superior political consideration at the moment was evidenced by the diplomats establishing themselves there, our own minister among them. The defeat of the Tycoon's forces in the field led to their abandoning the place, carrying off also the guards of the legations; a kind of protection absolutely required in those days, when the resentment against foreign intrusion was still very strong, especially among the warrior class. It was, after all, only fourteen years since Perry had extorted a treaty from a none too willing government. The fleeing Tycoon wished to get away from Osaka by a vessel belonging to him; but in the event of her not being off the bar – as proved to be the case – a party of two-sworded men, of whom he was rumored to be one, brought a letter from our minister asking any American vessel present to give them momentary shelter. It is customary for refugees purely political to be thus received by ships of war, which afford the protection their nation grants to such persons who reach its home territory; of which the ships are a privileged extension.

The minister's note spoke of the bearers simply as officers of the very highest rank. About three in the morning they came alongside of the *Iroquois*, their boatmen making a tremendous racket, awaking everybody, the captain getting up to receive them. When I came on deck before breakfast the poor fellows presented a moving picture of human misery, and certainly were under a heavy accumulation of misfortunes: a lost battle, and probably a lost cause; flying for life, and now on an element totally new; surrounded by those who could not speak their language; hungry, cold, wet, and shivering – a combination of major and minor evils under which who would not be depressed? At half-past seven they left us, after a brief stay of four hours; and there was much trouble in getting so many unpractised landsmen into the boats, which were rolling and thumping alongside in the most thoughtless manner, there being considerable sea. I do not remember whether the ladders were shipped, or whether they had to descend by the cleats; but either presented difficulties to a man clad in the loose Japanese garb of the day, having withal two swords, one very long, and a revolver. What with encumbrances and awkwardness, our seamen had to help them down like children. Poor old General Scott shuddering in a Key West norther, and these unhappy samurai, remain coupled in my mind; pendant pictures of valor in physical extremes, like Cæsar in the Tiber. For were not our shaking morning visitors of the same blood, the same tradition, and only a generation in time removed from, the soldiers and seamen of the late war? whose "fitness to win," to use Mr. Jane's phrase, was then established.

Between the departure of the Tycoon's forces and the arrival of the insurgent daimios, the native mob took possession of Osaka, becoming insolent and aggressive; insomuch that a party of French seamen, being stoned, turned and fired, killing several. The disposition and purposes of the daimios being uncertain, the diplomatic bodies thought best to remove to Kobé, a step which caused the exodus of all the new foreign population. Chiosiu and Satsuma, the leaders in what was still a rebellion, had not yet arrived, nor was there any assurance felt as to their attitude towards the foreign question. The narrow quarters of the *Iroquois* were crowded with refugees and fugitive samurai; while from our anchorage huge columns of smoke were seen rising from the city, which rumor, of course, magnified into a total destruction. Afterwards we were told that the Tycoon had burned Satsuma's palace in the place, in retaliation for which the enemy on entry had burned his. The Japanese in their haste left behind them their wounded, and one of the *Iroquois'* officers brought off a story of the Italian minister, who, indignant at this desertion, went up to a Japanese official, shouting excitedly, "I will have you to understand it is not the custom in Europe thus to abandon our wounded." This he said in English, apparently thinking that a Japanese would be more likely to understand it than Italian.

The embarkation was an affair of a short time, and the *Iroquois* then went to Kobé, where we discharged our load of passengers. The diplomats had decided that there, under the guns of the shipping, they would establish their embassies and remain; reasoning justly enough that, if foreigners suffered themselves to be forced out of both the ports conceded by treaty, there would be trouble everywhere, in the old as well as the new. So the flags were soon flying gayly, and all seemed quiet; but for the maintenance of order there was no assurance while the interregnum lasted, the Tycoon's authorities having gone, and Chiosiu or Satsuma still delaying. Officers on shore were therefore ordered to go armed. On February 4, 1868, two days after our return, a party of samurai, some five hundred strong, belonging to the Prince of Bizen, marched through the town by the Tokaido. As they passed the foreign concession, which bordered this high-road, they turned and fired upon the Europeans. The noise was heard on board the ships, and the commotion on shore was evident, people fleeing in every direction. The Japanese troops themselves broke and ran along the highway, abandoning luggage, arms, and field-pieces. The American and British ships of war, with a French corvette, manned and armed boats, landing in hot haste five or six hundred men, who pursued for some distance, but failed to overtake the assailants. At the same time the vessels sprang their batteries to bear on the town; a move which doubtless looked imposing enough, though we could scarcely have dared to

305

fire on the mixed multitude, even had the trouble continued.

When our seamen returned, a conference was held, wherein it was determined, as a joint international measure, to hold the concession in force; and as a further means of protection to close the Tokaido, which was done by occupying the angles of a short elbow, of two hundred yards, made by it in traversing the town. This step, while justifiable from the point of view of safety for the residents, was particularly galling to Japanese high-class feeling; for the use of the imperial road was associated with certain privileges to the daimios, during whose passing the common people were excluded, or obliged to kneel, under penalty of being cut down on the spot. Satsuma was reported to have remonstrated; but in view of the recent occurrence there could be no reply to the foreign retort, "You must secure our people." The custom-house, within the concession, was garrisoned, making a fortification very tenable against any enemy likely to be brought against it; while round it was thrown up a light earth-work, to which the seamen and marines dispersed in the concession could retire in case of need. But behind all, invulnerable, stood the ships, deterred from aggression only by fear for their own people, which would cease to operate if these had to be withdrawn.

The action of this body of samurai was probably unpremeditated, unless possibly in the mind of the particular officer in charge, who afterwards paid with his life for the misconduct of his men. While the state of siege continued a complete stop was put to our horseback excursions in the country, a deprivation the more felt because coinciding with an unusually fine spell of weather; but in a few days an envoy arrived from the insurgent daimios, with whom a settlement was speedily reached. Chiosiu and Satsuma had by this time succeeded in establishing themselves as the real representatives of the Mikado, an authority in virtue of which alone the Tycoon had ruled; the true headship of the Mikado being admitted by all. They undertook that foreigners should be adequately protected, and that the officer responsible for the late outrage should be punished with death. By the 20th of February Kobé was full of Chiosiu and Satsuma samurai, who were as courteously civil as those of the Tycoon had been; and after a conference with the special envoy of the Mikado the ministers returned to Osaka. We, too, resumed our country rides, but still weighted with a huge navy revolver.

No doubt on any hand was felt of the sincere purpose of the new government to fulfil its pledges; but their troops were still ill-organized, and it was impossible to rest assured that they might not here and there break bounds, as at Kobé. We were encountering the accustomed uncertainties of a period of revolutionary transition, intensified by prejudices engendered through centuries of national isolation, with all the narrowing and deepening of prepossession which accompanies entire absence of intercourse with other people. At this very moment, in March, 1868, the decree against the practice of Christianity by the natives was reissued: "Hitherto the

Christian religion has been forbidden, and the order must be strictly kept. The corrupt religion is strictly forbidden." Yet I am persuaded that already far-seeing Japanese had recognized that the past had drifted away irrevocably, and that the only adequate means to meet the inevitable was to accept it fully, without grudging, and to develop the nation to equality with foreigners in material resources. But such anticipation is the privilege of the few in any age or any country.

Very soon after the return of our men from their garrison duty, an outbreak of small-pox on board the *Iroquois* compelled her being sent to Yokohama, where, as an old-established port, were hospital facilities not to be found in Kobé, though we had succeeded in removing the first cases to crude accommodations on shore. The disease was then very prevalent in Japan, where vaccination had not yet been introduced; and to an unaccustomed eye it was startling to note in the streets the number of pitted faces, a visible demonstration of what a European city must have presented before inoculation was practised. One of our crew had died; and when we started, February 25th, we had on board some sick. These were carefully isolated under the airy topgallant forecastle, and with a good passage the contagion might not have spread; but the second day out the weather came on bad and very thick, ending with a gale so violent that to save the lives of the patients they had to be taken below, and then, for the safety of the ship, which was single-decked, the hatches had to be battened down. Conditions more favorable for the spread of the malady could not have been devised, and the result was that we were not fairly clear of the epidemic for nearly two months, though the cases, of which we had fifteen or twenty, were sent ashore as fast as they developed. At that period few ships on the station wholly escaped this scourge.

It was after we left Kobé that judicial satisfaction was given for the attack upon the foreign concession. My account depends upon the reports which reached us; but as the captain of the *Oneida* was one of the official witnesses, on the part of the international interests concerned, I presume that what we heard was nearly correct. The final scene was in a temple near Hiogo. Being of the class of nobles, the condemned had a privilege of the peerage, which insured for him the honorable death of the harakiri;[12] a distinction apparently analogous to that which our soldiers of European tradition draw between hanging and shooting. Having duly performed acts of devotion suited to the place and to the occasion, he spoke, justifying his action, and saying that, under similar circumstances, he would again do the same. He then partly disrobed, assisted by friends, and when all was ready stabbed himself; a comrade who had stood by with drawn sword at the same instant cutting off his head with a single blow. I was tempted by curiosity, once while on the station, to attend the execution of some ordinary criminals; and I can testify to the deftness and instantaneousness with which one head fell, in the flash of a sword or the twinkling of an eye. I did not care to view the fates of the three others condemned, but it was clear that no judicial death could be more speedy and merciful.

Nearly coincident with this exacted vengeance occurred an incident which demonstrated its policy. A boat's crew from a French ship of war had gone ashore to survey, unarmed. They were accosted by a well-dressed man, wearing two swords, who suggested to them going up to a village near the spot where they were at work. They accepted, and were led by him into an ambush where eleven of them – all but one – were slain. So there was another great funeral at Hiogo, but, one which excited emotions far otherwise mournful than the simple sorrow and sympathy elicited by the Bell disaster. The graveyard of the place had, indeed, a good start. The assassins in this case belonged to the troops of the insurgent daimios; and as the French already favored the Tycoon – which perhaps may have been one motive for the attack – some apprehension was felt that they might, in consequence, espouse his cause more actively. Nothing of the sort happened. I presume all the legations, and their nations, felt that at the moment the solidarity of the foreign interest was more important to be secured than the triumph of this or that party. By abstaining from intervention, all the embassies could be counted on to back a united demand for reparation for injuries to the citizens of any one.

With the arrival of the *Iroquois* at Yokohama the notable incidents of the cruise for the most part came to an end; there following upon it the routine life of a ship of war, with its ups and downs of more or less pleasant ports, good and bad weather, and the daily occupations which make and maintain efficiency. Yokohama itself was then the principal and most flourishing foreign settlement in Japan, the seat of the legations, and with an agreeable society sufficiently large. Among other features we here found again in force the British soldier; a battalion of eight hundred being permanently in garrison. The country about was thought secure, though for distant excursions, requiring a whole day, we carried revolvers; and I remember well the scuttling away of several pretty young women when one of these was accidentally discharged at a wayside tea-house. But while occasional rumors of danger would spread, it was hard to tell whence, I think nothing of a serious nature occurred. Nevertheless, albeit resentment and hostility were repressed in outward manifestation by the strong hand of the government, and by the examples of punishment already made, they were still burning beneath the surface. It was during this period that the British minister, visiting Kioto, a concession jealously resisted by conservative Japanese spirit, was set upon by some ronins while on his way to pay an official call. He was guarded by British cavalry and marines, and had besides an escort of samurai. It was said at the time that these fled, except the officers, who fought valiantly, slaying one and beating down the other of the two most desperate assailants. Considering the well-established courage of the Japanese, and that the attack was by their own people, sympathy with the attempt seems the most likely explanation of the faithlessness reported. The immediate effect of this was to curtail our privileges of riding about the country of Yokohama.

Perhaps the most notable incident, historically, of our stay in Yokohama was the arrival of the first iron-clad of the Japanese navy, to which it has fallen a generation later to give the most forcible lesson yet seen of iron-clads in battle. This vessel had been the Confederate ram *Stonewall*, and prior to her acquisition by Japan had had a curiously checkered career of ownership. She was built in Bordeaux, under the name *Sphinx*, by contract between a French firm and the Confederate naval agent in Europe; but some difficulty arose between the parties, and in 1864 Denmark, being then at war with Austria and Prussia concerning the Schleswig-Holstein duchies, bought her under certain conditions. With a view to delivery to the Danish government she was taken to a Swedish port, and after a nominal sale proceeded under the Swedish flag to Copenhagen, where she remained in charge of a banker of that city. Peace having been meanwhile declared, Denmark no longer wanted her. The sale was nullified under pretext of failure in the conditions, and she passed finally into the hands of the Confederacy,[13] sailing from Copenhagen January 7, 1865. Off Quiberon, in France, she received a crew from another vessel under Confederate direction, and thence attempted to go to the Azores, but was forced by bad weather into Ferrol. From there she crossed the Atlantic; but by the time of her arrival the War of Secession was ended by the surrenders of Lee and Johnston. Her commander took her to Havana, and there gave her up to the Spanish authorities. Spain, in turn, in due time delivered her to the United States, as the legal heir to all spoils of the Confederacy. Several years later, in 1871, I had a share in bringing home part of these often useless trophies; the ship in which I was having gone to Europe, without guns, loaded with provisions to supply the needs of the French poor, presumed to be suffering from the then recent war with Germany. Our cargo discharged, we were sent to Liverpool, and there took on board some rifled cannon and projectiles originally made for the South.

The *Stonewall* had been lying at the Washington Navy-Yard when I was stationed there in 1866. Measured by to-day's standards she was of trivial power, small in size, moderate in speed, light in armor and armament; but her ram was of formidable dimensions, and at that period the tactical value of the ram was estimated much more highly than it now is. The disastrous effect of the thrust, if successfully made, outweighed in men's minds the difficulty of hitting; an error of valuation similar to that which has continuously exaggerated the danger from torpedo craft of all kinds. After the sailing of the *Iroquois*, a deputation of Japanese officials came to the United States on a mission, part of which was to buy ships of war. In reply to their inquiries, Commander – now Rear-Admiral – George Brown, then ordnance officer of the yard, pointed out the *Stonewall* to them as a vessel suitable for their immediate purposes, and with which our government might probably part. He also expressed a favorable opinion of her sea-going qualities for reaching

Japan. A few days later they came to him and said that, as he thought well of her, perhaps he would undertake to carry her out; their own seamanship at that early date being unequal to the responsibility. This was more than was anticipated by Brown, interested in his present duties, but it rather put him on his mettle; and so he set forth, a satisfactory pecuniary arrangement having been concluded. She went by way of the Strait of Magellan and the Hawaiian Islands, reaching Yokohama without other incident than constant ducking. As one of her officers said, clothes needed not to be scrubbed; a soiled garment could be simply secured on the forward deck, and left there to wash in the water that came on board until it was clean. I have never known her subsequent fortunes in Japanese hands; but as the beginning of their armored navy she has a place in history – and here.

From Yokohama the *Iroquois* returned to Kobé, and there lay during July, August, and September; so that in our two visits I passed five months in this part of the Inland Sea. The summer, in its way, is there as pleasant as the winter in its. The highest thermometer I read was 87° Fahrenheit, and there was almost always a pleasant breeze. The country was now so far safe that we went everywhere within reasonable reach of the concession, and the scenery presented such variety in sameness as to be a perpetual source of enjoyment. The most striking characteristics are the views of the enclosed sea itself, ample in expanse, yet without the monotony attendant upon an unbounded water view; and, when that disappears, follows the succession of enclosed valleys, alike, yet different; a recurrent feature similar, though on another scale, to that presented by the valley of the Inn on the ride from Zurich to Innsbruck. How far away those days are is seen from my noting on one of them, while visiting what was known to us as the Moon Temple, that the ships of war below were dressed in honor of the first Napoleon's birthday, August 15th; an observance which ceased with the empire.

This time I managed an opportunity of seeing Osaka, which the disturbed conditions had prevented my doing during our winter stay. Description I shall avoid, as always; enough to say that the flatness of the site, in low land, six miles from the mouth of the narrow, winding river, makes the city one of canals, like Venice and Amsterdam. In visiting the great castle of the Tycoon, a stone fortification notable not only for its own size, but for the dimensions of the huge single stones of which it is built, we went by boat, following a sluggish watercourse, an eighth of a mile wide, and so shallow that we poled through it. The pull from the bar to the city was very tedious, and Kobé evidently had proved the better commercial situation; for even now, half a year after the opening of the port, we were looked upon with curiosity; were followed by crowds which stopped if we stopped, moved when we moved. To the children we were objects of apprehension; they eyed us fearfully, and scuttled away rapidly if we made any feint at rushing towards them. Nevertheless, the prevailing tone among the common people was now plainly kindly, although six months before they would at times spit at foreigners from the bridges which in great numbers span the streams. The temper of those who form mobs changes lightly. It is true that in our excursions we were accompanied by an armed guard, which would seem to indicate possibilities of danger; but these samurai themselves were not only courteous, but interested and smiling, and I thought gave good promise that their class in general was coming round to friendliness.

We left Kobé towards the end of September, in company with a new flag-ship which had arrived to take the place of the *Hartford*. This vessel rejoiced to call herself *Piscataqua*, which is worth recording as a sample of a class of name then much affected by the powers that were, presumably on account of their length; "fine flourishers," to quote the always illustrative Boatswain Chucks, "as long as their homeward-bound pendants, which in a calm drop in the water alongside." *Piscataqua*, however uncouth, most Americans can place; but what shall we say of *Ammonoosuc*, *Wampanoag*, and such like, then adorning our lists, which seem as though extracted by a fine-tooth comb drawn through the tangle of Indian nomenclature. Under the succeeding administration *Piscataqua* was changed to *Delaware*. The new commander-in-chief was among our most popular officers, distinguished alike for seamanship, courage, and courtesy; but he held to great secrecy as to his intentions, which caused officers more inconvenience than seemed always quite necessary. Questions of mess-stores, of correspondence, and other pre-arrangements, depend much upon

316

knowledge of future movements, as exact as may not interfere with service emergencies. These in peace times rarely require concealment. A characteristic story ran that, as the two vessels were leaving Kobé, when the flag-ship's anchor was a-weigh, her captain, still ignorant of her destination, turned to the admiral and said, "Which way shall I lay her head, sir?"

It turned out that we were bound to Nagasaki, on our way to China. The approaching northeast monsoon, with its dry, bracing air, dictates the period when foreign squadrons usually go south, having during the summer in Japan avoided the debilitating damp heat which those months entail in Shanghai, Hong Kong, and the Chinese ports generally. The *Iroquois*, however, had soon to separate from the flag-ship, owing to news received of a singular occurrence, savoring more of two hundred years ago, or of to-day's dime novel – "shilling shocker," as our British brethren have it – than of the prosaic nineteenth century. There had arrived at Hakodate, the northernmost of the then open Japanese ports, on the island of Yezo and Strait of Tsugaru, a mysterious bark, without name or papers, peopled only by Chinese of the coolie class, and bearing evident marks of foul play. From indications she was supposed to be American, and our ship, being the most immediately available, was ordered up to investigate; leaving Nagasaki October 24, 1868. Our course took us over the ground which has since become historic by the destruction of Rodjestvensky's fleet, as well as by other incidents of the Russo-Japanese war; and the weather we had, both going and returning, would justify the anxiety said to have been felt by the Japanese naval authorities, that Port Arthur should be taken before the winter set in. Like men, ships must do their work at whatever cost; but like men also, and perhaps even more, they should be spared needless strain, especially if they be few. A sick ship needs usually more time for recovery than a sick man.

Our orders directed a stop at a port called Niigata, on the west coast of Nippon. We must have communicated, for I thence despatched a letter; but at the time of our arrival a furious northwest gale was blowing, dead on shore. The ship, therefore, ran under a largish island called Sado, which much to our convenience lies a few miles to sea-ward of Niigata, and there anchored; quietly enough as to wind, though gusty willy-waws descending from the cliffs and swishing the water in petty whirlwinds testified to the commotion outside. We had quite the same experience returning to Shanghai; but at that time in mid-sea, where the *Iroquois*, powerless as to steam, but otherwise as much at home as the sea-fowl, rode it out gleefully, though I admit not luxuriously to flesh and muscles.

On November 1st we reached Hakodate, where our captain and consul, aided by the Japanese authorities, proceeded at once with their investigation. The strange vessel was in as distressed condition, almost, as that of the Ancient Mariner when he drew near "his own countree:" sails gone, rigging flying loose, one of her topgallant masts, if I remember right, snapped in two, and the exterior of her hull as though neither paint nor soap had known it for years. In her cabins were marks of blood not eradicated; and particularly on the transom over the stern windows was the print of a bloody hand, the fingers spread wide as they rested against the paint, suggesting resistance by one being thrust out. The story so far collected from the coolies was that they had sailed in her from Macao, a Portuguese port near Canton and Hong Kong, and that the captain and crew, after taking her far north in the ice, had abandoned her altogether. In support of this part of their story they showed furs procured from the natives. These gave plausibility to the ice experiences; but the rest of the account, unlikely in itself, had been disproved by inquiry in Macao, where nothing was known of any vessel answering to the descriptions. At last, however, a rumor had come, how conveyed I know not, that such a bark, with coolies and twelve thousand dollars in gold on board, had sailed from Callao, in Peru, the previous January, and had never since been heard from; that she had a Peruvian captain and crew, but carried American colors, probably merely as indicating American property. To claim full American privilege, ships must be American built; but one bought abroad and owned by Americans may carry the flag, in proof of nationality, though without the right of entering an American port like those to the manner born. They thus become entitled to the same national regard as any other possessions of American citizens under foreign jurisdiction.

So information stood when the *Iroquois* arrived – false on one hand, and on the other vague. Soon after the captain and consul began their investigation they stumbled upon the vessel's papers, concealed in a manner which had hitherto baffled careful search. These showed that she was the missing *Cayalti*, which on the previous January 18th had cleared from Callao for another Peruvian port; that she was American in ownership, while the captain and crew were Spanish in name. This fixed her identity; but how account for the disappearance of the ship's company, and for her presence in Hakodate, on the other side of the Pacific, three thousand miles north of Callao. To this inquiry the captain and consul addressed themselves in the cabin of the *Iroquois*. Two or three Japanese two-sworded officials were in attendance, and memory recalls their grave, impassive faces, as seen at times when some routine communication called me in to speak to our captain.

Contracted though the captain's quarters were, the unaccustomed scene, absent from their companions and from the familiar surroundings of their probable crime, was calculated to impress the culprits; and the methods pursued to instigate admissions savored, I fancy, more of the Orient than of modern Anglo-Saxon ideals. But the present functions of our officials corresponded to those of the French *juges d'instruction*; and, having to elicit the truth from a low class of Orientals, they dealt with them after the fashion which alone they would recognize as serious. The witnesses began, of course, by lying in the most transparent manner, but under judicious – or judicial – pressure a story was pieced together which in main outline probably corresponded with the truth; for in it three or four of them independently agreed. Two days out from Callao the coolies had risen against the whites, and after a short fight overpowered them. Of the crew, two jumped overboard; the rest submitted. A boat was then lowered, and the men in the water were killed; after which the others were tied together, made fast to an anchor, and so thrown into the sea, the mate, who had fought desperately, having first been mutilated by cutting off his ears. The captain and a Chinese steward were saved; the former to handle the ship, to which the coolies were unequal, and he was bidden to take her to China. I do not find in my contemporary letters the impression which remains on my mind, that they estimated his general observance of this order by the vague knowledge that China lay towards the evening sun. The history of that strange voyage would be interesting, but was scarcely recoverable in detail from the class of witnesses. It would be by no means certain that the master of a coastwise trader could navigate accurately; and, while he would always be sure of death if he brought the vessel within reach of China, it is not apparent why he should take her to the remote north in which the furs showed her to have been. I have never heard whether, as the evidence ran, he and the steward escaped alive, abandoning the ship.[14] He had disappeared when the Japanese found her drifting helplessly under her ignorant occupants.

While in Hakodate, I availed myself of the opportunity to visit a great lake and a volcano, not extinct, but not immediately active. They are distant about fifteen miles from the town, a position in which I see such a sheet of water on the maps of to-day. This was a long ride in the then state of the roads, after the autumn rains, and with nightly freeze sufficient continually to fix the moisture, and then to renew the dampness towards the noonday thaw. Transport was not by wheel, but by pack-animals; and as these marched in companies of a half-dozen or so, in single file, haltered one to the other, each as he stepped put his foot into the prints made, not merely by his immediate file-leader of the particular gang, but by all others going and coming for weeks before. The consequence was a succession of scallops, distributed over long stretches of mud, the consistency of which just sufficed to hold the shape thus impressed upon it. Japanese horses are small, and as a class quarrelsome; the one I rode on this occasion was little larger than a child's pony, and looked as if he had not been curried for a month. I hesitated to impose upon him my weight, a scruple which would have been intensified had I known the character of the pilgrimage through which he was to bear me. With his feet at the bottom of the scallop, the rounded top rose above his knee, nearly giving his patient nose the touch which his dejected mood and drooping head seemed to invite. At the first start he stumbled, nearly falling on me, but escaped with nostrils and mouth full of liquid dirt.

A day to go, a day to come, and one intervening to cross the lake and ascend the volcano, measured our excursion; through the whole of which we had sunny skies and exhilarating temperature till the last hour of our return, when a drizzling rain suggested what might have been our discomfort had the heavens above been as unpropitious as the roads beneath. Even the crossing of the lake and the ascent were particularly favored, the sky literally cloudless and water smooth; whereas the following morning, when we rose to depart, a fog had settled on the mountain, making movement upon it doubtful and even to a slight degree dangerous. The lake, some six miles by ten, and abounding in islets, lay smiling under the bright, wintry sun, its shores clad with leafless forests mingled with evergreens, save the barren slopes of the volcano itself; beneath the distant lava stream of which we were told seventeen hundred people lay, buried by the last eruption. The scene tempted me more than most to description, for the brilliant stillness of a clear November day, and the gaunt, bare trees, were strange to our long experience of verdure in southern Japan, and smacked strongly of home – Hakodate being in the latitude of New York; but, as always, the majority have their own vision, their own memory, of just such conditions and surroundings, more vivid for them than another's portrayal.

The two nights at the lake we slept in a Japanese tea-house, scrupulously clean and quite comfortable, but at that early date and remote region entirety primitive; I should rather say strictly native in all its arrangements. The kitchen was innocent of European suggestion; we ate with chopsticks, and fish from the lake were spitted and cooked around a fire in a sandy hearth, contrived below the middle of the room. Eggs were in abundance, but coffee was sorely missed at our chilly rising. At 9 A.M. we started for the volcano, getting back at 7 P.M. We landed at the foot of the lava stream and ascended by it through a picture of desolation. From shore to summit took us three hours, which confirmed to me a rough estimate of the height as about four thousand feet. The grade was not severe, some thirty or forty degrees; but by this time we had a brisk northwest wind blowing down our throats, and the latter part of the way our feet sank deep in volcanic dust. At the top the air was very cold, keen, and rare, but somewhat oppressive to the lungs. None of us cared to smoke, after eating and drinking, but the view afforded us was perfect; limitless, so far as atmospheric conditions went. In appearance the crater differed little, I presume, from others in a state of quiescence. Smoke and steam poured forth continually, in one spot in large volumes; while from many places issued little jets, such as puff from the out-door pipes of a factory, suggesting subterranean workmen. These were especially numerous from a large mound in the centre, which our guide told us was growing bigger and bigger with his successive visits, portending an outburst near. If his observation was accurate, it goes to show the coincident sympathetic movements which occur in volcanic regions remote from one another; for this year, 1868, followed one of great terrestrial disturbance. In 1867 two of our naval vessels had been carried ashore by a tidal wave in the West Indies; and of two others lying off Arica, Peru, one was dashed to pieces against the cliffs, while the other was carried over low, flat ground for a mile or so inland, where her dismantled hull was still lying when I was there in 1884.

Our starting when we did, as soon as possible, three days after arrival, justified the Nelsonian maxim not to trifle with a fair wind; for we just culled the three days which were the cream, and only cream, of our stay. From our return on the 6th, to sailing on the 12th, there was but one fair twenty-four hours – the rest from blustering to furious; and we went out with the promise of a gale which did not with evening "in the west sink smilingly forsworn." The *Iroquois* ran through Tsugaru Strait under canvas, with a barometer rather tumbling than falling, and an east wind fast freshening to heavy. We knew it must end at northwest; but it lasted till afternoon of the next day, so we got a good offing. The shift of the wind was in its accompaniments spectacular – and cyclonic. The morning of the 13th was among the wildest I have seen. Daylight came a half-hour late, with a lurid sky; the clouds, the confused, heaving water, the sails, spars, and deck of the ship herself, all as if seen in a Lorraine glass. It having become nearly calm, she lay thrashing aimlessly in the swell, unsteadied by the canvas. The barometer still fell slowly till two in the afternoon, when it stopped, and we began to look out.

"First rise, after very low Indicates a stronger blow."

At three it rose one one-hundredth of an inch, and almost simultaneously, looking over the weather rail, was to be seen the oncoming north-wester, never long in debt to a southeaster. First a gleaming white line of foam beneath the sombre horizon, gradually spreading to right and left, and visibly widening as it drew near. Soon its deepening surface broke to view into innumerable separate wave-crests, which advanced leaping in tumultuous accord, like the bounding rush of a pack of wolves, whom you may see, and whose howling you can imagine but do not yet hear. As Kingsley has said, "It looks so dangerous, and you are so safe" – all the thrill, yet none of the apprehension. The new gale struck the *Iroquois* in full force. Within twenty minutes it had reached its height, and so continued for near forty-eight hours, during thirty-six of which the hatches were battened down. For a time the two seas, the old and the new, fought each other to our discomfort; but the old yielded, and, as the new got its even, regular swing, the *Iroquois* agreed with its enemy of the moment and rode easily.

With our arrival at Shanghai we had left behind whatever in the cruise of the *Iroquois* could be considered exceptional as to incident; that is, while I remained with her. From December, 1868, we entered in China upon the usual routine of station movement; interesting enough at the time, but from which my memory retains nothing noteworthy. Subsequently we visited Formosa and Manila and Hong Kong; whence we were sent south for ten days to the Gulf of Hainan to search for a French corvette which had disappeared. We did not find her, nor was she again seen by mortal eyes. Returning to Hong Kong, we learned of the first election of General Grant to the presidency, and that a letter from him had reached the admiral asking that the captain of the flag-ship, who as a school comrade had once saved Grant's life, should be ordered home; the intention being to give him charge of an important bureau in the Navy Department. Under usual circumstances a relief would have been sent out; but as the request was from the expectant administration, not from the one still in power and antagonistic, a private letter was the chosen medium of action.

His departure made a vacancy, to which succeeded the captain of the *Iroquois*, a great favorite with the commander-in-chief. I was left in charge of the ship until we went back to Japan in May. There I fell ill at Nagasaki, and after recovery found myself at Yokohama, in command of a gunboat ordered to be sold. This consummation was reached in September, and I then started for home, having the admiral's permission to proceed by Suez to Europe, instead of by the usual route to San Francisco. My object was only to visit Europe; but on the way to Hong Kong a Parsee merchant, a fellow-passenger, suggested turning aside to India, which I had not contemplated. I shall not go into my brief India travel from Calcutta to Bombay, beyond mentioning the singular good-fortune, as it appeared to me, that I visited the ruined residence at Lucknow, and the remains of the memorable siege of twelve years before, in the company of an officer who had himself been a participant. His wife, still a very young and handsome woman, whom I had the pleasure of meeting, had been one of the children within the works, sharing the perils, if not the anxieties, of their mothers during that period of awful suspense.

Nor do I think my six months in Europe, leave for which met me on my arrival there, worthy of particular note, save in one incident which has always seemed to me curious. Landing at Marseilles, I found that intimate friends were then at Nice. I accordingly went there, instead of to Paris, as I had intended; and, like thoughtless young men everywhere, abandoned myself to pleasant society instead of to self-improvement by travel. My purpose, however, continually was to go directly to Paris when I did leave Nice, for my time was limited; but a middle-aged friend strongly dissuaded me. "You should by no means fail to visit Rome now," he said, "for, independently of the immortal interest of the place, of the treasures of association and of art which are its imperishable birthright, there is the more transient spectacle of the Papacy, in the pride, pomp, and circumstance of the temporal power. This may at any moment pass away, and you therefore may never have another opportunity to witness it in its glory. There is a vague traditional prophecy that, as St. Peter held the bishopric of Rome twenty-five years, any pope whose tenure exceeds his will see the downfall of the papal sovereignty over Rome. Such prophecies often insure their own fulfilment, and Pius IX. is now closely approaching his twenty-fifth year. Go while you can." So I went, in February, 1870; and before the next winter's snow the temporal power was a thing of the past.

XI
THE TURNING OF A LONG LANE
– HISTORICAL, NAVAL, AND PERSONAL

1870

In narrating the cruise of the *Iroquois* I have, as it were, laid the reins on the neck of my memory, letting it freely run away; partly because our track lay over stretches of sea even now somewhat unbeaten by travel, partly because the story of routine naval life and incidental experiences, in a time already far past, might have for the non-professional reader more novelty than could be premised by me, a daily participant therein. Moreover, there were in our cruise some exceptional occurrences which might be counted upon to relieve monotony. I purpose to observe greater restraint in what follows.

The year 1870, in which I returned home, was one of marked and decisive influence upon history, and in a way a turning-point in my own obscure career. As in February I witnessed the splendors of the papal city under its old régime, so in April and May I saw imperial Paris brilliant under the emperor. In the one case as in the other I was unconscious of the approaching *débâcle*; a blindness I presume shared by most contemporaries. Whatever the wiser and more far-seeing might have prophesied as to the general ultimate issues, few or none could then have foretold the particular occasion which so soon afterwards opened the floodgates. As the old passed, with the downfall of the French Empire and of the temporal kingdom, there arose a new; not merely the German Empire and the unity of Italy, crowned by the possession of its historic capital, but, unrecognized for the moment, then came in that reign of organized and disciplined force, the full effect and function of which in the future men still only dimly discern. The successive rapid overthrows of the Austrian and French empires by military efficiency and skill; the beating in detail two separate foes who, united, might have been too strong for the victor; the consequent crumbling of the papal monarchy when French support was withdrawn, following closely on the Vatican Decree of Infallibility; these things produced an impression which was transmitted rapidly throughout the world of European civilization, till in the Farther East it reached Japan. Into the current thus established the petty stream of my own fortunes was drawn, little anticipated by myself. To it was due my special call; for by it was created the predisposition to recognize the momentous bearing of maritime force upon the course of history, which insured me a hearing when the fulness of my time was come.

Until 1870 my life since graduation had been passed afloat almost without interruption. Soon afterwards I obtained command rank; and this promotion, combined with the dead apathy which after the War of Secession settled upon our people with regard to the navy, left me with relatively little active employment for several years. In America, the naval stagnation of that period was something now almost incredible. The echoes of the guns which from Königgrätz and a dozen battle-fields in France had resounded round the globe, awakening the statesmen of all countries, had apparently ricochetted over the United States, as fog sound-signals are noticed to rebound over-head, unheard through long stretches of the sea-level, until they again touch the water beyond. The nation slumbered peacefully in its "*petit coin*," to use the expressive phrase of a French admiral to me. Had even nothing been done, this inertness might have been less significant; but somewhere in the early seventies, despite all the progress elsewhere noticeable, there were built deliberately some half-dozen corvettes, smaller than the *Iroquois* class, mostly of wood. That a period of lethargy in action should steal over a government just released from strenuous exertion is one thing, and bad enough; but it is different, and much worse, that there should be a paralysis of idea, of mental development corresponding to the movement of the world.

I myself have always considered that the "right about" of policy came with the administration of President Arthur, when Mr. Chandler was Secretary of the Navy. It began with a work of destruction, an exposure of the uselessness of the existing naval material, due purely to stand-still; to being left hopelessly in the rear by the march of improvement elsewhere. Upon this followed under the same administration an attempt at restoration, gingerly enough in its conceptions. The vessels laid down were cruisers, the primary quality of which should be speed; but fourteen knots was the highest demanded, and that of one only, the *Chicago*. Unhappily, wherever the fault lay, the navy then had the habit of living from day to day on expedients, on makeshifts. Although deficiencies were manifest and generally felt, the prevailing sentiment had been that we should wait until the experiments of other peoples, in the cost of which we would not share, should have reached workable finalities. This is another instance of what is commonly called "practical;" as though mental processes must not necessarily antecede efficient action, and as though there was not then at hand abundant data for brains to work on, without any expenditure of money. Finality, indeed, had not been reached, and never will be in anything save death; but at that time it had been shown beyond peradventure that radically new conditions had entered naval warfare, and clearly the first most practical step was a mature official digestion of these conditions – a decision as to what types of vessels were needed, and what their respective qualities should be. In short, the first and perfectly possible thing was to evolve a systematic policy; a careful look, and then a big leap.

However, things rarely come about in that way. It involves getting rid of old ideas, which is quite as bad as pulling teeth, and much harder; and the subsequent adoption of new ones, that are as uneasy as tight shoes. We had then certain accepted maxims, dating mainly from 1812, which were as thoroughly current in the country – and I fear in the navy, too – as the "dollar of the daddies" was not long after. One was that commerce destroying was the great efficient weapon of naval warfare. Everybody – the navy as well – believed we had beaten Great Britain in 1812, brought her to her knees, by the destruction of her commerce through the system observed by us of single cruisers; naval or privateers. From that erroneous premise was deduced the conclusion of a navy of cruisers, and small cruisers at that; no battle-ship nor fleets.[15] Then we wanted a navy for coast defence only, no aggressive action in our pious souls; an amusing instance being that our first battle-ships were styled "coast defence" battle-ships, a nomenclature which probably facilitated the appropriations. They were that; but they were capable of better things, as the event has proved. But the very fact that such talk passed unchallenged as that about commerce-destroying by scattered cruisers, and war by mere defence – known to all military students as utterly futile and ruinous – shows the need then existent of a comprehensive survey of the contemporary condition of the world, and of the stage which naval material had reached. One such was made, which a subsequent secretary, Mr. Tracy, characterized to me as excellent; but the deficiencies and requirements exposed by it in our naval status frightened Congress, much as the confronting of his affairs terrify a bankrupt.

During the latter part of Secretary Chandler's term I was abroad in command of the *Wachusett*, on the Pacific coast. Besides her, the squadron consisted of the *Hartford*, Farragut's old flag-ship, the *Lackawanna*, and my former ship, the *Iroquois*. They all dated, guns as well, from the War of Secession, or earlier. Had they been exceptional instances, on a station of no great importance, it might not have mattered greatly; but in fact they still remained representative components of the United States navy. The squadron organization, too, was that which had prevailed ever since I entered the service, and so continued until a very few years ago. The rule was that the vessels were scattered, one to this port, another to that. They rarely met, except for interchange of duties; and when in company almost the only exercises in common were those of yards and sails, in which the ships worked competitively, to beat one another's time, – a healthy enough emulation. But this rivalry was no substitute for the much more necessary practice of working together, in mutual support; for the acquired habit of handling vessels in rapid movement and close proximity with fearless judgment, based upon experience of what your own could do, and what might be confidently expected from your consorts, especially your next ahead and astern. A new captain for the *Lackawanna* accompanied me to the station, where we found our ships in Callao, assembled with the other two. Within a week later we all went out together, performed three or four simple evolutions, and then scattered. This was the only fleet drill we had in the two years, 1883-1885.

In fact, from time immemorial the navy had thought in single ships, as the army had in company posts. To the several officers their own ship was everything, the squadron little or nothing. The War of Secession had broadened the ideas of the army by enlarging its operations in the field, although peace brought a relapse; but the navy having to fight only shore batteries, not fleets, was not forced out of the old tactical and strategic apathy. The huge accumulations of vessels under a single admiral entailed enlarged administrative duties; but the tactical methods, as shown in the greater battles, presented simply the adaptation of means to a particular occasion, and, however sagacious in the several instances – and they usually were sagacious – possessed no continuity of system in either theory or practice. Organic unity did not exist except for administration. There was an assemblage of vessels, but not a fleet. All this was the result, or at least the complement, of the theory of commerce destroying, which prescribed cruisers that act singly; and of war by defence only, which proscribed battle-ships, that act in unison and so compel unity.

A further incident of Mr. Chandler's tenure of office was the establishment of the Naval War College at Newport. This had its origin in the recognition of a defect in the constitution of the Navy Department, which was glaringly visible during the War of Secession. Immense and admirable as was the administrative work done by the Department during that contest, there did not exist in it then, nor did there for many years to come, any formal provision for the proper consideration and expert decision of strictly military questions, from the point of view of military experience and professional understanding. The head of the Department, invariably a civilian under our form of government, and therefore usually unfamiliar with naval matters, had not assured to him, at instant call, organized professional assistance, individual or corporate, prepared to advise him, when asked, as to the military aspect of proposed operations, what the arguments for or against feasibility, or what the best method of procedure. In other services, notably in the German army, this function is discharged by the general staff, nothing correspondent to which was to be found in our Navy Department. It is evident that the constitution of a general staff, or of any similar body called into being for such purpose, will be more broadly based, and sounder, as knowledge of the subjects in question is more widely distributed among the officers of the service; and that such knowledge will be imparted most certainly by the creation of an institution for the systematic study of military operations, by land or sea, applying the experiences of history to contemporary conditions, and to the particular theatres of possible war in which the nation may be interested.

Such studies are the object of the Naval War College, which was established upon the report of a board of officers, at the head of which was the present Rear-Admiral Stephen B. Luce, to whose persistent initiative must be attributed much of the movement which thus resulted. The other members of the board were the late Admiral Sampson, and Commander – now Rear-Admiral – Caspar F. Goodrich. Luce became the first president of the institution, for which the Department assigned a building, once an almshouse, situated on Coaster's Harbor Island, in Narragansett Bay, then recently ceded to the United States government. It remained still to get together a staff of instructors, and he wrote me to ask if I would undertake the subjects of naval history and naval tactics. The proposition was to me very acceptable; for I had found the Pacific station disagreeable, and, although without proper preparation, I believed on reflection that I could do the work. During my last tour of shore duty I had read carefully Napier's *Peninsular War*, and had found myself in a new world of thought, keenly interested and appreciative, less of the brilliant narrative – though that few can fail to enjoy – than of the military sequences of cause and effect. The influence of Sir John Moore's famous march to Sahagun – less famous than it deserves to be – upon Napoleon's campaign in Spain, revealed to me by Napier like the sun breaking through a cloud, aroused an emotion as joyful as the luminary himself to a navigator doubtful of his position.

"Then felt I as some watcher of the skies When a new planet swims into his ken; Or like stout Cortez, when with eagle eyes He stared at the Pacific."

Following this I had written by request a volume on the Navy in the War of Secession, entitled *The Gulf and Inland Waters*; my first appearance as an author. Herein also I had recognized that the same class of military ideas took possession of my mind. I felt, therefore, that I should bring interest and understanding to my task, and hoped that the defects of knowledge, which I clearly realized, would be overcome. I recalled also that at the Military Academy my father, though professor only of engineering, military and civil, had of his own motion introduced a course of strategy and grand tactics, which had commended itself to observers.

I trusted, therefore, that heredity, too, might come to my aid.

As acceptance placed me on the road which led directly to all the success I have had in life, I feel impelled to acknowledge my indebtedness to Admiral Luce. With little constitutional initiative, and having grown up in the atmosphere of the single cruiser, of commerce-destroying, defensive warfare, and indifference to battle-ships; an anti-imperialist, who for that reason looked upon Mr. Blaine as a dangerous man; at forty-five I was drifting on the lines of simple respectability as aimlessly as one very well could. My environment had been too much for me; my present call changed it. Meantime, however, there was delay. A relief would not be sent, because the ship was to go home; and the ship did not go home because there was, first, a revolution in Panama, and then a war between the Central American states, both which required the *Wachusett's* presence. Mr. Cleveland was elected at this time; there was a change of administration, and with a new Secretary a lapse of Departmental interest. The ship did not go to San Francisco till September, 1885, nearly a year after the admiral's proposition reached me.

The year had not been unfruitful, however. Naturally predisposed, as I have said, my mind ran continually on my subject. I imagined various formations for developing to the best effect the powers of steamships, and sudden changes to be instituted as the moment of collision approached, calculated to disconcert the opponent, or to surprise an advantage before he could parry. Spin-

338

ning cobwebs out of one's unassisted brain, without any previous absorption from external sources, was doubtless a somewhat crude process; yet it had advantages. One of my manoeuvres was to pass a column of ships by an unexpected flank movement across the head of an enemy's column. This I have since heard called "capping;" if, at least, I correctly understand that word. Putting it afterwards before a body of officers attending the College course, all men of years and experience, one said to me, derisively, "Do you suppose an enemy would let you do that?" "It is a question of how quick he is," I replied. "In these days of twelve or fifteen knots he will have no time to ponder, and scarcely time to act." The query illustrates a habit of mind frequently met. It is like discussing the merits of a thrust *en carte*. If the other man is quick enough, he will parry; if not, he will be run through: sooner or later the more skilful usually will get in.

Naval history gave me more anxiety, and I afterwards found it was that which Luce particularly desired of me. I shared the prepossession, common at that time, that the naval history of the past was wholly past; of no use at all to the present. I well recall, during my first term at the College, a visit from a reporter of one of the principal New York journals. He was a man of rotund presence, florid face, thrown-back head, and flowing hair, with all that magisterial condescension which the environment of the Fourth Estate nourishes in its fortunate members; the Roman citizen was "not in it" for birthright. To my bad luck a plan of Trafalgar hung in evidence, as he stalked from room to room. "Ah," he said, with superb up-to-date pity, "you are still talking about Trafalgar;" and I could see that Trafalgar and I were thenceforth on the top shelf of fossils in the collections of his memory. This point of view was held by very many. "You won't find much to say about history," was the direct discouraging comment of an older officer. On the other hand, Sir Geoffrey Hornby, less well known in this country than in Great Britain, where twenty years ago he was recognized as the head of the profession, distinctly commended to me the present value of naval history. I myself, as I have just confessed, had had the contrary impression – a tradition passively accepted. Thus my mind was troubled how to establish relations between yesterday and to-day; so wholly ignorant was I of the undying reproduction of conditions in their essential bearings – a commonplace of military art.

He who seeks, finds, if he does not lose heart; and to me, continuously seeking, came from within the suggestion that control of the sea was an historic factor which had never been systematically appreciated and expounded. Once formulated consciously, this thought became the nucleus of all my writing for twenty years then to come; and here I may state at once what I conceive to have been my part in popularizing, perhaps in making effective, an argument for which I could by no means claim the rights of discovery. Not to mention other predecessors, with the full roll of whose names I am even now unacquainted, Bacon and Raleigh, three centuries before, had epitomized in a few words the theme on which I was to write volumes. That they had done so was, indeed, then unknown to me. For me, as for them, the light dawned first on my inner consciousness; I owed it to no other man. It has since been said by more than one that no claim for originality could be allowed me; and that I wholly concede. What did fall to me was, that no one since those two great Englishmen had undertaken to demonstrate their thesis by an analysis of history, attempting to show from current events, through a long series of years, precisely what influence the command of the sea had had upon definite issues; in brief, a concrete illustration. In the preface to my first work on the subject, for the success of which I was quite unprepared, I stated this as my aim: "An estimate of the effect of Sea Power upon the course of history and the prosperity of nations; ... resting upon a collection of special instances, in which the precise effect has been made clear by an analysis of the conditions at the given moments." This field had been left vacant, yielding me my opportunity; and concurrently therewith, untouched from the point of view proposed by me, there lay the whole magnificent series of events constituting maritime history since the days of Raleigh and Bacon, after the voyages of Columbus and De Gama gave the impetus to over-sea activities, colonies, and commerce, which distinguishes the past three hundred years. Even of this limited period I have occupied but a part, though I fear I have skimmed the cream of that which it offers; but back behind it lie virgin fields, in the careers of the Italian republics, and others yet more remote in time, which can never be for me to narrate, although I have examined them attentively.

I cannot now reconstitute from memory the sequence of my mental processes; but while my problem was still wrestling with my brain there dawned upon me one of those concrete perceptions which turn inward darkness into light – give substance to shadow. The *Wachusett* was lying at Callao, the seaport of Lima, as dull a coast town as one could dread to see. Lima being but an hour distant, we frequently spent a day there; the English Club extending to us its hospitality. In its library was Mommsen's *History of Rome*, which I gave myself to reading, especially the Hannibalic episode. It suddenly struck me, whether by some chance phrase of the author I do not know, how different things might have been could Hannibal have invaded Italy by sea, as the Romans often had Africa, instead of by the long land route; or could he, after arrival, have been in free communication with Carthage by water. This clew, once laid hold of, I followed up in the particular instance. It and the general theory already conceived threw on each other reciprocal illustration; and between the two my plan was formed by the time I reached home, in September, 1885. I would investigate coincidently the general history and naval history of the past two centuries, with a view to demonstrating the influence of the events of the one upon the other. Original research was not within my scope, nor was it necessary to the scheme thus outlined.

Perhaps it is only a subtle form of egotism, but as a condition of my life experience I could wish

to convey to others an appreciation of my profound ignorance of both classes of history when I
began, being then forty-five; not that I mean to
imply that now, or at any time since, I have de-
luded myself with the imagination that I have
become an historian after the high modern pattern. I tackled my job much as I presume an im-
migrant begins a clearing in the wilderness, not
troubling greatly which tree he takes first. I laid
my hands on whatever came along, reading with
the profound attention of one who is looking for
something; and the something was kind enough
to acknowledge my devotion by shining forth in
unexpected ways and places. Any line of investigation, however unsystematic in method, branches out in many directions, suggests continually
new sources of information, to one interested in
his work; and I have felt constantly the force of
Johnson's dictum as to the superior profit from
time spent in reading what is congenial over the
drudgery of constrained application. Every faculty
I possessed was alive and jumping. Incidentally, I
took up the study of land warfare, using Jomini
and Hamley. For naval history the first book upon
which I chanced – the word is exact – was just
what I needed at that stage. It was a history of the
French navy, by a Lieutenant Lapeyrouse-Bonfils,
published about 1845. As naval history pure and
simple, I think little of it; but the author had a
quiet, philosophical way of summing up causes
and effects in general history, as connected with
maritime affairs, which not only corresponded
closely with my own purpose, but suggested to
me new material for thought – novel illustration.

Such treatment was with him only casual, but it opened to me new prospects.

It would be difficult to define precisely to what degree the art of naval warfare had been formulated, or even consciously conceived, in 1885. There could scarcely be said to exist any systematic treatment, or extensive commentary by acknowledged experts, such as for generations had illuminated the theory of land warfare. Naval histories abounded, but by far the most part were simply narratives. Some valuable research, however, had then recently been done; notably by Captain Chevalier, of the French navy, who had produced from French documents a history of the maritime war connected with the American struggle for independence. This he followed with a less exhaustive account of the wars of the French Revolution and Empire, which also appeared in time for me to use. These were marked by running comment, rather than by a studied criticism such as that of Jomini or Napier. In Great Britain, James held, and I think still holds, the field for exhaustive collection of information, documentary or oral in origin, during the period treated by him, 1793-1815; but he has not a military idea in his head beyond that of downright hard fighting, punishing and being punished. In his pages, to take a tactical advantage seems almost a disgrace. The Navy Records Society of Great Britain had not then begun the fruitful labors which within the last decade and a half has made accessible in print a very large amount of new matter; nor had the late Admiral Colomb published his comprehensive book, *Naval Warfare*. So far as I was concerned, the old works of Lediard, Entick, Campbell, Beatson, – in French, Paul Hoste, Troude, Guérin, and others equally remote, – had to be my main reliance; though numerous modern scattered monographs, English and French, were existent. In connection with these one of my most interesting experiences was lighting upon a paper in the *Revue Maritime et Coloniale*, describing in full the Four Days' battle between the English and Dutch in 1666. It purported to be, and I have no doubt was, from a personal letter recently discovered; but I subsequently found it almost word for word in the *Mémoires du Comte de Guiche*, also a participant, printed in 1743. This *Revue* contained many able and suggestive articles, historical and professional, as did the British *Journal of the United Service Institution*; each being in its own country a principal medium for the exchange of professional views. Conspicuous in these contributions to naval history and thought, in England, were Admiral Colomb and Professor Laughton; upon the last named of whom, since these words were first written, has been bestowed the honor of knighthood, a recognition in the evening of life which will be heartily welcomed by his many naval friends on both sides of the Atlantic. In short, apart from the first-hand inquiry which I did not yet attempt, the material available in 1885 was chiefly histories written long before, supplemented by a great many scattered papers of more recent date.

Before leaving this part of my experience I will say a good word for Campbell's *Lives of the Admirals*, so far as his own work – down to 1744 – is concerned. Under this title it is really a history of the British navy, very well done for enabling a professional man to understand the naval operations; but, more than this, maritime occurrences of other sorts, commercial movement, and naval policy, are presented clearly, and with sufficient fulness to illustrate the influence of sea power in its broadest sense upon the general history. Bearing, as it does, strong indications of a full use of accessible accounts, contemporary with the events narrated, I know no naval work superior to it for lucidity and breadth of treatment. Campbell was he of whom Dr. Johnson said: "Campbell is a good man, a pious man; I am afraid he has not been inside a church for many years; but he never passes a church without pulling off his hat. This shows he has good principles."

In history other than naval I was for my object as fortunate as I had been in Lapeyrouse-Bonfils. An accident first placed in my hands Henri Martin's *History of France*. I happened to see the volumes, then unknown to me, on the shelves of a friend. The English translation of Martin covered only the reigns of Louis XIV. and XV., and of Louis XVI. to 1783, the close of the War of American Independence. The scope of my first book, *The Influence of Sea Power upon History*, coincides precisely with this period, and may thus have been determined. I think, however, that the beginning of the work was fixed for me by the essentially new departure in the history of England and France, connoted by the almost simultaneous accession of Charles II. and Louis XIV.; while the end was dictated by the necessity to stop and take breath. Besides, I had to lecture, which for the moment interrupted both reading and writing. The particular value of Martin to me was the attention paid by him to commercial and maritime policy, as shown in those frank methods of national regulation which in the seventeenth and eighteenth centuries characterized all governments, but were to be seen in their simplest and most efficient executive operation in an absolute monarchy. A more advanced age may doubt the wisdom of such manipulation of trade; but in the hands of a genius like Colbert it became a very active and powerful force, the workings of which were the more impressive for their directness. They could be easily followed. Whatever Martin's views on political economy, he was in profound sympathy with Colbert as an administrator, and enlarged much on his commercial policy as conducing to the financial stability upon which that great statesman sought to found the primacy of his country. To one as ignorant as I was of mercantile movement, the story of Colbert's methods, owing to their pure autocracy, was a kind of introductory primer to this element of sea power. Thus received, the impression was both sharper and deeper. New light was shed upon, and new emphasis given to, the commonplace assertion of the relations between commerce and a navy; civil and military sea power. While I have no claim to mastery of the arguments for and against free trade and protection, Colbert, as expounded by Martin, sent me in later days to the study of trade statistics; as indicative of naval or political conditions deflecting commercial interchange, and influencing national prosperity. The strong interest such searches had for me may show a natural bent, and certainly conduced to the understanding of sea power in its broadest sense. Martin set my feet in the way, though Campbell helped me much by incidental mention.

It is now accepted with naval and military men who study their profession, that history supplies the raw material from which they are to draw their lessons, and reach their working conclusions. Its teachings are not, indeed, pedantic precedents; but they are the illustrations of living principles. Napoleon is reported to have said that on the field of battle the happiest inspiration is often but a recollection. The authority of Jomini chiefly set me to study in this fashion the many naval histories before me. From him I learned the few, very few, leading considerations in military combination; and in these I found the key by which, using the record of sailing navies and the actions of naval leaders, I could elicit, from the naval history upon which I had looked despondingly, instruction still pertinent. The actual course of the several campaigns, or of the particular battles, I worked out as one does any historical conclusion, by comparison of the individual witnesses presented in the several accounts; but the result of this constructive process became to me something more than a narrative. Both the general outcome and the separate incidents passed through tests which formed in me an habitual critical habit of mind. My judgments, one or all, might be erroneous; but, right or wrong, what I brought before myself was no mere portrayal, accurate as I could achieve, but a rational whole, of composite cause and effect, with its background and foreground, its centre of interest and argument, its greater and smaller details, its decisive culmination; for even to a drawn battle or a neutral issue there is something which definitely prevented success. It was the same with questions of naval policy. Jomini's dictum, that the organized forces of the enemy are ever the chief objective, pierces like a two-edged sword to the joints and marrow of many specious propositions; to that of the French postponement of immediate action to "ulterior objects," or to Jefferson's reliance upon raw citizen soldiery, a mob ready disorganized to the enemy's hands when he saw fit to lay on. From Jomini also I imbibed a fixed disbelief in the thoughtlessly accepted maxim that the statesman and general occupy unrelated fields. For this misconception I substituted a tenet of my own, that war is simply a violent political movement; and from an expression of his, "The sterile glory of fighting battles merely to win them," I deduced, what military men are prone to overlook, that "War is not fighting, but business."

It was with such hasty equipment that I approached my self-assigned task, to show how the control of the sea, commercial and military, had been an object powerful to influence the policies of nations; and equally a mighty factor in the success or failure of those policies. This remained my guiding aim; but incidentally thereto I had by this determined to prepare a critical analysis of the naval campaigns and battles, a decision for which I had to thank Jomini chiefly. This would constitute in measure a treatment of the art of naval war; not formal, nor systematic, but in the nature of commentary, developing and illustrating principles. I may interject, as possibly suggestive to professional men, that such current comment on historical events will lead them on, as it led me irresistibly, to digest the principles thus drawn out; reproducing them in concise definitions, applicable to the varying circumstances of naval warfare, – an elementary treatise. This I did also, somewhat later, in a series of lectures; which, though necessarily rudimentary, I understand still form a groundwork of instruction at the War College. For the framework of general history, which was to serve as a setting to my particular thesis, I relied upon the usual accredited histories of the period, as I did upon equally well-known professional histories for the nautical details. The subject lay so much on the surface that my handling of it could scarcely suffer materially from possible future discoveries. What such or such an unknown man had said or done on some back-stairs, or written to some unknown correspondent, if it came to light, was not likely to affect the received story of the external course of military or political events. Did I make a mistake in the detail of some battle, as I got one fleet on the wrong tack in Byng's action, or as in the much-argued case of Torrington at Beachy Head, it would for my leading purpose do little more harm than a minor tactical error does to the outcome of a large strategic plan, when accurately conceived. As a colleague phrased it to me, speaking of the cautious deliberation of some men, "A second-best position to-day is better than a first-best to-morrow, when the occasion has passed." Strike while the iron is hot! and between reading and thinking my iron was very hot by the time I laid it on the anvil. Moreover, I had to meet the emergency of lecturing, one of the main reliances of our incipient undertaking.

I had begun my reading with Lapeyrouse-Bonfils, in October, 1885. The preceding summer at Panama had so far affected my health as to cause a month's severe illness in the winter; and when recovered I unguardedly let myself in for another month's work, on naval tactics, which might have been postponed. Hence the end of the following May had arrived before I began to write; but I was so full of matter, absorbed or evolved, that I ran along with steady pace, and by September had on paper, in lecture form, all of my first *Sea Power* book, except the summary of conclusions which constitutes the final chapter. Before publication, in 1890, the whole had been very carefully revised; but the changes made were mostly in the details of battles, or else verbal in character, to develop discussions in amplitude or clearness. Battles had been to me at first a secondary consideration; hence for revision I had accumulated many fresh data, notably from two somewhat scarce books: *Naval Battles in the West Indies*, by Lieutenant Matthews, and *Naval Researches*, by Captain Thomas White, British officers contemporary and participant in the events which they narrate of the War of American Independence.

A lecturer is little hampered by the exactions of style; indeed, the less he ties himself to his manuscript, the more he can talk to his audience rather than read, and the more freely his command of his subject permits him to digress pertinently, the better he holds attention. When I found after my first course that the treatment was to my hearers interesting as well as novel, the thought of publishing entered my mind; and while I had no expectation or ambition to become a stylist, the question of style gradually forced itself on my consideration. I intend to state some of my conclusions, because the casual remarks of others, authors or critics, have been helpful to me. Why should not style as well as war have its history and biography, to which each man may contribute an unpretentious mite? Notably, I got much comfort from Darwin's complaint of frequent recurrences of inability to give adequate expression to thoughts, which he could then put down only in such crude, imperfect form as the moment suggested, leaving the task of elaboration to a more propitious season. If so great a man was thus troubled, no strange thing was happening to me in a like experience. Such good cheer in intellectual as well as moral effort is one of the best services of biography and history, raising to the rank of ministering spirits the men whose struggles and success they tell. Was not Washington greater at Valley Forge than at Yorktown? and Nelson beating against a head wind than at Trafalgar? Johnson has anticipated Darwin's method in advice given in his Gargantuan manner: "Do not exact from yourself, at one effort of excogitation, propriety of thought and elegance of expression. Invent first, and then embellish. The production of something, where nothing was before, is an act of greater energy than the expansion or decoration of the thing produced. Set down diligently your thoughts as they arise in the first words that occur, and, when you have matter, you will easily give it form." To Trollope I owed a somewhat different practical maxim. His theory Was that a man could turn out manuscript as steadily as a shoemaker shoes – his precise simile, if I remember; and he prided himself on penning his full tale each day. I could not subscribe to this, and think that Trollope's work, of which I am fond, shows the bad effect; but I did imbibe contempt for yielding to the feeling of incapacity, and put myself steadily to my desk for my allotted time, writing what I could. Whether the result were ten words or ten hundred I tried to regard With equanimity.

I have never purpose attempted to imitate the style of any writer, though I unscrupulously plagiarize an apt expression. But gradually, and almost unconsciously, I formed a habit of closely scrutinizing the construction of sentences by others; generally a fault-finding habit. As I progressed, I worked out a theory for myself, just as I had the theory of the influence of sea power. Style, I said, has two sides. It is first and above all the expression of a man's personality, as characteristic as any other trait; or, as some one has said – was it Buffon? – style is the man himself. From this point of view it is susceptible of training, of development, or of pruning; but to attempt to pattern it on that of another person is a mistake. For one chance of success there are a dozen of failure; for you are trying to raise a special product from a soil probably uncongenial, or a fruit from an alien stem – figs from vines. But beyond this there is to style an artificial element, which I conceive to be indicated by the word *technique* as applied to the arts; though it is possible that I misapprehend the term, being ignorant of art. In authorship I understand by *technique* mainly the correct construction of periods, by the proper collocation of their parts. I subscribe heartily to the opinion I have seen attributed to Stevenson, that everything depends upon the order of the words; and this, in my judgment, should make the sentence as nearly as possible independent of punctuation.

Further, there are many awkwardnesses of expression which proper training or subsequent practice can eliminate; and in proportion as a writer attains the faculty of instinctively avoiding these, his technique improves. Perfected, he would never use them, and his sentences would flow untaught from his pen in absolutely clear reflection of his thought. As an example of what I mean by awkwardnesses, I would cite the use of "whose" as the possessive of "which." I know that adequate authority pronounces this correct, so it is not on that score I reject it. Moreover, I recognize that in myself the repulsion is somewhat of an acquired taste. When I began to write I thus employed it myself, but its sound is so inevitably suggestive of "who" as to constitute an impertinence of association. I have lately been reading a very excellent history of the United States, in which the frequent repetition of "whose" in this sense causes me the sensation of perpetually "stubbing" my toe; an Americanism, which, I will explain to any British reader, means stumbling over roots or on an unequal pavement, the irritation of which needs not exposition.

In the matter of natural style I soon discovered that the besetting anxiety of my soul was to be exact and lucid. I might not succeed, but my wish was indisputable. To be accurate in facts and correct in conclusions, both as to appreciation and expression, dominated all other motives. This had a weak side. I was nervously susceptible to being convicted of a mistake; it upset me, as they say. Even where a man writes, this is a defect of a quality; in active life it entails slowness of decision and procrastination, failure "to get there." I have no doubt that much contemporary writing suffers delay from a like morbid dread as to possibility of error. The aim to be thus both accurate and clear often encumbered my sentences. My cautious mind strove to introduce between the same two periods every qualification, whether in abatement or enforcement of the leading idea or statement. This in many cases meant an accumulation of clauses, over which I exercised my ingenuity and lavished my time so to arrange them that the whole should be at once apprehended by the reader. It was not enough for me that the qualifications should appear a page or two before, or after, and in this I think myself right; but in wanting them all in the same period, as I instinctively did, – and do, for nature is obstinate, – I have imposed on myself needless labor, and have often taxed attention as an author has no right to do. Unless under pressing necessity, I myself will not be at pains to read what I can with difficulty understand.

It is to this anxiety for full and accurate development of statements and ideas that I chiefly attribute a diffuseness with which my writing has been reproached; I have no doubt justly. I have not, however, tried to check the evil at the root. I am built that way, and think that way; all round a subject, as far as I can see it. I am uneasy if a presentment err by defect, by excess, or by obscurity apparent to myself. I must get the whole in; and for due emphasis am very probably redundant. I am not willing to attempt seriously modifying my natural style, the reflection of myself, lest, while digging up the tares of prolixity I root up also the wheat of precision. The difference emphasized by Dr. Johnson, "between notions borrowed from without and notions generated within," seems to me to apply to the mode of expression as well as to the idea expressed. The two spring from the same source, and correspond. You impress more forcibly by retaining your native manner of statement; chastened where necessary, but not defaced by an imitation, even of a self-erected, yet artificial, standard. It does not do to meddle too much with yourself. But I do resort to a weeding process in revising; a verb or an adjective, an expletive or a superlative, is dragged out and cast away. Even so, as often as not, I have to add. The words above, "as far as I can see it," have just been put in. Of course, in the interest of readers, I resort to breaking up sentences; but to me personally the result is usually distasteful. The reader takes hold more easily, as a child learns spelling by division into syllables; but I am conscious that instead of my thoughts constituting a group mutually related, and so reproducing the essential me, they are disjointed and must be reassembled by others.

A man untrained in youth, and who has never systematically sought to repair the defect, can scarcely hope fully to compass technique in style. He will thus lose some part of that which he may gain by being more nearly his natural self; for there is a real gain in this. Such advance as I have made in technique – and I trust I have made some – I have owed to the critical running analysis of the construction of sentences, which has been my habit ever since I began to write. That this is constant with me, subconsciously, is shown by the frequency with which it passes into a conscious logical recasting of what I read. To get antecedents and consequents as near one another as possible; qualifying words or phrases as close as may be to that which they qualify; an object near its verb; to avoid an adjective which applies to one of two nouns being so placed as to seem to qualify both; such minute details seem to me worthy of the utmost care, and I think I can trace advance in these respects. My experiments tend to show that the natural order of nominative, verb, object, is usually preferable; and as a rule I find that adverbs and adverbial phrases fall best between nominative and verb. Still, the desirability of tying each period to its predecessor, as does the rhyme of the fourth and fifth lines of a sonnet, will modify arrangement. In reading another author, where such precaution as I name is neglected, a word misplaced in its relation to the others of the sentence runs my mind off the track, like an engine on a misplaced switch, and I dislike the trouble of backing to get on the right rails. It is the same with my own work, if time enough elapses between composition and subsequent reading. Generally I make such time, either in manuscript or proofs; but I am chagrined when I meet slips in the printed page, as I too often do. There is no provision against such fault equal to laying the text aside till it has become unfamiliar; but even this is not certain, for construction, being consonant to your permanent mode of thinking, may not when erroneous jar upon you as upon another.

In acquiring an automatic habit, which technique should become, principles tend to crystallize into rules, and a few such I have; counsels of perfection many of these, too often unrealized. I do not like the same word repeated in the same paragraph, though this lays a heavy tax on so-called synonymes. Assonances jar me, even two terminations "tion" near together. I will not knowingly use "that" for "which," except to avoid two "whiches" between the same two periods. The split infinitive I abhor, more as a matter of taste than argument. I recognize that it is at times very tempting to snuggle the adverb so close to the verb; but I hold fast my integrity. Once, indeed, I took it into my head not to split compound tenses, and carried this fad somewhat remorselessly through a series of republished articles; but the result has not pleased me. Boswell tells us that Johnson would have none of "former" and "latter;" that he would rather repeat the noun than resort to this subterfuge. I see no good reason for rejecting these convenient alternatives; but nevertheless I have obsequiously bowed to the autocrat and taken a skunner to the words – the only literary snobbishness of which I am conscious. I can stand out against Macaulay's proscription of prepositions ending sentences. Although I generally twist them round, they often please my ear there. It is not exactly in point, but I have always rejoiced over "Silver was nothing accounted of" in the days of King Solomon; indeed, I was brought to book by a proofreader for concluding a sentence with "accounted of." I let it stand, so taking was it to me.

The question doubtless occurs to most authors how far they are under bonds to the King's English. As to grammar, I submit; the consequences of anarchy dismay me; but I question whether in words coinage is an attribute of sovereignty. There is, of course, plenty of false money going around, current because accepted; but I think a man is at liberty to pass a new word, a word without authority in dictionaries, if it be congruous to standard etymology. I once wrote "eventless;" but, on looking, found it not. Yet why not? "Homeless," "heartless," "shoeless," etc.; why merely "uneventful," a form only one letter longer, it is true, but built up to "eventful" to be pulled down to "uneventful"? Besides, "uneventful" does not mean the same as "eventless." "Doubtless" and "undoubtedly" differ by more than a shade in sense, and we have both. So we have "anywhere," "nowhere," "somewhere," "everywhere;" why not "manywhere," if you need it? Again, if "hitherto" be good – and it is – why not "thitherto"? In the case of "eccentric" as a military term, I felt forced to frame "ex-centric;" the former – I ask Dr. Johnson's pardon – has, in America at least, become so exclusively associated with the secondary though cognate idea of singularity that it would not convey its restricted military significance to a lay reader.

I had been assigned to the War College in October, 1885, Admiral Luce being still its president, but I did not go into residence until the end of the following August. Luce had then been for some months detached, to command the North Atlantic fleet, and I had succeeded him by default, without special orders that I can remember. He was anxious for me to live on the spot, to be "on deck," as he phrased it, for the College had many enemies and few friends; and matters were not helped by a sharp official collision that summer between him and Secretary Whitney, who from indifference passed into antagonism. I cannot say that his change was due to this cause, and for a long time his hostility did not take form in act. Now that the College, after twenty years, has had the warm encomium of the President of the United States in his message to Congress, it is interesting to a veteran recipient of its early buffets to recall conditions. In my two years' incumbency we got decidedly more kicks than halfpence. Yet in retrospect it gains. A prominent New York lawyer once told me of a young man from a distant State consulting him with a view to practising in the city. In response to some cautious warning as to the difficulties, he said: "Do you mean that with my education and capacity I cannot expect rapid success?" "I fear not," replied the mentor. A few months later they met casually. "Are you getting on as fast as you had hoped?" asked the older man. "No," admitted the other, "but it's heaps of fun." He doubtless got on, and so did the College. I at the time was less appreciative of the fun, but I liked the work, and now I see also the comical side.

Between the early favor of the Department and his own energy, Luce had given the College a good send-off, like a skiff shoved by hand from the wharf into mid-stream. There remained only to keep it moving. We had an appropriation, and a building that was ready for lecturing; with also two as yet uncompleted suites of quarters, for myself and one other officer. We had also a very respectable library, in which, among many valuable works, conspicuously selected with an eye to our special objects, I recall with amusement certain ancient encyclopædias, contributed apparently by well-wishers from stock which had begun to encumber their shelves. Howbeit, like Quaker guns, these made a brave show if not too closely scrutinized, and spared us the semblance of poverty in vacant spaces. Every military man understands the value of an imposing front towards the enemy. When I arrived, I was the sole occupant of the building; and except an army officer – now General Tasker Bliss – was the only *attaché*. As I walked round the lonely halls and stairways, I might have parodied Louis XIV., and said, "*Le Collège, c'est moi.*" I had, indeed, an excellent steward, who attended to my meals and made my bed. There was but one lamp available, which I had to carry with me when I went from room to room by night; and, indeed, except for the roof over my head, I might be said to be "camping out." There was yet a month before the class of officers was to arrive. This interval was more than occupied preparing the necessary maps for my lectures, much of the time by my lonely light. Owing to lack of regular assistance, a great part of the map work was done by my own hands, often sprawled on the floor as my best table; though I was fortunate in receiving much voluntary help from a retired lieutenant, now Captain McCarty Little, then and always an enthusiastic advocate of the College, who did some of the drafting and all the coloring. Thus were put together three of the four maps which afterwards appeared in my first book. The fourth, of the North Atlantic Ocean, was begged of the hydrographer of the navy; a friendly Rhode Island man.

Besides the maps, there were to be produced some twenty or more battle plans. For these I hit on a device which I can recommend. I cut out a number of cardboard vessels, of different colors for the contending navies, and these I moved about on a sheet of drawing-paper until satisfied that the graphic presentation corresponded with facts and conditions. They were then fastened in place with mucilage. This saved a great deal of drawing in and rubbing out, and by using complementary colors gave vivid impression. In combats of sailing fleets you must look out sharp, or in some arrangement, otherwise plausible, you will have a ship sailing within four points of the wind before you know it. Nor is this the only way truth may be insulted. Times and distances also lay snares for incautious steps. I noticed once in an account of an action two times, with corresponding positions, which made a frigate in the meanwhile run at eighteen knots under topsails.

By such shifts we scrambled along as best we could our first year, content with beef without horseradish, as Sam Weller has it; hitching up with rope when a trace gave way, in the blessed condition of those who are not expecting favors. But worse was to come. Besides the general offence against conservatism by being a new thing, the College specifically had poached its building from another manor. It stood upon the grounds of the Naval Training Station, for apprentices, which considered itself defrauded of property and intruded upon by an alien jurisdiction – an *imperium in imperio*. The two were not even under the same bureau, so the antagonism existed in Washington as well as locally; and now a Secretary of malevolent neutrality. Truly some one was needed "on deck;" though just what he could do with such a barometer did not appear, unless he bore up under short canvas, like Nelson, who "made it a rule never to fight the northwesters." And such was very much our policy; reefed close down, looking out for squalls at any moment from any quarter, saying nothing to nobody, content to be let alone, if only we might be so let. Small sail; and no weather helm, if you please. One most alleviating circumstance was the commandant of the training station, the local enemy, one of the born saints of the earth, Arthur Yates. Officially, of course he disapproved of us; professional self-respect and precedent, bureau allegiance, and all the rest of it, were outraged; but when it came to deeds, Yates could not have imagined an unkind act, much less done it. Nor did he stop there; good-will with him was not a negative but an active quality. What we wanted he would always do, and then go one better, if he could find a way to add to our convenience; and when we ultimately came to grief, after his departure, he wrote me a letter of condolence. Altogether, while clouds were gathering in Washington, it was perpetual sunshine at home as to official and personal relations. I have no doubt he would have drawn maps for me had I asked it.

None the less, trouble was at hand. In 1886 we had a session which by general consent was very successful in quality, if not in quantity, lasting little over two months. Our own bureau controlled the ordering of officers, so it swept together a sufficient number to form a class. We had several excellent series of lectures: on Gunnery in its higher practical aspects, by Lieutenant Meigs, who has since left the navy for a responsible position in the Bethlehem Iron Works; on International Law, by Professor Soley, who under the next administration became Assistant-Secretary of the Navy; on Naval Hygiene, by a naval surgeon, Dr. Dean; together with others less notable. All these had been contracted for by Luce. Captain Bliss and myself, as yet the only two permanent *attachés*, of course took our share. So much was new to the officers in attendance, not only in details but in principle, that I am satisfied nine-tenths of them went away friendly; some enthusiastic. The College had steered clear of any appearance of scientific, or so-called post-graduate, instruction, consecutive with that given at Annapolis; and had demonstrated that it meant to deal only with questions pertinent to the successful carrying-on of war, for promoting which no instrumentality existed elsewhere. The want had been proved, and a means of filling it offered. The listeners had been persuaded.

I well remember my own elation when they went away in the latter part of November. Success had surpassed expectation. But in a fortnight Congress met, and it soon became evident that we were to be starved out, – no appropriation. It was a short session, too; scant time for fighting. I went to Washington, and pleaded with the chairman of the House naval committee, Mr. Herbert; but while he was perfectly good-natured, and we have from then been on pleasant terms, whenever he saw me he set his teeth and compressed his lips. His argument was: Once establish an institution, and it grows; more and more every year. There must be economy, and nowhere is economy so effectually applied as to the beginnings. In vain did I try to divert his thoughts to the magnificent endings that would come from the paltry ten thousand the College asked. He stopped his ears, like Ulysses, and kept his eyes fixed on the necessity of strangling vipers in their cradle. In vain were my efforts seconded by General Joe Wheeler, also a representative from Alabama, and strongly sympathetic with military thought. No help could be expected from the Secretary, and we got no funds.

The fiscal year would end June 30, 1887. It was of no use to try saving from the current balance, for by law that must be turned in at the year's end.

So we shrugged our shoulders and trusted to luck, which came to our assistance in a comical manner. For summer we were all right, or nearly so; but winter might freeze us out. Still, unless the Secretary saw fit to destroy the College by executive order, it had a right to be warm; so we sent in our requisition for heating the building. It went through the customary channels, was approved, and the coal in the cellars before the Department noticed that there was no appropriation against which to charge it. Upon reference to the Secretary, he decided that the coal had been ordered and supplied in good faith, and should be left and paid for. In fact, however, if the building was used it would have to be heated; the decision practically was to let the College retain the building. It was an excellent occasion to wipe us out by a stroke of the pen, but Mr. Whitney had not yet reached that point. The fuel, I think, was charged to the bureau to which the Training Station belonged, which would not tend to mollify its feelings.

Coal was our prime necessity, but it was not all. The hostile interest now began to cut us short in the various items which contribute to the daily bread of a government institution. We lived the year from hand to mouth. From the repairs put on the building a twelvemonth before there was left a lot of refuse scrap lying about. This we collected and sorted, selling what was available, on the principle of slush-money. Slush, the non-professional may be told, is the grease arising from the cooking of salt provisions. By old custom this was collected, barrelled, and sold for the benefit of the ship. The price remained in the first lieutenant's hands, to be expended for the vessel; usually going for beautifying. What we sold at the College we thus used; not for beautifying, which was far beyond us, but to keep things together. This proceeding was irregular, and for years I preserved with nervous care the memoranda of what became of the money, in case of being questioned; although I do not think the total went much beyond a hundred dollars. It is surprising how much a hundred dollars may be made to do. For our lectures the hydrographer again made for the College two very large and handsome maps.

The session of 1887 was longer and more complete than the year before; but specifically it increased our good report in the service and added to us hosts of friends. Many were now ready to speak in our favor, if asked; and some gave themselves a good deal of trouble to see this or that person of importance. This was a powerful reinforcement for the approaching struggle; but with the Secretary biassed against us, and resolute opposition from the chairman of the committee, the odds were heavy. Mr. Whitney showed me a frowning countenance, quite unlike his usual *bonhomie*; and yielded only a reluctant, almost surly, "I will not oppose you, but I do not authorize you to express any approval from me." With that we began a still hunt; not from policy, but because no other course was open, and by degrees we converted all the committee but three. This was quite an achievement in its way; for, as one of the members said to me, "It is rather hard to oppose the chairman in a matter of this kind. Still, I am satisfied it is a good thing, and I will vote for it."

So we got our appropriation by a big majority. Mr. Herbert was very nice about his discomfiture. That a set of uninfluential naval officers should so unexpectedly have got the better of him, in his position, had a humorous side which he was ready to see; though it is possible we, on whose side the laugh was, enjoyed it more. He afterwards, when Secretary of the Navy, came to think much better of the College, which flourished under him.

I had soon to find that my mouth had more than one side on which to laugh. Confident that we were out of the woods, I proceeded to halloo; for in an address made at the opening of the session of 1888, alluding to the doubt long felt about the appropriation, I said, "That fear has now happily been removed." I reckoned without the Secretary, who issued an order, a bolt out of the blue, depriving the College not only of its building, but of its independent existence; transferring it to the care of the commander of the Torpedo Station, on another island in Narragansett Bay. This ended my official existence as president of the College, and I was sent off to Puget Sound; one of a commission to choose a site for a navy-yard there. I never knew, nor cared, just why Whitney took this course, but I afterwards had an amusing experience with him, showing how men forget; like my old commodore his moment of despondency about the outcome of the war. In later years he and I were members of a dining club in New York. I then had had my success and recognition. One evening I chanced to say to him, apropos of what I do not now recall, "It was at the time, you know, that you sent Sampson to the Naval Academy, and Goodrich to the Torpedo Station." "Yes," he rejoined, complacently; "and I sent you to the War College." It was literally true, doubtless; his act, though not his selection; but in view of the cold comfort and the petard with which he there favored me, for Whitney to fancy himself a patron to me, except on a Johnsonian definition of the word,[16] was as humorous a performance as I have known.

So I went to Puget Sound, a very pleasant as well as interesting experience; for, having a government tender at our disposal, we penetrated by daylight to every corner of that beautiful sheet of water, the intricate windings of which prepare a continual series of surprises; each scene like the last, yet different; the successive resemblances of a family wherein all the members are lovely, yet individual. Then was there not, suburban to the city of Seattle, Lake Washington, a great body of fresh water? Of this, and of its island, blooming with beautiful villas, a delightful summer resort in easy reach of the town by cars, we saw before our arrival alluring advertisements and pictures, which were, perhaps, a little premature and impressionist. How seductive to the imagination was the future battle-ship fleet resting in placid fresh water, bottoms unfouled and little rusted, awaiting peacefully the call to arms; upon which it should issue through the canal yet to be dug between sound and lake, ready for instant action! Great would have been the glory of Seattle, and corresponding the discomfiture of its rival Tacoma, which undeniably had no lake, and, moreover, lay under the stigma of having tried, in such default, to appropriate by misnomer another grand natural feature; giving its own name Tacoma to Mount Rainier, so called by Vancouver for an ancient British admiral. A sharp Seattleite said that a tombstone had thus been secured, to preserve the remembrance of Tacoma when the city itself should be no more. The local nomenclature affixed by Vancouver still remains in many cases. Puget, originally applied to one only of the many branches of the sound, was among his officers. Hood's Inlet was, doubtless, in honor of the great admiral, Lord Hood; while Restoration Point commemorates an anniversary of the restoration of Charles II. As regarded Lake Washington, our commission was a little nervous lest an injury to the canal might interfere at a critical moment with the fleet's freedom of movement, leaving it bottled up, and wired down. We selected, therefore, the site where the yard now stands, in a singularly well-protected inlet on the western side of the main arm, with an anchorage of very moderate depth and easy current for Puget Sound. There, if my recollection is right, it is nearly equidistant from the two cities. Our judgment was challenged and another commission sent out. This confirmed our choice, but very much less land was secured than we had advised.

XII
EXPERIENCES OF AUTHORSHIP

Before my return from Puget Sound a new administration had come in with President Harrison, and the War College was once more in favor. But its organization had been destroyed, and some time must elapse before it could get again on its legs. In the summer of 1889 a course was held at the Torpedo Station, where I lectured with others. The following winter an appropriation of one hundred thousand dollars was made for a College building; the old one being confirmed to the training station, which continued, however, strongly to oppose any use of its grounds for the new venture. In this it was overruled, and in 1892 the College started afresh in what has since been its constant headquarters, two hundred yards from its original position.

In the mean time my first series of lectures had been published in book form, under the title *The Influence of Sea Power upon History, 1660-1783*. This was in May, 1890. That it filled a need was speedily evident by favorable reviews, which were much more explicit and hearty in Europe, and especially in Great Britain, than in the United States. The point of view apparently possessed a novelty, which produced upon readers something of the effect of a surprise. The work has since received the further indorsement of translation into French, German, Japanese, Russian, and Spanish; I think into Italian also, but of this I am not certain. The same compliment has, I believe, been paid to its successor, which carried the treatment down to the fall of Napoleon. Notably, it may be said that my theme has brought me into pleasant correspondence with several Japanese officials and translators, than whom none, as far as known to me, have shown closer or more interested attention to the general subject; how fruitfully, has been demonstrated both by their preparation and their accomplishments in the recent war. As far as known to myself, more of my works have been done into Japanese than into any other one tongue.

In 1890 and 1891 there was no session of the College. During this period of suspended animation its activities were limited to my own preparations for continuing the historical course through the wars of the French Revolution and Empire, with a view to the resumption of teaching. I was kept on this duty; and I think no one else was busy in direct connection with the institution, though the former lecturers were for the most part available. It is evident how particularly fortunate such circumstances were to an author. For the two years that they lasted I had no cares beyond writing; was unvexed by either pecuniary anxieties or interference from my superiors. The College slumbered and I worked. My results, after one season's use as lectures, were published in two volumes, under the title *The Influence of Sea Power upon the French Revolution and Empire*.

Of this work it may accurately be said that in order of composition it was begun with its final chapter. The accumulation and digestion of material had been spasmodic and desultory, for I had hesitated much whether to pursue the treatment after 1783. The instability of the College fortunes had irritated as well as harassed me. If the navy did not want what I was doing, why should I persist? Nothing having been given to the world, I had had no outside encouragement; and little from within the profession, save the cordial approval of a very few officers. However, during the two years of doubtful struggle I had read quite widely upon the general history of the particular period, as well as upon the effects of sea power in the Peloponnesian War; together with such details as I could collect from Livy and Polybius of naval occurrences while Hannibal was in Italy. My outlook was thus enlarged; not upon military matters only, but by an appreciation of the strength of Athens, broad based upon an extensive system of maritime commerce. This prepared me to see in the Continental System of Napoleon the direct outcome of Great Britain's maritime supremacy, and the ultimate cause of his own ruin. Thus, while gathering matter, a conception was forming, which became the dominant feature in my scheme by the time I began to write in earnest. Coincidently with these studies, and with my other occupations when at first president of the College, two introductory chapters had been written; one bridging the interval between 1783 and 1793, so as to hitch on to my first book, the other dealing with the state of the navies at the opening of the French Revolution.

There Mr. Whitney's action brought me up with a round turn. When I resumed, late in 1889, I extended my reading by Jomini's *Wars of the French Republic*, a work instructive from the political as well as military point of view; concurrently testing Howe's naval campaign of 1794 by the principles advanced by the military author, which commended themselves to my judgment. In connection with this study of naval strategy, I reconstructed independently Howe's three engagements of May 28th and 29th, and June 1st, from the details given by James, Troude, and Chevalier, analyzing and discussing the successive tactical measures of the opposing admirals; in the battle of June 1st going so far as to trace even the tracks of the fifty-odd individual ships throughout the action. This, the most complicated presentation I ever attempted, was a needless elaboration, though of absorbing interest to me when once begun. A comparison between it and the bare conventional diagram of Trafalgar in the same volumes, which has been criticised as not reproducing the facts, may serve to show how far multiplicity of minutiæ conduces to clearness of perception. From the Trafalgar plan a reader, lay or professional, can grasp readily the underlying conceptions upon which the battle was fought, and the manner in which they were executed, as commonly received; but who ever has tried to comprehend the movements of the vessels on June 1st, as I elicited them? Assuming their correctness, it was a mere mental diversion, in result rather confusing than illuminative to a student; whereas ships arranged like beads on a string can give an impression fundamentally correct, and to be apprehended at a glance. So far from tending to lucidity, accumulation of detail in pursuit of minute accuracy rather obscures. Nelson himself indicated his intentions sufficiently by straight lines. One merit my June 1st plan may possibly possess; the perplexing optical effect may convey better than words the intricacy of a naval *mêlée*.

Coincidently with the study of military events, connoted by Howe's campaign and Jomini, I of course did a good deal of reading which here can be described only as miscellaneous; prominent amid which was Thiers's *History of the Consulate and Empire*, Napoleon's *Correspondence and Commentaries*, and the orations of Pitt and Fox. From Thiers, confirmed by contemporary memoirs and pamphlets and other incidental mention, I gained my conviction that the Continental System was the determinative factor in Napoleon's fortunes after Tilsit. Pitt's speeches, taken with his life, seemed to me conclusive as to his policy, despite the evil construction placed upon his acts by Frenchmen of his day, which Thiers has perpetuated. I saw clearly and conclusively, as I thought, apparent in his public words and private letters, a strong desire for peace, and a hand forced by a wilful spirit of aggression which momentarily had lost the balance of its reason. Making every allowance for the extravagances of the French rulers, unpractised in government and driven by a burning sense of mission to universal mankind, it was to me evident that their demands upon other nations, and notably upon Great Britain, were subversive of all public order and law, and of international security.

Pitt's proud resolution to withstand to the uttermost this tendency, coupled with his evident passionate clinging to peace as the basis of his life

ambition, constituted to my apprehension a tragedy; of lofty personal aim and effort wrestling
with, and slowly done to death by, opposing conditions too mighty for man. The dramatic intensity
of the situation was increased by the absence of
the external dramatic appeal characteristic of his
father. It carried the force of emotion suppressed.
The bitter inner disappointment is veiled under
the reserve of his private life and the reticence of
his public utterance, which give to his personality
a certain remoteness from usual joys and sorrows;
but, the veil once pierced by sympathy, the human side of the younger Pitt stands revealed as of
one who, without complaint, bore no common
burden, did no common work, and to whom fell
no common share of the suffering which arises
from disappointment and frustration, in ideals
and achievement. The conflict of the two motives
in the man's steadfast nature aroused in me an
enthusiasm which I did not seek to check; for I
believe enthusiasm no bad spirit in which to realize history to yourself or others. It tends to bias;
but bias can be controlled. Enthusiasm has its
place, not for action only, nor for speaking, but in
writing and in appreciation; quite as critical analysis and judicial impartiality have theirs. To deny
either is to err. The moment of exaltation gone, the
dispassionate intellect may sit in judgment upon
the expressions of thought and feeling which have
been prompted by the stirring of the mind; but
without this there lacks one element of true
presentation. The height of full recognition for a
great event, or a great personality, has not been
reached. The swelling of the breast under strong

emotion uplifts understanding. Under such influence a writer is to the extent of his faculties on the level of his theme. As for biography, I would no more attempt to write that of a man for whom I felt no warm admiration, than I would maintain friendship with one for whom I had no affection.

Doubtless there also was in Pitt's manner of speech, in the cast of his sentences, – the style that is the man himself, – something which appealed especially to me. Often, when reading in the Public Library of New York a passage of unusual eloquence, I would be strongly moved to rise on the spot and give three cheers; and I heartily subscribed to a Latin motto on the title-page of the edition I was using: If you could but have heard himself. But it was more than that. The story increasingly impressed itself upon me. I saw him conscious of great capacities for the administration of peace, an inner conviction of far less ability for war; with a vision of Great Britain happy and prosperous beyond all past experience under his enlightened guidance, of which already the plans had been revealed and proof been given, and over against this the palpable reality of a current too powerful to be resisted, sweeping her into a conflict, the end of which, amid such unprecedented conditions, could not be foreseen. Also, despite all his deficiencies for a war ministry, as I read and studied the general features of the situation with which he had to deal, I became convinced that the broad lines of his policy coincided with the military necessities of the case, to an extent that he himself very possibly did not realize. For as the Directory outlined Napoleon's Continental System, so Pitt, unknowingly perhaps, pursued the methods, as he definitely predicted the means – exhaustion – by which his successors brought to a stop the mischievous energies of France under the great emperor.

Thus, before I began to write, my leading ideas for the historical treatment of the influence of sea power during the period 1793-1814 rested upon an approval of the main features of Pitt's war policy, and sympathy with his personal position; upon a clear conviction of the weight of the Continental System as a factor in the general situation, and of its being a direct consequence from British maritime supremacy; and upon a sufficiently comprehensive acquaintance with the operations of the land warfare up to the Peace of Amiens. Having as yet written only the two introductory chapters, and Howe's campaign being strictly episodical, the work as an organic whole was still before me when the summer of 1890 arrived. It was then thought probable that the College would at once resume, and in order to be at hand I settled my family in Newport, there addressing myself to my new lectures. Considering the mass of detail through which my hearers must be carried, I thought advisable to begin with an outline statement of the general political and military conditions, and of their sequences; a rudimentary figure, a skeleton, the nakedness of which should render easy to understand the mutual bearings of the several parts, and their articulations. So most surely could the relation of sea power to the other members be seen, and its influence upon them and upon the ultimate issue be appreciated. Before I began, I remember explaining to a brother officer my conception of the Continental System as the culmination of the maritime struggle, which in a narrowly military sense had ended with Trafalgar. The light thus cast would illuminate afterwards each of the several sections of the history, treated circumstantially in order of time. In short, I here applied to the whole the method of my diagram for Trafalgar, and not of that for June 1st. The result was the chapter last in the work, as it now stands, but the first to be composed.

A few months before book publication this chapter appeared in the *Quarterly Review*, under the title "Pitt's War Policy," chosen by me to express my recognition that the grand policy was his; that in it he was real as well as titular premier; and that in my judgment, despite the numerous errors of detail which demonstrated his limited military understanding, the economical comprehension of the statesman had developed a political strategy which vindicated his greatness in war as in peace. The article ended, as the chapter then did, with the well-known quotation, particularly apt to my appreciation, "The Pilot had weathered the storm." The few subsequent pages were added later. By an odd coincidence, just as I had offered the paper to the *Quarterly*, one under the same title, "by a Foxite," came out in another magazine. Somewhat discomposed, I hurried to look this up; but found, as from the *nom de plume* might be presumed, that it did not take my line of argument, but rather, as I recall, that of Pitt's opponents, which Macaulay has developed with his accustomed brilliancy, although to my mind with profound misconception and superficial criticism. Fox's speeches had made upon me the impression of the mere objector. Indeed, I felt this so strongly that I had written of him as "the great, but factious, leader of the opposition." In proofreading I struck out "factious;" as needless, and as a generalization on insufficient premises.

It was not till the following December – 1890 – that I began the two chapters next in order of composition, on "The Warfare against Commerce." These occupied me late into the winter, covering as they did the entire period 1793-1814, and embracing a great deal of detail. Taken together, these three chapters, final but first written, contain the main argument of the book. The naval occurrences, brilliant and interesting as they were, are logically but the prelude to the death grapple. Pitt's policy stood justified, because naval supremacy, established by war, secured control of the seas and of maritime commerce, and so exhausted Napoleon. Not till this demonstration had been accomplished to my own satisfaction did I take up the narrative and discussion of warfare, land and sea. Thus the prelude followed the play. My memory retains associations which enable me definitely to fix the progress of the work. Thus the chapter on "The Brest Blockade," from its characteristics, long continuance, and incidents, one of the most interesting of the purely naval operations, was composed in the summer of 1891, at Richfield; while the campaign and battle of Trafalgar, the last done of all, passed through my hands in April, 1892, in Richmond, Virginia, where I then was on court-martial duty.

This second book was written under much more encouraging circumstances than its predecessor, and with much greater deliberation. The first occupied me little over one year; the second, though covering only one-fifth the time, was in hand three. There were long interruptions, it is true; the Puget Sound business, and the writing of a short *Life of Farragut*. But the chief cause of delay was a much more extensive preparation. This was owing largely to the crowded activities of the brief twenty years treated, and still more to wider outlook. I attempted, indeed, nothing that could be called original research. I still relied wholly upon printed matter, but in that I wandered far. The privilege was accorded me of free access to the alcoves of what was then the Astor Library, now, while keeping its name, incorporated with the New York Public Library; and I rummaged its well-stocked shelves, following up every clue, especially memoirs, pamphlets, and magazines, contemporary with my period. From the estimate I had formed of the effect of commerce upon the outcome of the hostilities, it was necessary to digest the statistics of the times, much of which existed in tabulated form; and, for commercial policy, the State Papers, and debates in Parliament, as well as in the French National Convention. I now had not only interest in my task, but pride; for the favorable criticism upon the first sea-power book not only had surprised me, but had increased my ambition and my self-confidence. It was a distinct help that there was no expectation of pecuniary advantage; no publisher or magazine editor pressing for "copy," on which dollars depended. I now often recall with envy the happiness of those days, when the work was its own reward, and quite sufficient, too, almost as good as a baby; when there were no secondary considerations, however important, to dispute for the first place. I have never knowingly let work leave my hands in shape less good than the best I can turn out; but I have often felt the temptation to do so, and wished – almost, not quite – that there was no money in it. I recast Dr. Johnson's saying: "None but a blockhead would write unless he needed money." None but a blockhead would write for money, unless he had to.

Though not embarrassed by publishers, I found a more formidable enemy on my tracks in 1892. There had been a change in the Bureau of Navigation, and the new chief, under whom the College was, thought my help to it less necessary than my going to sea. To an advocate of allowing me time, he replied, summarily, "It is not the business of a naval officer to write books." As an aphorism the remark is doubtless unassailable; but, with a policy thus defined, my position, again to quote Boatswain Chucks, became "precarious and not at all permanent." That my turn for sea service had come was indisputable. I could pretend to no grievance, but I did want first to finish that book. Yet I have recalled with happiness that I was enabled to work steadfastly on, my pulse beating no quicker for fear I should be interrupted and my task left unfinished. I remember a Boston publisher telling me of the anxiety felt by one of his distinguished clients, lest death should overtake him before that which he had planned was completed. The feeling is common to man, and one is touched by the apparent tragedy when men of promise and achievement are so removed, their aims unaccomplished, as were recently Professor Rawson Gardiner and Sir William Hunter; but it was given me early to realize that there is no such thing as being cut off unbetimes. If I were called at the end of a day's stint, or the pen fell from my hand in the midst of it, that which was appointed me was done; if well done, what mattered the rest? This quietness came to me through a chain of thought. I had been experiencing, as many others have, the weariness of a long-winded job, the end of which seemed to recede with each day's progress; and there came to my mind Long-fellow's "Village Blacksmith:"

"Toiling, rejoicing, sorrowing, Onward through life he goes; Each morning sees some task begin, *Each evening sees it close.*"

Would it were so with me! And a voice replied, "Is it not so with you? with all?" Since then I have understood; though the flesh is often weak, and even the calm of the study cannot always exclude the contagious fever of our American pace. In the particular juncture, the Secretary of the Navy, Mr. Tracy, took my view of relative importances, and time was secured me. The manuscript was complete by the late spring of 1892, and the book published in December, having meantime been used for lectures in the first session of the College in its new building; a renewal of life which has since proved continuous.

During this interval occurred another presidential campaign. Mr. Harrison was defeated and

Mr. Cleveland elected. I was now ready to go to sea, but by this time had decided that authorship had for me greater attractions than following up my profession, and promised a fuller and more successful old age. I would have retired immediately, had I then fulfilled the necessary forty years' service; but of these I still lacked four. My purpose was to take up at once the War of 1812, while the history of the preceding events was fresh in my mind; and in this view I asked to be excused from sea duty, undertaking that I would retire when my forty years were complete. The request was probably inadmissible, for I could have given no guarantees; and the precedent might have been bad. At any rate, it was not granted, luckily for me; for by a combination of unforeseen circumstances the ship to which I was ordered, the *Chicago*, was sent to Europe as flag-ship of that station, and on her visit to England, in 1894, occasion was taken by naval officers and others to express in public manner their recognition of the value they thought my work had been to the appreciation of naval questions there. This brought my name forward in a way that could not but be flattering, and affected favorably the sale of the books; the previous readers of which had seemingly been few, though from among those few I had received pleasant compliments. Upon this followed the conferring upon me honorary degrees by the two universities; D.C.L. by Oxford, and LL.D. by Cambridge. After my return, in 1895, LL.D. was extended also by Harvard, Yale, and Columbia, in the order named, and by McGill in Montreal.

Another very pleasing and interesting experience while in London was dining with the Royal Navy Club. This is an ancient institution, dating back to the middle of the eighteenth century. Its list of members carries many celebrated names, among others Nelson. It has no club-house, and exists as an organization only; meeting for dinners on or near the dates of some half-dozen famous naval victories, the anniversaries of which it thus commemorates yearly. There is by rule one guest of the evening, and one only, who is titularly the guest of the presiding officer; but on this occasion an exception was made for our admiral and myself. Unfortunately, he, who was much the better after-dinner speaker, was ill and could not attend. The rule thus remained intact, and I have understood that this was the first time in the history of the club that the guest had been a foreigner.

The *Chicago* had left England and was lying at Antwerp when the time for conferring degrees arrived. My attendance in person was requisite, but only a week could be spared from the ship for the purpose. This made it impossible for me to be present in both cases at the high ceremonial, where the honors are bestowed upon the full group of recipients. Oxford had been first to tender me her distinction, and I accordingly arranged my journey with a view to her celebration; two days before which I went down to Cambridge, and was there received and enrolled at a private audience, before the accustomed officials and some few visitors from outside. What the circumstances lacked in the pomp of numbers and observance, and in the consequent stimulus to interest which a very novel experience arouses, was compensated to me by the few hours of easy social intercourse with a few eminent persons, whom I had the pleasure of then meeting very informally.

The great occasion at Oxford presents a curious combination of impressiveness and horse-play, such as is associated with the Abbot of Misrule, in the stories of the Middle Ages. It is this smack and suggestion of antiquity, of unnumbered such occasions in the misty past, when the student was half-scholar and half-ruffian, which make the permitted license of to-day not only tolerable, but in a sense even venerable. The good-humor and general acceptance on both sides, by chaffers and chaffed, testified to recognized conditions; and there is about a hoary institution a saving grace which cannot be transferred to *parvenus*. Practised in a modern Cis-Atlantic seat of learning, as I have seen it done, without the historical background, the same disregard of normal decorum becomes undraped rowdyism – boxing without gloves. The scene and its concurrences at Oxford have been witnessed by too many, and too often described, for me to attempt them. I shall narrate only my particular experiences. I had been desired to appear in full uniform – epaulettes, cocked hat, sword, and what is suggestively called "brass-bound" coat; swallow-tailed, with a high collar stiffened with lining and gold lace, set off by trousers with a like broad stripe of lace, not inaptly characterized by some humorist as "railroad" trousers. The theory of these last, I believe, is that so much decoration on hat and collar, if not balanced by an equivalent amount below, is top-heavy in visual effect, if not on personal stability. Whatever the reason, it is all there, and I had it all at Oxford; all on my head and back, I mean, except the epaulettes. For to my concern I found that over all this paraphernalia I must also wear the red silk gown of a D.C.L. It became evident, immediately upon trial, that the silk and the epaulettes were agreeing like the Kilkenny cats, so it was conceded that these naval ornaments should be dispensed with; the more readily as they could not have been seen. In the blend, and for the occasion, my legal laurels prevailed over my professional exterior.

In the matter of dress my life certainly culminated when I walked up – or down – High Street in Oxford with cocked hat, red silk gown, and sword, the railroad trousers modestly peeping beneath. It must be admitted that the townsmen either had more than French politeness, or else were used to incongruities. I did not see one crack a smile; whether any turned to look or not, I did not turn to see. My hospitable escort and myself joined the other expectants before the Sheldonian Theatre, where the ceremonies are held. The audience, of both sexes, visitors and students, had already crammed the benches and galleries of the great circular interior when we marched to our seats, in single file, down a narrow aisle. The fun, doubtless, had been going on already some time; but for us it was non-existent till we entered, when the hose was turned full upon us and our several peculiarities. I am bound to say that to encourage us we got quite as many cheers as chaff, and the personalities which flew about like grape-shot were pretty much hit or miss. I noticed that some one from aloft called out, "Why don't you have your hair cut?" which I afterwards understood was a delicate allusion to my somewhat unparalleled baldness; but it happened that two behind me in the procession was a very distinguished Russian scientist, like myself a D.C.L. *in ovo*, whose long locks fell over his collar, and I innocently supposed that so pertinent a remark was addressed to him on an occasion when *im*pertinence was lord of the ascendant. Thus the shaft passed me harmless, or fell back blunted from my triple armor of dulness.

Although in itself in most ways enjoyable, the cruise of the *Chicago* while it lasted necessarily suspended authorship. I heard intimations of the common opinion that the leisure of a naval officer's life would afford abundant opportunity. Even I myself for a moment imagined that time in some measure might be found for accumulating material, for which purpose I took along several books; but it was in vain. Neither a ship nor a book is patient of a rival, and I soon ceased the effort to serve both. Night work was tried, contrary to my habit; but after a few weeks I had to recognize that the evening's exertion had dulled my head for the next morning's duties.

My orders not only interrupted writing, but changed its direction for a long while. I had foreseen that the War of 1812, as a whole, must be flat in interest as well as laborious in execution; and, upon the provocation of other duty, I readily turned from it in distaste. Nine years elapsed before I took it up; and then rather under the compulsion of completing my Sea Power series, as first designed, than from any inclination to the theme. It occupied three years – usefully, I hope – and was published in 1905. Regarded as history, it is by far the most thorough work I have done. I went largely to original documents in Washington, Ottawa, and London, and I believe I have contributed to the particular period something new in both material and interpretation. But, whatever value the book may possess to one already drawn to the subject, it is impossible to infuse charm where from the facts of the case it does not exist. As a Chinese portrait-painter is said to have remonstrated with a discontented patron, "How can pretty face make, when pretty face no have got?"

Thus my orders to the *Chicago* led to dropping 1812, and to this my *Life of Nelson* was directly due. The project had already occurred to me, for the conspicuous elements of human as well as professional interest could not well escape one who had just been following him closely in his military career. *Sea Power in the French Revolution* having been published less than six months before, the framework of external events, into which his actions must be fitted, was fresh in my recollection, as was also the analysis of his campaigns and battles, available at once for fuller treatment, more directly biographical. After consultation with my publishers I decided to undertake the work, and with reference to it chiefly I provided myself reading-matter. I have already said that the experiment of writing on board did not succeed. I composed part of the first chapter and then stopped; but the purpose remained, and was resumed very soon after leaving the *Chicago*, in May, 1895.

For the writing of biography I had formed a theory of my own, a guiding principle, closely akin to the part which sea power had played in my treatment of history. This leading idea was not intended to exclude other points of view or manners of presentation, but was to subordinate them somewhat peremptorily. As defined to myself, my plan was to realize personality by living with the man, in as close familiarity as was consistent with the fact of his being dead. This was to be done first, for myself, as the necessary prelude to transmission to my readers. When there remains a huge mass of correspondence, by one as frank in utterance and copious in self-revelation as was Nelson, the opportunity to get on terms of such intimacy is unique, one-sided though the communication is. Besides, companions and subordinates have left abundant records of their association with him, which constitute, as it were, the other side of conversation; relieving the monologue of his own letters. The first thing in order is to know the living man; and it seemed to me that, with such materials, this could be accomplished most fully by steeping one's self in them, creating an environment closely analogous to the intercourse of daily life. I believed that passive surrender to these impressions, rather than conscious labored effort, would gradually produce the perceptions of immediate contact, to the utmost that the nature of the case admitted. Johnson doubtless was right in naming personal acquaintance as chief among the qualifications of a biographer; failing that, one must seek the best substitute. By either method the conception of character and temperament is formed; its reproduction to readers is a matter of power of expression, and of capacity to introduce aptly, here and there, the minute touches by which an artist secures likeness and heightens effect.

Whatever the worth of this theory, it was due in large measure to revulsion from a form of biography, to me always displeasing and essentially crude, which gives a narrative of external life-events, disjointed continually by letters. Profuse recourse to letters simply turns over to the reader the task which the biographer has undertaken to do for him. Perhaps the biographer cannot do it. Then he had better not undertake the job. A collection of letters is one thing, a biography another; and they do not mix well when a career abounds in incident. Letters are material for biography, as original documents are material for history; but as documents are not history, so letters are not biography. The historian and biographer by publishing virtually contract to present their readers with a digested, reasoned whole; the best expression, full yet balanced, that they can give of the truth concerning a period, or a man. It is a labor of time and patience, and should be also of love; one which the reader is to be spared, on the principle that a thousand men should not have to do, each for himself, the work the one writer professes. It is no fair treatment to tumble at their feet a basketful of papers, and virtually say, "There! find out the man for yourself."

The interest of lives, of course, varies, and with it the opportunity of the biographer. I do not mean in degree, which is trite to remark, but in kind, which is less recognized. There are men the value of whose memory to their race lies in their thought and words, whose career is uneventful. Yet even with them the impression of personality is not as vividly produced by masses of correspondence as it may be by the petty occurrences of daily life, which for them are the analogues of the stirring incidents that mark the course of the man of public action, statesman or warrior. The reason is plain; the character of few rises to the height of their words, written or spoken. These show their wisdom, or power, and are uplifting; but their shortcomings, too, have a virtue. We fight the better for appreciating that victors have known defeat. The supreme gift of biography to mankind is personality; not what the man thought or did, but what he was. Herein is inspiration and reproof; motive force, inspiring or deterrent. If nothing better, mere recognition, or exultation in an excellence to which we do not attain, has a saving grace of its own.

For the purposes of his biographer, Dr. Johnson scarcely left London. Beyond a brief visit to Paris, only a tour through the Hebrides; this an event so colossal in its elevation above the flat level of his outward existence, like the church towers in a Dutch landscape, that it is treated as a thing quite apart, has a volume to itself, severed from its before and after. Boswell gives letters, certainly, and many; yet, in the matter of character portrayal, what are they alongside of the talk?

And also, more pertinent, what to Boswell was even the talk, compared with the intercourse to which the talk was incident? In this he immersed himself and his strong receptive powers, absorbing the impression which he has so skilfully reproduced. Such apprehension as Boswell thus gained for himself is no neutral acquirement; it is a working force, instinctively selective from that on which it feeds, and intuitive in its power of arrangement. To copy his result is futile. Like Nelson, there is but one Boswell; but it may be permitted to believe that lesser men will profit to the extent of their capacities by adopting his method. This possibly he never formulated, in that again proving his genius, the unconscious faculty of a very self-conscious man; but I conceive the process to have been, first know your subject yourself thoroughly by close contact and sympathy, and then so handle your material as to bring out to the reader the image revealed to you.

This is, in a measure, a plea for picturesque treatment of biography and of history; not by gaudy coloring and violent contrasts, striving after rhetorical effect, but in the observance of proportion, of grouping, of subordination to a central idea; not content with mere narration, however accurate in details. A narrative which fails in portrayal, in picturesque impression, is not accurate; and a biography which presents a man's thoughts and acts, yet does not over and above them fashion his personality to the reader, is a failure. How much conscious effort may be necessary to the due handling of materials, I certainly cannot undertake to say; but persuaded I am that the utmost results possible to any particular man can be attained only by passive assimilation, and that so they will be attained to the measure of his individual capacity. By such digestion a theme apparently dry may be quickened to interest. Though not a lawyer, nor a student of constitutions, I found Stubbs's *Constitutional History of England* fascinating. I have not analyzed my pleasure, but I believe it to have been due to portrayal; to arrangement of data by a man exceptionally gifted for vivid presentation, who had so lived with his subject that it had realized itself to him as a living whole, which he successfully conveyed to his readers. There is no disjointment. The result is a great historical picture; or a biography, of law as a benevolent developing personality, moving amid the struggles and miseries of the human throng, healing and redressing.

To *The Life of Nelson* I applied the idea of this method, which I thought to be helped rather than hindered by my warm admiration for him, little short of affection. I had faith in the power of attachment to comprehend character and action; and because of mine I believed myself safer when necessary to censure. I grieved while I condemned. I was sure also that, however far below an absolute best I might fall, the best that I could do must thus come out. Amid approval sufficient to gratify me, I found most satisfaction in that of a friend who said he felt as if he had been living with my hero; and of another who told me that after his day's work, which I knew to be laborious, he had refreshed his evenings with *Nelson*. In the first edition I fell into two mistakes of some importance, as well as others in small details, the effect of which was to confirm me in my theory; for while they were blemishes, and needed correction, they did not, and do not, to my mind affect the portrait – the conveyance of true personality.

Of these errors the most serious, regarded as a fault, was an inadequate study of Nelson's course at Naples in 1799, so sharply challenged at that time and afterwards. I recognized the justice of a criticism which alleged that I had not sufficiently examined the other side of the case, as presented by Italian authors. This I now did, rewriting my account for the second edition. I found no reason to change my estimate of Nelson's conduct, but rather to confirm the favorable aspects; but what was more instructive to me was that even so large an oversight did not when remedied affect the portrait. The personality remained as first conceived; Nelson had acted in character. The same was substantially true of a more pregnant incident, the discovery of a number of his letters to his wife, which had escaped the diligent search made by the editor of his correspondence, Sir Harris Nicolas. After lying concealed for the half-century between Nicolas and myself, they turned up shortly after my book was in print. Here was more self-revelation; how might it modify my picture? The event was ushered in with a great flourish of trumpets, the walls of Jericho were about to fall, and I own I felt anxious. Some of the letters were published; permission to see the others was refused me. As these have not since been given to the world, I fancy that they sustain the opinion expressed by me on those that were; that beyond emphasizing somewhat his hardness to Lady Nelson during the period of his growing alienation, they add little to the impression before formed. A slight touch of the brush, another line in the face, that is all.

The question of Nelson's action at Naples was brought forward in a way which required from me some controversial writing. To this I have no intention of alluding here, beyond stating that up to the present my confidence has not been shaken in my defence of the main lines of his conduct, clearing him of the deceit and double-dealing alleged against him. I say this because there may be some who have thought me silenced by argument, in that I have not seen fit to rise to such crude taunts as that, "After this Captain Mahan will not undertake," etc. What Captain Mahan will or will not do is of no particular importance; but when the repute of such an one as Nelson is at stake, burdened by the weight of calumny laid upon him by Southey's ill-instructed censures, it is right to repeat that nothing I have seen since I last wrote, about 1900, has appeared to me to call for further answer.

The Life of Nelson, and *The War of 1812*, of which I have already spoken, remain my last extensive works. In the interval between them, 1897-1902, I was engaged mostly in occasional writing, for magazines or otherwise. From time to time these papers have been collected and published, under titles which seemed appropriate. Concerning them, for the most part, there is one general statement to be made. With few exceptions, they have been written to order. Partly from indisposition to this particular activity, partly from indolence, ultimately from conviction that editors best know – or should know – what the public want, I have left them to come to me. When expedient, I have taken a subject somewhat apart from that suggested, but usually akin. Speaking again generally, the field of thought into which I have been thus drawn has been that of the external policy of nations, and of their mutual – international – relations; not in respect to international law, on which I have no claim to teach, but to the examination of extant conditions, and the appreciation of their probable and proper effect upon future events and present action. In conception, these studies are essentially military. The conditions are to my apprehension forces, contending, perhaps even conflicting; to be handled by those responsible as a government disposes its fleets and armies. This is not advocacy of war, but recognition that the providential movement of the world proceeds through the pressure of circumstances; and that adverse circumstances can be controlled only by organization of means, in which armed physical power is one dominant factor.

In direct result from the line of thought into which I was drawn by my conception of sea power, and which has inspired my subsequent magazine writing, I am frankly an imperialist, in the sense that I believe that no nation, certainly no great nation, should henceforth maintain the policy of isolation which fitted our early history; above all, should not on that outlived plea refuse to intervene in events obviously thrust upon its conscience. The world of national activities has become crowded, like the world of professions; opportunity, consequently, has diminished, and possibilities must be cultivated and husbanded. This is the primary duty of a government to its own people and to their posterity. But there are other duties which must be accepted, even though they entail national sacrifice, because laid at the nation's door, like Cuba, or forced upon its decision, like the Philippines. I see too clearly in myself the miserable disposition to shirk work and care, and responsibility, to condone the same in nations. I once heard a preacher thus parody effectively the words of the prophet – "Here am I, send *him*!" And I have heard attributed to the late Mr. John Hay an equally telling allusion to certain of our moralists, who would discard the Philippines on the score of danger to the national principles. Said a pious girl, "When I realized that personal ornaments were dragging my immortal soul to hell, I gave them to my sister." Still less, let us hope, will one of the wealthiest of nations, almost alone in the possession of an abundant surplus income, desert a charge on the poor plea of economy; or so far distrust its fate, as to turn its back upon a duty, because dangerous or troublesome. If the political independence of the Philippine Islands bid fair to result in the loss, or lessening, of the safeguards of personal freedom to the private Philippine islander, the mission of the United states is at present clear, nor can it be abandoned without national discredit; nay, national crime. Personal liberty is a greater need than political independence, the chief value of which is to insure the freedom of the individual.

Similarly, not only for the sake of its own citizens, but for the world at large, each country should diligently watch and weigh current external occurrences; not necessarily to meddle, still less to forsake its proper sphere, but because convinced that failure to act when occasion demands may be as injurious as mistaken action, and indicates a more dangerous condition, in that moral inadequacy means ultimately material decline. When the spirit leaves the body, the body decays.

In these subjects and my way of viewing them, I suppose that ten years ago, before our war with Spain, I was ahead of the times, at least in my own country, and to some extent helped to turn thought into present channels; much as to my exposition of sea power has been credited a part of the impulse to naval development which characterizes to-day. Immediately after the Spanish War I seemed to some, if I may trust their words, to have done a bit of prophecy; while others laid to my door a chief share in the mistaken direction they considered the country to be taking. Of course, I was pleased by this; I have never pretended to be above flattery judiciously administered: but, while confident still in the main outlook of my writing, I know too well that, when you come to details, prediction is a matter of hit or miss, and that I have often missed as well as hit in particulars. "It is all a matter of guess," said Nelson, when tied down to a specific decision, "but the world attributes wisdom to him who guesses right." This is less true of the big questions and broad lines of contemporary history. There insight can discern really something of tendencies;

enough to guide judgment or suggest reflection. But I am now sixty-seven, and can recognize in myself a growing conservatism, which may probably limit me henceforth to bare keeping up with the procession in the future national march. Perhaps I may lag behind. With years, speculation as well as action becomes less venturesome, and I look increasingly to the changeless past as the quiet field for my future labors.

FOOTNOTES:

[1] Worcester, quoting from *Falconer's Marine Dictionary*, defines "Grommet" as "a small ring or wreath, formed of the strand of a rope, used for various purposes."

[2] J. R. Soley, The Blockade and the Cruisers, 1883. Scribner's, Navy in the Civil War.

[3] This statement when written rested on my childhood's memory only. A few months later there came into my hands a volume of the publications of the British Navy Records Society, containing the Recollections of Commander James Anthony Gardner. 1775-1814. Gardner was at one time shipmates with Culmer, who it appears eventually received a commission. By Gardner's reckoning he would have been far along in the forties in 1790. The following is the description of him. "Billy was about five feet eight or nine, and stooped; hard features, marked with the small-pox; blind in an eye, and a wen nearly the size of an egg under his cheek-bone. His dress on a Sunday was a mate's uniform coat, with brown velvet waistcoat and breeches; boots with black tops; a gold-laced hat, and a large hanger by his side like the sword of John-a-Gaunt. He was proud of being the oldest midshipman in the navy, and looked upon young captains and lieutenants with contempt."

[4] The *Navy Register* of 1842 shows the number appointed in 1841 to have been two hundred and nineteen.

[5] That is, within a quarter of a point on either side of her course. A "point" of the compass is

one-eighth of a right angle; e.g., from North to East is eight points.

[6] *Naval Letters of Captain Percival Drayton.* Edited by Miss Gertrude L. Hoyt. 1906. Pages 10, 3, 4.

[7] The anchoring chains pass from inboard through the hawse-holes to the anchor. When left bent on soundings, the sea, if rough, will rush through them copiously. To prevent this in part, conical stuffed canvas bags were dragged in from outside. These were called "jackasses."

[8] Acknowledgment is here due to Mr. Thomas G. Ford, once a professor at the Naval Academy, cordially remembered by the midshipmen who knew him there in the fifties. His article is in the issue of the *Naval Institute Proceedings* for June, 1906, which has just reached me. He attributes his information to the late Admiral Preble, almost the only American officer within my time who has had the instincts of an archæologist.

[9] Perhaps it is better to explain that there are three watches from 8 P.M. to 8 A.M.; the two watches into which the crew were divided had on alternate nights one watch, or two watches, on deck. This sybarite was foretasting two watches below.

[10] On referring to the file of the *Times*, I find that the forecast concerning Vicksburg occurred in the issue of July 1st. "It is not improbable we may hear that General Grant has been obliged to raise the siege of Vicksburg." It is surprising to note of how secondary importance the Vicksburg issue appears to have been thought at the time.

[11] Rhodes's *History of the United States*, vol. V., p. 99.

[12] I have here used the expression "harakiri," because so commonly understood among English – speaking readers. A Japanese correspondent has informed me that it is never used among the Japanese, with the signification we have attached to it. The proper word is "Seppuku."

[13] Official Record of the Union and Confederate Navies, Series I., iii., p. 722.

[14] Since this was written, I have been told by one of the officers of the *Iroquois*, Lieutenant – now Rear-Admiral – Nicoll Ludlow, that many years afterwards he saw the story of the *Cayalti's* captain, told by himself, in the *Overland Monthly*, of San Francisco. He had been allowed to go ashore to get provisions, and of course did not return.

[15] This is not the place for a discussion of commerce-destroying as a method of war; but having myself given, as I believe, historical demonstration that as a sole or principal resource, maintained by scattered cruisers only, it is insufficient, I wish to warn public opinion against the reaction, the return swing of the pendulum, seen by me with dismay, which would make it of no use at all, and under the plea of immunity to "private property," so called, would exempt from attack the maritime commerce of belligerents.

[16] "Is not patron, my lord, one who looks with unconcern on a man struggling for life in the water, and, when he has reached ground, encumbers him with help?" – Johnson to the Earl of Chesterfield.